THE PRINCIPLES OF
BRAZILIAN
SOCCER

by

José Thadeu Goncalves

in cooperation with Professor Julio Mazzei

Published by REEDSWAIN INC

Library of Congress Cataloging - in - Publication Data

Goncalves, José Thadeu
    The Principles of Brazilian Soccer

ISBN No. 1-890946-06-0
Library of Congress Catalog Card Number 97-75741
Copyright © April 1998

Reedswain books are available at special discounts for bulk purchase. For details, contact the Special Sales Manager at Reedswain at 1-800-331-5191.

Art Direction, Design and Layout
Kimberly N. Bender
Editing and Proofing
Bryan R. Beaver

Printed by:
DATA REPRODUCTIONS, Auburn Hills, Michigan

)OKS and VIDEOS
612 Pughtown Road
Spring City, Pennsylvania 19475 USA
1-800-331-5191 • www.reedswain.com

Acknowledgments

Thank you to Jesus, for his guidance everyday.

To my family: Teka, Thulio and Thadeuzinho
My parents, Manoel and D. Etelvina and my brothers and sister, Fatima and My best teammate Sanzio

My Special Team

Miguel de Lima: My keeper - guiding always from the back as a friend, father, brother and teammate.

Skip Grossman: The Center Midfield Defensive - always marking and helping to build the attack.

Chuck Emling: The Forward - always playing aggressively.

Bernice Teegarden: My special thanks for helping to transform my notes and dreams for this book.

Special People in my Life

Prof. Julio Mazzei: My dear friend and advisor.

Ramona Barber, Alaercio Borelli, Mike Carrier, Dalmo Gaspar, Mark Hammon, Adailton Ladeira, Ricart Pidelasierra, Neil and Fran Roberts, Bob Shoemaker, Donald Wedgebury, and Bill Wimmer.

Special Recognition

Rick Miller: For helping me to believe that dreams are the first step of reality. We did. Thank you very much, my first Brazilian - American dreamer.

Phil Stevens: Through his photos he has captured some unforgettable moments of passion.

Finally, thanks to the hundreds of coaches and players who have played a huge part in my education in soccer and in life.

Table of Contents

Preface

We believe the selling of soccer as only business and only about winning has to stop.

The game of soccer was created in England and played for fun among friends. This same feeling has to come back to our children.

Just think about having fun at something. The more fun you have at doing something, the more you will want to keep doing it. As with soccer, the more fun you have the more you keep doing it, the better you become, to the point you can start to win, and win and win!

The Principles of Brazilian Soccer offers the opportunity to share with the North American soccer community a few ideas about the way we develop our educational methodology, based on the Brazilian soccer style. The book discusses the importance of not pushing players by trying to identify the Michael Jordan, Tiger Woods or Joe Montana of soccer. Young players have heroes, good examples of men and women and of competitive athletes, and finally, and the most important, they must have the right education.

We are committed to help build the new North American soccer generation, combined with experience of the past, dreams of the present and hope for the future. Miguel de Lima - José Thadeu Goncalves

Foreword

It is a pleasure for me to do the forward for this book, especially because of the person behind it. I had an opportunity to meet José Thadeu Goncalves for the first time back in 1984. During all these years we have built a relationship very deep in identifying the best way to promote Brazilian soccer in all parts of the world.

I have traveled in more than 65 countries together with Péle, introducing this philosophy.

For a few years I had the opportunity to direct the New York Cosmos and again the seed was planted; this time to the North American soccer community.

"The Principles of Brazilian Soccer" is the first book published about the methodology of the most successful style of playing in the world. I am very excited about this historic moment for soccer. "The Principles of Brazilian Soccer" is a guide that any coach or player must read. Reading this book will clarify and answer all the questions you may have about Brazilian soccer. It is not just about technical and tactical strategies, but stresses the importance of respect, discipline and commitment to this wonderful game.

I have a dream of coaching a team where politics, race, religion, socio-economic status and gender are not a factor. The team will be unified by the power of love and the name of the team will be "The Mankind Soccer Team".

We want to invite you to be part of this team.

Prof. Julio Mazzei

Pioneers in the development of the Brazilian soccer philosophy.

Péle and Prof. Julio Mazzei

Introduction

I n 1994 Brazilian soccer again burst onto the international scene in the World Cup finals. The style was so unique that traditional soccerphiles everywhere sat up and took notice. Rather than the long, predictable passes and running, the Brazilians virtually danced down the field, moving the ball quickly with short passes and constant movement. Their game had a rhythm and grace that seemed natural; the style was simply a manifestation of the players' pure delight at finding themselves on the soccer field again. The seriousness of the World Cup did not seem to weigh heavily on the Brazilians; they laughed and rejoiced all the way to the championship. They were having fun.

There is no great mystery to understanding the Brazilian style of soccer. It is a combination of quickness in their touch and the ability to play without the ball, using the open spaces well. It can be readily taught, but it is vital to approach the learning process as a cycle of education with progressive challenges as skills increase. Before a coach can set about instructing players in this style, he must truly understand how to instill a love of the game in a player and how to avoid the pitfalls which plague coaches and drive far too many youngsters from the game at an early age.

The primary objectives of Brazilian soccer are scoring goals, applying the necessary creativity, and making brilliant defensive moves, and this is very simple and enjoyable because it is fun. This philosophy is deeply ingrained in each game. When players are enjoying themselves, they come to practice early and leave grudgingly when it's time to go. And as their skills and confidence increase, so grows their love and commitment to the game.

In this book we will examine the concepts which make Brazilian soccer so unique and successful, and take you step-by-step through the progressive cycle of education. We will provide strategies for planning your season and setting goals for various age groups and skill levels. We will examine specific elements of the Brazilian game, such as the Brazilian 4-4-2 and the tactical adjustment to any system or style of pressure; circuit training; training with and without the ball; specific Brazilian technical skills in progressive development; and psychological aspects of the game. We will show how careful analysis of players can provide invaluable data for enhancing your team's performance.

It is our sincere wish that this book gives you an understanding and appreciation of this unique and thrilling style of soccer so that you, too, may take the Brazilian Challenge!

References to the male gender in this book with respect to players and coaches are for simplification only and apply to both males and females.

The Most Influential Soccer Philosophies in the World

England won the World Cup in 1966 and a year later North America started its own Division One level professional league. This new league, the NASL, attracted some of the world's best players, as well as many others with professional experience, mostly players from the English leagues. The American clubs invested heavily in an attempt to make the league successful, and names like Péle, Franz Beckenbauer, Johan Cruyff, Carlos Alberto, George Best, and other greats, appeared daily in American newspapers. But after a few years of tremendous fan fervor and immense club investment, the big clubs couldn't replace or support its aging stars with players of the same brilliance. As a result, the once attractive game played here lost its finesse and much of its excitement, and the league soon folded.

The American soccer community continued to grow and flourish in the years that followed. However, it continued to need role models and experienced players for its young soccer generation to idolize and learn from. Many of the league's name players, particularly those from England who shared a common language, found themselves out of jobs as players but with a chance to influence and profit from the American youth program through other avenues. Thus, the early mission of promoting soccer in North America fell largely to the British.

As youth players and teams increased in numbers across the country, parents and parent-coaches alike, most with little or no background in soccer, hungered for more information. Consequently, the British Football Association (FA) and the now local, immigrant British soccer community started to write books, produce videos and educate parent-coaches about teaching the game to their future soccer stars. College programs were created and many British coaches were hired. Thus, for many years in North America the British soccer philosophy and style of play largely influenced soccer communities.

It was not until West Germany won the World Cup in 1974 and Argentina's victory in 1978 that the United State Soccer Federation and its coaching school began to embrace other European and South American influences and styles. In fact, successive World Cup champions repeatedly influenced North American soccer education.

The next key event influencing contemporary American soccer education came in 1990 when the United States qualified for the final stage of the World Cup held that year in Italy. With the USA national team participating, the growing American soccer population took notice and began to observe and appreciate the soccer styles played in other parts of the world, i.e., in Germany, Holland, Italy, Argentina, Brazil, and Africa.

Up to this point, American television had shown little interest in televising soccer, the viewership and economics were not there for the major networks.

In 1994, however, soccer in North America was forever changed. The USA hosted World Cup '94 and, for the first time, with the interest of network and cable television, the entire population had an opportunity to watch and embrace a very different methodology and philosophy of soccer from the championship Brazil team.

Philosophy of Brazilian Soccer

Carlos Alberto Parreira, Brazil's World Cup winning coach, said in an interview leading up to the Cup finals that for his team to do well it had to be "defensively organized, as fit or fitter than its opponents, and offensively express themselves in the 'Brazilian way'".

What are the characteristics of modern Brazilian soccer? To play fast and secure with unpredictable and creative offensive attacking movement. How does the Brazilian approach differ from that of the English? The Dutch? the German? Let's start by describing the individual Brazilian player and then his team play.

First, the individual Brazilian player is technically very sound; every player on the field plays comfortably with the ball at his feet. Additionally, he is creative by nature, and while tactically very astute, he also likes to do the simple things with flair. We've all learned to expect the unexpected in Brazil's attacking area of the field.

The Brazilian player works hard and is physically trained in highly scientific, closely monitored methods. This high level of fitness enables him to do the work necessary to supply positive numbers around the ball-- both offensively and defensively. Combine fitness with this mix of individual skill, creativity and tactical awareness and you create special players and remarkable teams.

Brazil's team tactics further distinguish Brazilian play. Again Parreira said, "I didn't have to teach our players how to play soccer, but I did have to help them develop as a unit. That is not easy for Brazilian players because they are all such individuals." (Reported in Paul Gardner's Soccer Talk column in the October 9, 1995 issue of Soccer America.)

First, the Brazilian approach is to keep the ball moving on the ground whenever possible, except when crossing, shooting or sometimes when exploiting an opening up front or changing the point of attack from one flank to the other with a single pass. The necessary touch is developed early by training barefoot, when a miss-kick or long ball physically hurts. Frequently, too, small rubber balls and futsal balls are used to develop better touch.

Next, the point of attack is constantly switched away from pressure through a series of short passes on the ground. Possession is insured by the proper positioning of supporting players. Brazil's 4-4-2 scheme of play (diagram 1) emphasizes diagonal support on both the attacking and defensive sides of the player in possession: the offensive center midfielder supporting both strikers; the defensive center midfielder supporting both outside midfielders; and one of the inside defenders supporting both out-side defenders and the other inside defender. We call these three positions the 911 of the team and they function similarly to point guards in bas-ketball. They are always there in case of emergency and available to quick-ly switch the point of attack. We refer to this network of supporting play from diagonally positioned players as 'triangulation'.

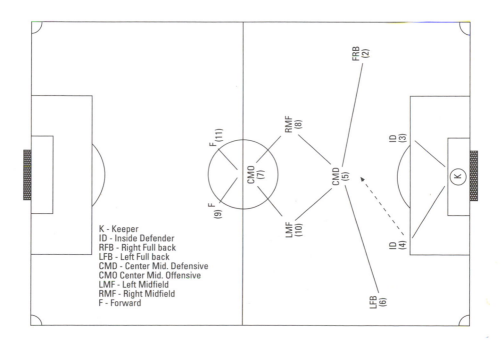

K - Keeper
ID - Inside Defender
RFB - Right Full back
LFB - Left Full back
CMD - Center Mid. Defensive
CMO Center Mid. Offensive
LMF - Left Midfield
RMF - Right Midfield
F - Forward

Diagram 1: *South American Philosophy: Brazilian Style.*

Diagram 1 shows Brazil's tentative 4-4-2 scheme of play applying an offensive midfield with its World Cup players identified by position. Brazil's teams generally play a flat-back four defensive scheme with two inside defenders having the same function. This scheme requires great understanding and experience among the back players, which may not always be successful with your players and teams. We will utilize the sweeper/stopper combination as a simpler alternative.

Finally, there is this sense of constant movement--constant player circulation--in the Brazilian game. A player from the back makes a pass, then runs into space to create further options or to support the play of others. At the same time, another player drops to cover the space just vacated. There is this constant circulation of players through Brazil's scheme of play.

Contrasts of Schools

Let's now contrast four different schools of play: the Brazilian, the English, the Dutch and the German. Each has been influenced and shaped by many factors: climate, national characteristics of the players, and national views on coaching, to name a few. Each has been successful, dominating the world at different points in time. Let's look at how the four differ in their preferred approaches to moving the ball from their defensive-to-attacking thirds. Four basic factors will be analyzed to compare these schools:

1. Speed of the ball from the defense to the attack sector.
2. Possession or safe play of the ball.
3. Safety of the players (minimize the number of situations which could generate injuries).
4. The key surprise - the ability to play the ball in situations that are unpredictable to the opponent.

The Brazilian team (diagram 2) likes to build fast in short passes from the back with safe play so as not to risk losing possession, creating unpredictable attacking situations. It switches early and often away from pressure in its defensive half and looks to penetrate from the opposite flank. If the opponent adjusts defensively, another switch can precede its penetration of the final third. Most often the final penetration stays on the ground with the creative flair we're all so familiar with. Short passing, player circulation, player positioning in support, individual technical skill and creativity and finesse are all characteristic.

The British Philosophy (diagram 3) by contrast, plays more directly out of its back as it looks to enter its attacking third with as few passes as possible. Often its midfield has primarily defensive responsibilities and the play from the back is to target front runners who hold possession or lay the ball off.

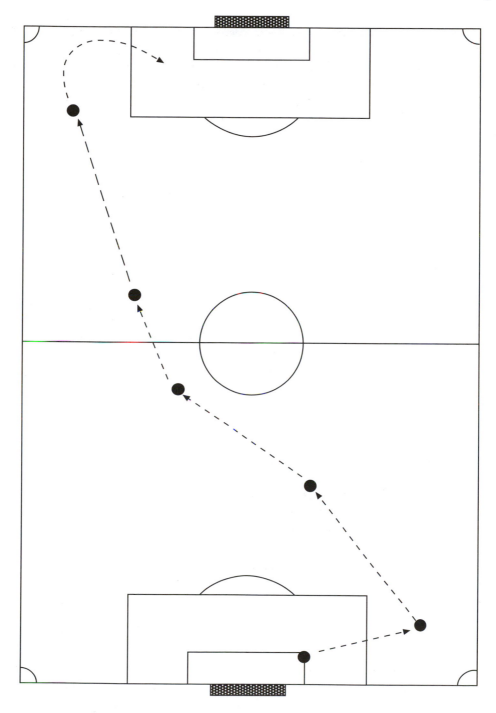

Diagram 2: *South American Philosophy: Brazilian Style.*

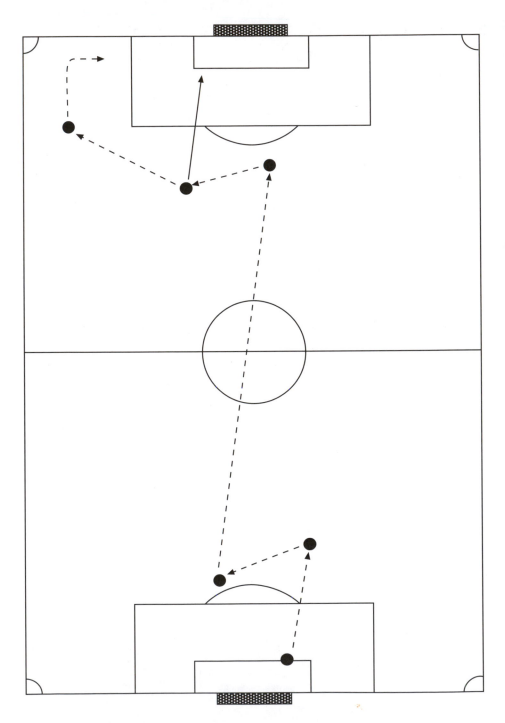

Diagram 3: *European Philosophy: British Style.*

The English don't feel as comfortable in holding possession with short passing sequences so they get the ball from the back to front as directly as possible. Balls in the air, attacks from the flank, fitness, work rate and player toughness are characteristic along with powerful shooting from outside the penalty area and strong offensive heading. These are very predictable attacking patterns and very unsafe to the players.

The Dutch team (diagram 4) on the other hand, likes to take the ball down one flank with a series of short passes, then switch the point of attack to the other flank on entering its attacking half. Usually the switch is made with longer passing. The Dutch don't wish to expose the ball in front of their own goal or take the time to switch early to allow the defense that extra time to recover. Conversely, the Dutch will risk possession with longer balls in the attacking half. Short passing in the defensive half growing longer in the attacking half and strong individual technical skills are again characteristic. They have recently shown the capability to penetrate successfully through the middle with short passes during the qualification games for the World Cup finals in France in 1998.

The German teams (diagram 5) like to attack down the center, maintaining possession with short passing options and the dribble, then look to a flank in their attacking half. Again they're looking to play both more directly and to eliminate the time given the defense to recoup. Flank crossing, work rate, fitness, methodical play, and perfection of individual and group tactics are characteristic.

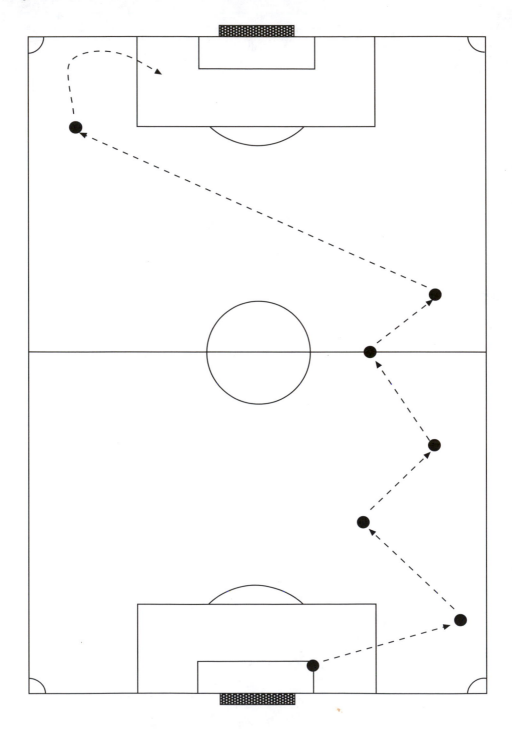

Diagram 4: *European Philosophy: Dutch Style.*

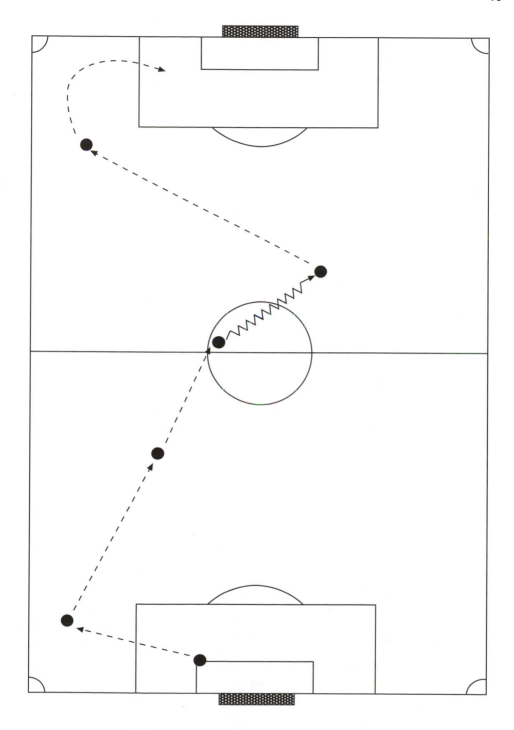

Diagram 5. *European Philosophy: German Style.*

Seasonal Planning

Why should coaches plan their soccer season? Every soccer organization from the youth level to the pro-level should develop
proper planning skills in order to facilitate constant player and
team evaluation and to organize the areas of training that need to be
done.

An important responsibility of the coach is to identify the problems the
team experienced in the last week, last month, and even last year. It is
critical that the coach helps the team to adjust, to improve and to learn
from previous experiences. Success comes from intensive planning and
constant evaluation of results.

Planning enables a coach to verify the quality of practice sessions, apply
a correct ratio of fitness training, avoid boring and repetitive practices,
and observe individual development or lack of development.

Planning means success.

Planning includes comprehensive game analysis addressing the many factors that could interfere with a team achieving its top performance.

Planning does not simply mean setting the time and place that players and coaching staff will meet to cover some of the weak tactical/technical problems the group recently experienced. Planning must be a full analysis of the factors that can change the safe and comfortable pace of operation of the group, which, as we described in the Brazilian philosophy, is a critical ingredient in increasing the probability of success. By the way, success is not an accident; success is work, study, and work, work, work!

Four major considerations must be properly factored in the planning process:

1. Financial resources: At any level the tactics and strategy of team development will be based on the financial resources of the team or club. Technical or tactical development are affected if there is not enough financial support for fields, equipment, accommodations, meals, transportation, salary (Pro-level), and quality of competition to be played. A successful coach must prioritize his plan based on the resources available. Only with proper planning is this possible.

2. Teamwork on and off the field: Each person within the team or club has an ability to contribute to the program. It is important to identify a specific job for each member of the organization. This will increase commitment to the program and allow the coach to focus on team training and development. But this coalition only comes from planning and coordination.

3. Educational philosophy of the organization: Planning should be based on the needs of the soccer organization. For example, the goals of an AYSO youth team are to develop an understanding and love for the game. Its planning must be structured towards long term results; this differs from an MLS team, which needs immediate results.

At the professional level planning is of course quite different. The operation runs as a business. Planning is based on achieving short-range success; winning games, tournaments, and league championships as well as developing players (who can be sold in order to generate income for the organization).

A good example of one of Brazil's most successful coaches is Tele Santana, former coach of Brazilian National Team (1982, 1986) and Sao

Paulo F.C. He won 2 World Club championship titles and numerous national and league tournaments but all the while he never gave up his philosophy of educating young players (on and off the field). Mr. Santana was committed to his plan and worked hard to achieve his results. He used to stay hours after the regular practice sessions teaching and correcting technical and tactical points of the game to any player in need. In addition, he took one of the most exciting teams to the World Cup in 1982, always playing very offensive soccer. His philosophy was a very positive influence on the quality of the Brazilian game today.

4. The fans: Part of successful planning must be to take into consideration the people who support the team or club organization. Many organizations hire great field coaches but do not address the character of the coach. How often do we see teams demonstrate lack of sportsmanship, respect, discipline and, not coincidentally, also a lack of quality soccer.

In today's world of business dominating sport, the financial interest of the player often is more powerful than his love of the game and club jersey, but the fan is the one who will perpetually support the team or club. The fans must be a top priority of the planning of the organization's coach and technical directors.

In addition, there are several other important factors to be analyzed in the coach's season planning:

a. Control the expectations. Many club, high school, college and pro-level teams establish higher goals than realistically can be attained. It is important to not have unreasonable expectations before the pre-season starts because this can jeopardize the full season's planning. The players, fans, directors, media and everybody else will expect results commensurate with these expectations.

Many organizations promise more than the group of players can accomplish, creating further problems for the players because of the excessive pressure.

b. Set realistic goals. Only after the selection process is finished and the weak and strong points of the group are identified will the coach be able to establish the realistic goals of the team for the season.

It is very important to have full control of the activities on and off the field.

SEASON: _____

CHART 1 • MACRO CYCLE

YEAR _____

MONTHS	1	2	3	4	5	6	7	8	9	10	11	12
ACTIVITIES												
Pre-season												
Qualification Season												
Finals												
Post-Season												
Games												
Vacation												
Physical Condition												
Technical Development												
Tactical												
Organizational Period												
Recruiting												
Tryouts												
Int. Competition												
Community Services												
Educational Programs												

NOTE: Month 1 must always be your initial planning period.

This control can be covered in 6 major charts:

1. Chart #1: Macro cycle - Monitoring the frequency of games, practices, and extra activities during the full year, subdivided in monthly activities.

It is important for everybody involved in the soccer organization to know the complete annual schedule. This will:

- Create a very professional understanding about the commitment, peak periods, vacation, trips, etc.

- Help bring together all the members of the soccer organization and always review the plan.

- Provide information on the following year's planning, identifying the positive and negative aspects and come to the right decision.

- Reduce the risk of having excessive or not enough practices or games.

- Help the organization's financial, marketing and promotion planning.

2. Chart #2: Medium cycle. Monitoring the full monthly activities subdivided into weekly scheduling.

Allow the organization to focus closer on the thirty days operation.

3. Chart #3: Micro cycle. Monitoring the weekly activities with daily scheduling. Very important, especially in terms of the coaching staff, observing the day by day problems.

4. Chart #4: Injury/Excuse/Absence. Chart players' absences from practices, games or off field activities, and identify the reasons. At the professional level significant sums of money are invested in players with good technical/tactical abilities who often allow off field problems to interfere with their individual and team performance. At the youth level a common problem is a lack of commitment. In many cases it is better for a coach to select a player with less technical/tactical ability who is highly committed and reliable over a highly skillful player without the desire to improve and make the team better.

Often, a player may lose interest in soccer because of the lack of coaching, conflicting philosophies within the coaching staff or

Year:_____

Season_____

CHART 2
Medium Cycle - 30 (31) Days Planning
Team's Practice Control

Month:_____

	1	2	3	4	5	6	7	8	9	10	11	12	13	14	15	16	17	18	19	20	21	22	23	24	25	26	27	28	29	30	31
Game																															
Days Off																															
Aerobic Resistance																															
Muscle Resistance																															
Agility																															
Flexibility																															
Speed																															
Coordination (Capoeira)																															
Acrobatic Exercises																															
Anaerobic Activity																															
Power of Speed																															
Relaxation Exercises																															
Finishing																															
Ball Control (Trapping)																															
Passes																															
Dribbling																															
Heading																															
Shooting																															
Improvisation																															
Goal Keepers																															
Tactical - Individual																															
Tactical - Group																															
Tactical - Team																															
1. Other Activity																															
2. Other Activity																															

NOTE: Other activities could include vacation, community service and educational programs.

CHART 3 • MICRO CYCLE
Weekly Schedule

Week: 1 - 2 - 3 - 4

Year _____

CLUB: _____

DAYS	Monday		Tuesday		Wednesday		Thursday		Friday		Saturday		Sunday	
	A.M. / P.M.		A.M. / P.M.		A.M. / P.M.		A.M. / P.M.		A.M. / P.M.		A.M. / P.M.		A.M. / P.M.	
ACTIVITIES														
Medical Dept. - Check Out														
Game Day														
Day Off														
Physical Condition														
Physical Tech														
Technical														
Technical - Tactical														
Tactical														
Scrimmaging														
Lecture														
Community Service														
Educational Program														

BRUSA INTERNATIONAL SOCCER INSTITUTE

Chart 4 - Injury / Excuse / Absence

MONTH:

Player	1	2	3	4	5	6	7	8	9	10	11	12	13	14	15	16	17	18	19	20	21	22	23	24	25	26	27	28	29	30	31

lack of consistent and challenging practice intensity. Absenteeism may result. It is important to identify these characteristics during the pre-season and plan accordingly.

To help control this problem of absenteeism in Brazil many teams at the professional level create the "Caixinha" or little safe deposit box. The team selects a 'president' and 'treasurer' from among the coaching staff and players to manage the Caixinha. Before the pre-season starts, all the members pay a deposit fee and a bank account is opened with that money.

The directors of the Caixinha will establish a number of rules. If a rule is broken, such as tardiness or absenteeism, a portion of his monthly salary will be taken away and deposited in the Caixinha account. By the end of the year all the money accumulated will be divided among all the members or used for a team event.

5. Chart #5: Game analysis-monitoring all the factors during the competition.
These factors are subdivided into 4 aspects:
General information:

    a. Competition day: Location, referees number of attendants, weather, etc.
    b. Analysis of your own team.

All of this information will be a great asset as you go through the season.

Starting team, playing time, cards, technical performance and tactical participation.

The left column shows the player's name and number (Eg. 2 to 11) and the substitutions. Your assistant coach will make notes, adding a check mark every time the technical skill is done right or wrong. The ball must switch the speed of the game, offensively, finding a penetration, or defensively, when a mistake is made and the speed of the game will change in favor of the opposite team, ending in counter-attack.

- Right technical performance (R)

- Wrong technical performance (W)

- The right side column will show two soccer fields. The field above will be all of the tactical aspects of the first half from both teams.

- The five aspects to be analyzed are positioned in rows.

- 'Player' row will show the number of the player who took the action.

- "Time" row will show the time during the game when the action happened. Go from minute (1) to (90) or the time used by your team age group.

- R (right)/W (wrong) row will show the result of the action.

- It will be right if the ball took the goal direction and was saved (good keeper performance), the continuity of that play ends in a goal or the goal was scored in that action.

- It will be wrong if the end of the action did not show any positive result. Could be a good shot close to the bar, but only an action requiring the interception of the keeper/defender or a score will be a right result.

- 'Kind of shot' • The part of the body which took the last touch on the ball in that final action.

  eg: Shot with the right leg, (rf) right foot, (h) heading etc.
  It is very important to report the kind of penetration before the action, eg: The ball was passed, or individual penetration. It is important to register from where the action started and ended.

Studying the game analysis.
Remember: Recording the number of victories and losses is easy. The difficult and more important task is evaluating and identifying the reasons for the results.

The coaching staff must meet as soon as the first half is over and briefly go through the important factors that can help during the second half. The meeting will give the head coach a realistic situation, and he must be the one to communicate the problems to the players.

    Note: Technical problems require a private meeting with the player or players involved.

    Tactical problems are addressed to the full team together. Open discussion with the team is fundamental.

    It is important in Chart #5 that we monitor and record the playing time, goals, ball 'steals', cards and off sides. This data will help a coach to have a better understanding of the offensive and defensive performance of his players. This information and the information above will help a coach plan functional training and specific areas (sectors) of team development.

    Prepare game analysis that monitor individual technical performance (Chart #5). Technical skills to be evaluated include passing, trapping, shooting, tackling and heading. These analyses will help a coach to identify the technical problems experienced by each player. Based on these evaluations, an individual training program should be set up and each player should be responsible to devote personal practice time to address these weaknesses. Individual progress must be observed and expected in subsequent games.

Chart #5 • Tactical aspects:

Prepare tactical game evaluation and analysis: The final analysis to be done is related to the team performance. A coach must observe player movement, positioning and timing of penetration with each movement of the ball in play. It is very important for players to understand the concept of unified team play. Team unity will help to generate faster pace of the ball and speed of play while still allowing for possession and the creation of unpredictable options in the attack.

Points to be analyzed:
- Position to the ball. Is there a diagonal angle of support?

- Showing to the ball. Has the player identified the correct reception position?

- Number of touches a player uses.

- Number of consecutive passes among the players without loss of possession.

- Build up from the defense. Is the defense playing fast and safe? Identify where the ball is losing the speed of transition.

- Are possessions and passes leading to unpredictable and effective offensive penetrations?

Implementation of any soccer program depends on an organization with expertise in the different areas of the game.

Chart 5
Game Analysis

Date:____/____/____

Location:_____

Weather:_____Temp:_____

Championship:_____

Game:_____

Time:_____

Of Expect.:_____

Referee:_____

Linesman 1:

Linesman 2:

Note:

1st Half

#	Player's Name	Shoot R W	Pass R W	Track R W	Head R W	F	OS	G	N
2									
3									
4									
5									
6									
7									
8									
9									
10									
11									
( )									
( )									
( )									

Player

Time

R / W

Kind Sh.

| 11 | 10 | 9 | 8 | 7 | 6 | 5 | 4 | 3 | 2 | 1 | Sh. Number |

Player

Time

R / W

Kind Sh.

| 11 | 10 | 9 | 8 | 7 | 6 | 5 | 4 | 3 | 2 | 1 | Sh. Number |

2nd Half

Notes:

Keeper	R.S. R W	L.S. R W	BW R W	Pass R W	PK	F	P	G	N

Opponent:

1- (K) _____   _____   _____

_____   _____   _____

_____   _____   _____

_____   _____   _____

_____   _____   _____

Summary: _____

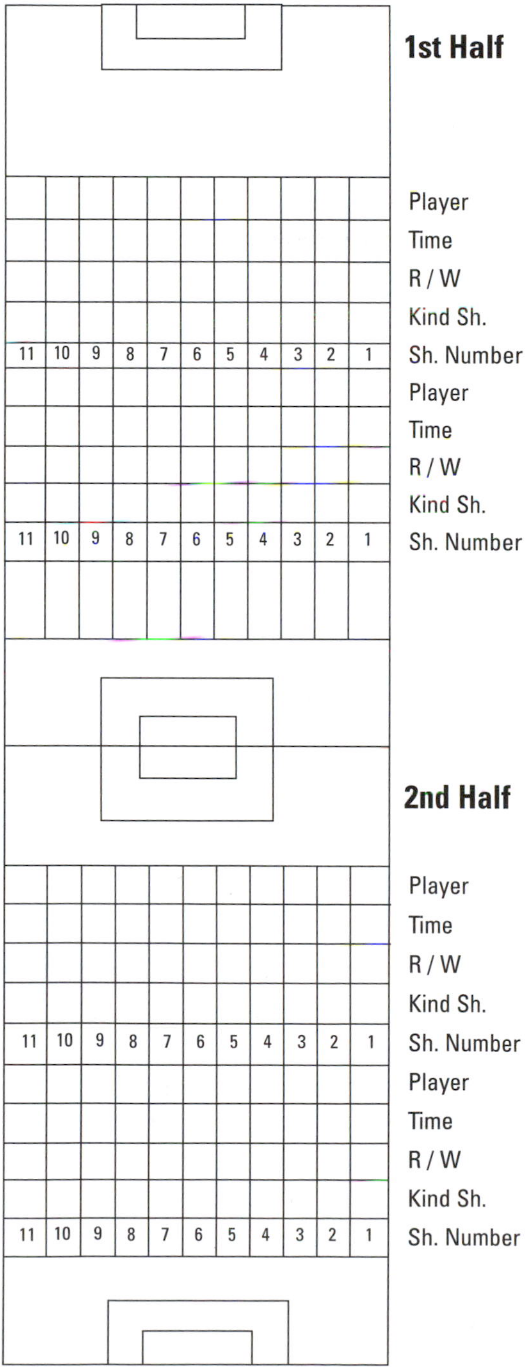

_____

_____

_____

Player

Time

R / W

Kind Sh.

| 11 | 10 | 9 | 8 | 7 | 6 | 5 | 4 | 3 | 2 | 1 | Sh. Number |

Player

Time

R / W

Kind Sh.

| 11 | 10 | 9 | 8 | 7 | 6 | 5 | 4 | 3 | 2 | 1 | Sh. Number |

General Manager: The responsibility of the general manager is to manage all outside of the field activities and commitments such as financial planning, sponsorships, fund raising, public relations and community support. At the professional level, the general manager normally sets the budget available for coaching and player contracts, and represents the coaching staff and players to the board of directors in any matter.

Technical (Coaching) Director: The coaching director is responsible for establishing the philosophy of the soccer organization from the development level (6 to 10 years old) to the competitive and select program (11 through 19 years old) to the pro-level. Normally the coaching director is also directly responsible for coaching the oldest age group of the soccer organization (youth programs) or for the pro-team in the case of professional clubs.

The technical (coaching) director should be responsible for establishing the curriculum and educating the coaches responsible for the progressive education at the different levels.

Assistant Coaches: At the professional clubs assistant coaches are responsible for overseeing and implementing all the coaching director functions. They provide the supplementary training to the players when special sessions are required. Also, assistant coaches scout teams to be played and target players who might be contracted by the club.

At the youth level, assistant coaches are responsible for team training and maintaining the consistency of the philosophy and methodology of the technical (coaching) director. Assistant coaches also help chart and record required game and player data (as discussed above).

Goalkeeper Coach: This important function is of course responsible for the development of the goalkeepers at all levels. It is important that the goalkeeper coach train the older club keepers and enlist them in the training of the younger goalkeepers.
(Chart #6 Goalkeepers schedule control)

Physical Conditioning Trainer - Chart 7: This position is responsible for physical fitness evaluation, design and implementation of fitness training programs, and supporting each player in their specific needs during the season. They will be assisting with the speed and coordination to the technical skills.

YEAR

SEASON

BRUSA INTERNATIONAL SOCCER INSTITUTE

Monthly Control

Chart 6 - Goalkeepers Schedule Control

	1	2	3	4	5	6	7	8	9	10	11	12	13	14	15	16	17	18	19	20	21	22	23	24	25	26	27	28	29	30	31
Power and Strength																															
Coordination & Agility																															
Flexibility																															
Reaction Speed																															
Stance																															
Catching																															
Footwork																															
Deflective																															
Diving																															
Crossed Balls																															
Boxing																															
Shot Handling																															
Mental Discipline																															
Courage																															
Confidence																															
Leadership																															
Concentration																															
Training Ethics																															
Throw & Roll																															
Shooting																															
Punt																															
Drop Kick																															
Goal Kick																															
Controlling Tempo																															
Break - Away																															
Positioning																															
Positioning and Angle																															
Restarts and Wall Sit.																															
Communication and Defender Org.																															
Anticipation																															
Initiating the Offense																															
Constructive Possession																															

BRUSA INTERNATIONAL SOCCER INSTITUTE

Chart 7 - Physical Conditioning Capacity

YEAR

SEASON

	1	2	3	4	5	6	7	8	9	10	11	12	13	14	15	16	17	18	19	20	21	22	23	24	25	26	27	28	29	30	31
Speed																															
Agility																															
Aerobic Training																															
Muscular Resistance																															
Leaping Ability																															
Flexibility																															
Joint Flexibility																															
Stretching																															
Coordination																															
Acrobatic Exercises																															
10 Laps																															
Respiratory Exercises																															
Power with Speed																															
Relaxation Exercises																															
Courage																															
Ball Control (Trapping)																															
Passes																															
Dribbling																															
Heading																															
Shooting																															
Other Activities																															
Goal Keepers																															
Tactical																															

E.C. Vitoria 1996 Dallas Cup Champion. E.C. Vitoria is among the top 3 worldwide soccer clubs in successful planning at the youth level.

Organization of a Soccer Club

A common approach to the organization of the soccer education curriculum within a club is to divide the club or soccer organization into four departments.

1. Development Dept. 6 to 9 years old. This department must have some of the best educator coaches of the organization. The major responsibility of coaches at this level is keeping the game fun, and developing body coordination and a sound foundation of ball control.

The curriculum at this age should be primarily based on fun. Enjoying the game is always a great motivation. Practice sessions should have exercises to develop coordination, agility, and speed of reaction (developed through circuit training with the ball). Training with small rubber balls is utilized and helpful in all the body coordination drills. The curriculum for 6 year olds is developed with the participation of the parents in practices; they play together.

The continuity of the technical development is based on fun educational games and small sided games with small goals (no keepers). Specific keeper training can be provided to all the children in this age group.

2. Competitive Dept. 10 to 16 years old. This group of players will be given extra supervision and assistance to increase the speed of their learning process.

3. Select Players Dept. U11 through U19. For players at a serious level of development and competition. This group will usually train at least 3 times a week giving them 6 hours of education. Training will be devoted to physical conditioning with the ball, technical skills and tactical concepts and strategies.

4. Professional Level Dept. Ideally, a successful club will be able to utilize a significant number of players generated from their youth program. If a specific position can not be filled adequately with players from the youth level, an outside player must be hired.

A good example of this organization is the E.C. Vitoria Club in Brazil. In the last two years the club has been dedicated to the development of the youth program while at the same time trying to keep the professional team among the top 10 teams in Brazil. E.C. Vitoria has recently won several top youth tournaments around the world such as the Phillips Cup (Holland) 95-96, the Dallas Cup (USA) 96-97, and the Mannheim Cup (Germany) 97. In the next three years the Club will be able to export the older, more experienced players to many countries and replace them with younger, well prepared players of similar quality. This structure and cycle of education allows the club the time to properly prepare the players, the players the time to develop, and the club the ability to profit financially from the sale of players and the corresponding influx of sponsors and advertisers resulting from quality performances and successful competitions.

Development Objectives

Competitive Dept. The objectives at the Competitive level are the same for the select level at these ages - the emphasis is on technical skills. This group is considered the B level team for each age group. The reason to maintain the competitive level is that many players will have a late development. With good supervision and training many players will progress and tryout the following year and make the Select team (A team).

A good soccer organization must develop specific age group Depts. to really establish the objectives to be accomplished in each one, and be able to better monitor the player-coaching development.

U11/12 Dept. The major goal for this group is to develop the basic technical skills of the game:
- Ball control
- Dribbling (both feet)
- Shooting (driving/curve) (from outside the box)
- Passing inside-outside of the foot (also with curve)
- Crossing (short/long)
- Defensive and offensive heading
- Finishing (inside penalty area)
- Anticipation
- Improvisation

Apply these technical skills in game situations against pressure and defenders.

Positioning for both the defense and offense will be introduced at this age level.

Local and state competitions will be entered for match experience.

U13/U14 Dept. The development at this age level will focus on speed of reaction of all technical skills in game situations from 2 v 1 through 6 v 5. Concentrate on developing equal technical skill with both feet.

It is customary at all levels of Brazilian soccer, even professional, to review and practice the technical skills as a routine part of training.

Intensive training in the 4 basic aspects of Brazilian soccer is part of U13/U14. These must become automatic decisions.

1. Playing the ball on the ground.

2. Minimizing the number of touches.

3. Receiving the ball and switching the point of attack.

4. Diagonal positioning - defensive and offensive. Showing for the ball.

Intensity of training in both offense and defense will increase. In addition, the players at this level should begin to learn how to play in all the sectors of the field. (Defensive - Midfield - Attacking) The different pressures on the ball, circulation of the ball and rotation of the players (defensive) are also introduced at this level.

Local and state level competition with some national competitions should be entered for match experience.

U15/16 Dept. The major developmental goal at this level is the technical and tactical training for both the individual player and the team.

- As we said, always review the technical skills.

- Identify the best sector (defense/midfield/forward) for each one of the players and develop his expertise in that sector.

- Intensive tactical planning (patterns).

- Reinforce the cycle of the game in different situations and types of pressure, and different strategies.

- Total understanding of how to build from the back with inside/outside penetration.

Local, state and national competitions and some international tournaments should be entered for match experience.

U17/U19 Dept. The major goal at this level is to develop the tactical knowledge and strategies to be applied in different systems (3-5-2/4-4-2/4-2-4).

Develop an understanding of the different kinds of pressure and the corresponding movement and circulation of the midfielders. Full cycle of the game must be understood by the team.

Full schedule of local, national, and international competition is advised. Participate in competitions with Brazilian teams.

Player Selection

The next step is to identify and select the best group of players that will fit your coaching philosophy and organizational needs.

At the youth level a coach has the opportunity to access players through parent networks and advertisements in the newspapers. It is important to explain your major goals and the benefits of participation in your soccer program.

At the college level the evaluation is often made only after a commitment has been made to the player. References from competent and honest coaches can save much time and money for the college coaches. College coaches often discover attitude and commitment problems with new players which can jeopardize a successful season. References should include an evaluation of a player's maturity, attitude and character.

At the professional level the budget again is a big factor. Players come from different sources. Many countries such as Brazil, Holland, England, and Germany are developing professional-ready players very young. These systems allow coaches an opportunity to develop the players' soccer skills along with the players' attitude and character.

Clubs like E.C. Vitoria have scouts all over the country selecting the youth players with the abilities to play at the club. The child must pass the first tryout in his city. If approved, the second step will be to go to Salvador, Bahia to train and play with his age group team. If approved, the player will move to Vitoria's center of training and become part of the Club.

The number of players per team is around 28 players. This means that when a better player is discovered, an existing player may be asked to leave the club. Developing youth players in these systems have a big risk of failure if the coaching is not done correctly because of the inescapable pressure put on these

Bebeto (1994 World Champion) is one of the players that started his soccer career in the youth development program at the E.C. (Esporte Clube) Victoria.

young players to succeed. The youngest age recommended to move to a pro-club is 14 years of age.

Tryouts

It is very important that you, as the head coach, be careful to not jeopardize the unity of your team. Many times excessive rotations of players can create a lack of the development of the tactical concepts. If a new player is coming to the tryouts to replace somebody who knows your coaching philosophy, understands the concepts and has a positive attitude; you should definitely think twice before replacing him. This new player must really have better technical skills and some qualities for the specific position you are looking for.

IMPORTANT QUALITIES TO IDENTIFY BY POSITION

Capacities Positions	Technical	Leadership	Body type	Speed
Keeper	3	3	3	3
Outside F. Backs	2	2	1	3
Libero (Sweeper)	3	3	3	3
Stopper	2	2	2	2/3
C.M.defensive	2/3	3	2	2
C.M.Offensive	3	2	1-2	2/3
Outside Midfields	2/3	2	1-2	2/3
Forwards	2	1-2	2-3	2-3

You should plan your tryouts upon your needs.

It is important that you understand the characteristics of each position, and how to evaluate the players available correctly. You can always develop technical skills, improve tactical concepts and physical conditioning aspects, but be careful with the personality and the attitude of the player towards the group.

Explanation of the qualities:

Technical: Ability to perform the skills correctly, making the right decisions under pressure.
   1. In the development process.
   2. Must have the ability to perform in many pressure situations.
   3. Must be able to perform in any pressure situation.

Leadership:
   1. It is not required from this player.
   2. It is important this player have some communication. skills, and be able to help the team, especially when in high pressure situations.
   3. Player with the capacity to lead the team during the competition. He is able to communicate and support the coach's requests.

Body type: The physical characteristics of the player:
1. Any athletic body condition is acceptable.
2. Require some specific aspects such as: Tall, strong body, short and strong, thin etc.
3. A player will fit the necessary needs as a good athlete in terms of size, strength, etc. It is important we mention that in our methodology the size and speed are factors for the inside defensive positions such as: Sweeper, stopper (inside defenders) and defensive midfielder.

Speed:
1. Does not need to be very fast in decisions, with and without the ball.
2. Regular speed.
3. Speed is a big factor to accomplish this style of game.

A well-planned technical/tactical evaluation is necessary to give the coaches a fair opportunity to observe all the players interested in his program.

You should have a minimum number of participants to create the environment of challenge and competition necessary to put some pressure on all the participants.

The minimum number of players for an effective tryout is:

U11 and above through pro - 20 field players and 2 keepers.

U10 - 16 players and 2 keepers. (no tryouts, only placement) team A/B.

U 8 - 10 players (everybody tries as keeper) (no tryouts, only placement) Team A/B.

In college or upper level tryouts it is useful to have older, more experienced players involved to provide proper challenge and player numbers.

Players go through the registration and receive a number that is placed on the front or back of their shirt.

The coaching staff will receive a sheet with the following information:
- Name of the player
- Date of birth
- Preferred positions
- Registration number

Stations should be set up for evaluation. Each coach responsible for a station should be able to explain:
- **How to do it?**
- **When to apply it?**
- **Why to use it?**

In terms of technical or tactical aspects of the game.

The stations should be divided based on the number of players to be evaluated.

Never allow more than 10 players per station and do not let your try-out sessions be longer than 3 hours for U15 and above (including pro) and 2 hours for U14 and below. The quality of performance of the players will decrease and wrong judgments and decisions could be made.

At each station keep the quality of players balanced during game conditions.

The best players should be put together at the end of the evaluation to play a full-sided game without restrictions. This is the time when the final decisions are to be made.

Warm up - 15 min.

Brazilian warm-up without the ball and stretching. Younger ages need more explanation of the proper warm up movements and sequences. A good warm-up is fundamental before starting the tryout. Coaches will be better able to evaluate body coordination.

Station #1:

1 v 1 with two goals. The objective is to evaluate the technical skill and decision making (both defensive and offensive) in the most common pressure situation. Use two regular size goals for the age group of players you are evaluating. Each player should have his own ball.

For duration, we recommend:
- a. U10 and below - 10 sec.
- b. U14 and below - 15 sec.
- c. U15 and above - 20 sec.

The time is based on the level of ability to keep possession of the ball and scoring or defending the ball. Maximum time to be allowed is 20 sec.

Points to observe: Individual offensive and defensive aspects. It is important to explain and demonstrate which aspects you will be observing.

Defensive:
- When the player should tackle or delay.
- The defensive line (the player should be between the center of the goal and the ball).
- Body position: one leg forward, knees must be bent, upper body down and arms up.

Offensive:
Option #1 - If the defender comes with the proper pressure, delaying the attack, the attacker should:
- Use outside foot in the direction of the attacker's weak leg
- Then cut inside and take a shot.

Option #2 - If the defender comes too fast, without any control, the forward should:
- Maneuver past the defender as fast as possible using his individual ball skills.

Option #3 - If the defender comes too slowly to pressure, the forward should:
- Take a shot immediately.

Station #2:
Regular or smaller-sided game with three goals. The objective of this station is to evaluate the natural positioning where the players feel most comfortable. Set up three goals or flags. Use 1/2 field of the age group field size.

Rules:
1. A team must score in 2 other goals and defend their own goal.
2. No consecutive goals at the same goal.
3. Count goals against and goals for.
4. Introduce 2 balls into the game.

As soon as the game starts each player will move to the attack, midfield or defensive zone naturally without being asked. The forwards will be moving from goal to goal asking for the ball. The midfielders will be dropping to the defense to receive the ball and start the attack. The defenders will stay in the back and rarely will move to the attack.

This station is very important to identify a player's level of tactical experience and ability. Observe where each player is most comfortable.

Station #3:

Game Condition: 2 full teams - 11 v 11, 8 v 8, 5 v 5. The primary objective is to evaluate the speed of decision making of the players when in possession of the ball.

Rules:
3 touches - 5 to 10 min. (all the groups).
2 touches - 5 min. (U11 and above and U10).
1 touch - 3 min. (only for U11 and above).

Good players are the ones that make the best decision available when in possession of the ball and take the minimum time possible. Remember, our philosophy is premised on safety of possession, speed of the ball and constantly surprising counter-attacks.

The coach will probably observe that almost all the players can play comfortably when playing 3 touches. The number of players playing successfully will be reduced when play goes to 2 touches. The players that play with one touch without difficulty should be your play makers, the spine of the team (sweeper (libero) - center midfield defensive (CMD) - outside midfield - offensive midfield - and one attacker (+ keeper).

Station #4:

Regular game. The objective is to evaluate the players' understanding of the 4 basic aspects of the Brazilian soccer approach.
  • Use 2 goals or flags marking the goals.

  • The time in this station will be divided into 4 segments: Start a new segment every 5 minutes.

  a. Ball on the ground. Players must keep the ball on the ground except for crossing from the end line or shooting from outside the penalty area.

  b. Playing 2 touches. Players must keep the ball on the ground while playing with a two touch maximum restriction.

  c. Receiving and switching to the opposite side from where the ball was passed. The players should show to the ball, always turning the body to the opposite side to avoid playing back to the pressure zone and, therefore, be able to restart a fast counter-attack through the opposite side.

  d. Players must show only in diagonal to the ball. The players with the ball can only pass the ball in (offensive or defensive) diagonal.

Station #5:

Regular field with the maximum number of players allowed for that age group.

- The objective is to evaluate the players in different game situations.

- The time in this station will be divided into 3 segments:

a. Play only with the weak foot when passing or shooting.

b. Play with 2 balls at the same time. Concentrate on marking and attacking simultaneously.

c. Outside of the foot passing and constant support.

Station #6:

Speed. The objective is to identify the speed of the player. Correct the arms' movement. 50 yards against the clock.

It is important to identify the fastest player of the group and use this player as a reference point for the rest of the group.

Station #7:

Shooting. The objective is to evaluate the correct technique, accuracy and power of the shooter. Use 2 goals facing each other at a distance of 1/4 of the soccer field relative to the players' age group.

Players start from the side of the opposite goal, penetrate and take the shot.

Aspects to be observed:

- Penetration with the ball using the outside of the foot.

- Placement of the ball at a diagonal at the correct distance from the opposite foot.

- Proper bending of the knee of the planting leg.

- Adequate distance from the opposite foot to the ball.

- Correct technique of striking the ball.

The players should change goal lines after shooting. Players should take shots for at least 10 minutes with each foot.

After the tryouts it is important to explain to the players not selected the reason(s) they have not been chosen and give each one of them suggestions for improvement and encouragement to try again in the future. Even at the pro-level it is always important to be fair, honest and friendly

c. Basic Education. This is the base principle that builds the character of the person. It has a very heavy influence from the family environment. Identification of the character of the individual through his personality.

d. Excessive expectations from media, fans, parents, agents, club directors and finally the player and coach himself.

e. Cultural Education. The level of formal school education and specific soccer/sports education will greatly influence the behavior of each player or coach. Players are constantly challenging the expertise of the coaches and in many cases coaches expect perfection without teaching or sharing adequate information with the players.

f. Social and financial aspects. Often coaches or managers do not confront problems with the players, especially the stars, because they are intimidated and afraid of losing their jobs and their stable financial situation (pro-level). Or, in the case of youth players, coaches will compromise their beliefs and philosophy in order to appease a player or his parents (youth soccer in North America).

Youth players, particularly from under-developed nations, come from very poor families. In many cases the family will direct the best way that is possible in their attitudes (basic education) but unfortunately the lack, of parenthood supervision does not provide the cultural education, and the possibility to play soccer professionally becomes the only option and induces them to dedicate all of their time and effort towards this goal. Often as a result these young players will give up school and education. Unfortunately, in many cases their success in soccer ends before achieving professional success and their future opportunities outside of soccer are limited.

In more developed countries the social and financial influences take the players in a different direction. The players who are playing soccer normally come from the middle and upper income segments of the society. The parents will prioritize the cultural education (school) and strong parental supervision. The desire to make the commitment to become a successful college or professional player is found in only a small number of youth players. Too many other sports and alternative activities are available. There is little incentive to jeopardize a comfortable living environment for the challenge and demands to be a high-level soccer athlete.

g. Superstitions: Superstitions, regardless of the silliness or oddity of the belief or behavior, can affect a player's mental readiness for the game. A player must possess first the belief that he can be successful. A player's mental state, though not as quantifiable as technical ability, is as important, if not more so, than that player's technical skill or the team's tactical plan.

In Brazil, I was part of championship teams whose coaching staff met at midnight before every match so that the head coach could place salt in the field's corners. I played for coaches who wore the same shirt all season, who didn't change socks. Silly as these rituals might seem, if they reassure a belief or instill a confidence, they can impact a player's or team's ability to perform at peak levels.

Prior to entering the field of play, it is common to see Brazilian teams form a circle where players and coaches hold hands, touch feet, and pray together, asking for protection against injuries. This practice builds team unity, respect, and focus, and acknowledges that nothing worthwhile can be accomplished without God guiding us. Soccer offers an opportunity to learn about life's challenges and lessons and to develop spiritually. The game is more than just a win or loss, it is a chance to grow by experiencing life's highest highs and lowest lows - frequently within the span of the same match - and reacting to these moments and learning from your experiences and emotions in these situations.

Importance of the Coach as a Role Model

The coach is an educator, a guide, a friend, and sometimes a father or mother. It is important that he or she exhibit good, positive behavior for his players. No matter what the age of the players, the actions and words of that coach influence players and are noticed by others. The coach should set the right example in his attitudes toward the team, toward opponents, toward parents and officials. Avoid the use of profanity at all times, especially during practices and games, and require the same standards from your players, directors, parents and fans. Avoid emotional outcries deriding opponents or officials. Players follow your example. When you exhibit this negative type of behavior they are likely to challenge your authority and lose respect.

Importance of the relationship between coach, player and parents

In any part of the world and in any sport you normally will find very strong family support behind a successful athlete. Soccer is no different.

Parents seek the best opportunities for their children. Usually to parents this means playing on the best team (normally the ones that win the most) or playing for the best coach (again the one producing winning teams).

It is important that parents understand that winning does not always equate with proper fundamental development of young players. Pressure at a young age often intimidates the player from trying new challenges and taking risks during the game, thereby limiting his self-confidence and creativity. At the youth level the soccer experience should be focused on:

a. The fun of playing. Interest will naturally increase if the young player is having fun and with that interest will come the desire and commitment to improve. One of the primary reasons the child decided to start playing was because of the social activity, in other words, enjoying the experience with his friends.

b. Skills development. Develop the technical skills sufficient enough to generate the interest and confidence to continue participation in the sport. Having fun and young player's progressive developments are closely tied together. If the child is enjoying the experience that child will come early to practice and will complain when the soccer activity is over.

The concept of winning and successful tactical play will be a consequence of patient technical development. An emphasis on winning and the corresponding team tactics does not allow time to learn the basic skills and principles of the game.

Unfortunately, more than 50% of the children in North America leave soccer during the transition from 10 to

The fun of playing - the goal celebration.

11/12 years old or from recreational to traveling, 'select' programs. Of course, other sports and the increased costs to families are factors as well. However, the early excessive pressure to win regardless of the ability or capacity of each individual or team are important influences, often intimidating or demoralizing the young player and consequently decreasing his fun and interest. It is not common to find this type of organized, competitive system at the youth level in other parts of the 'soccer world'. Something to think about!

Any information a child receives must go through a proper learning process. **This process has four major phases:**

Phase 1 • Introduction of the fundamentals.

Phase 2 • Experience through repetitions without pressure initially and progressing to low intensity pressure with frequent explanations, demonstrations and corrections.

Phase 3 • Progress to match conditions, increasing the pressure. Explain the likelihood of frequent mistakes and emphasize that this experience is a normal part of the learning process.

Phase 4 • Post-game evaluation. Repeat this cycle of progressive education. Only when the proper level of understanding and proficiency of that fundamental skill is achieved for that specific age group can a new fundamental be introduced. Each child has a unique personality, level of coordination and pace of understanding. A coach must be able to identify the best way to approach and positively influence each one of them.

Many North American parents have grown up appreciating the long pass and the long kick in American football, the long home run in baseball, and the long three-point shot in basketball. Consequently, they often think successful soccer is kicking the ball hard and long. Parents often don't appreciate the difference between kicking the ball and passing it. Teaching parents the game and educating them as to your philosophy of play is often as important to building a successful program as coaching the players.

At the youth level we recommend that the coach give an explanation of the educational process to parents and players. We recommend:

a. Game analysis. Early in the season videotape one of your games and then schedule a meeting with all the players and parents. Review your team's style in the last season (maximum 10 minutes) outlining the strengths and weaknesses. Then for the next 10 minutes show a tape of the Brazilian team playing, observing the basic aspects of this style: balls on the ground, minimum number of touches (short or long when necessary, and why), positioning always in diagonal, and finally receiving balls with an orientation towards the opposite side.

Explain that the long ball tactic is fast but can be physically unsafe and becomes too predictable, as the defenders are able to anticipate the attacks and counterattacks. The short pass strategy is still a fast game but much safer while allowing an unpredictable attack.

Finally, show the game you just videotaped and explain the steps you are introducing related to the new philosophy and the goals you expect to achieve. Ask for patience and understanding. Everybody must learn how to mark and defend and players will be put in different positions to foster total development. Keeping the parents informed and well educated will enhance team commitment and foster overall support of the program.

Patience is critical to this first phase of education. The team will lose some games, probably because they will try to build from the back, to play a more controlled game, and to pass the ball instead of just kicking it. They will be predictable in their decisions and slow in their pace of play.

You will start to see some success after 6 to 7 games. If possible, try to schedule easy games early in the season. This allows the players to focus on reception and passing (technical points). After the 3rd game they are probably ready to concentrate on the diagonal positioning to receive the ball. With more education and experience, gradually increase the level of challenge. Soon players, coaches and parents will experience tremendous joy and excitement over the quality and style of soccer demonstrated. However, your next coaching challenge will be the players' Wall of Frustration.

Wall of Frustration

Wall of frustration is a normal consequence that happens to many young players as they get older and transition to a more challenging environment. Many of these players used to be the 'stars' on their team, generally because of their physical size and speed. Because of these early developmental advantages these players never had to focus on their technical skills. This transition to a new style asks for more team unity, ball control and creativity.

This unseen wall is created by players to justify their mistakes. Leaving the field a player will often blame the field, the referees, or the lack of team unity. He might even criticize teammates for their excessive mistakes. All of this provides a convenient excuse for his own poor performance or the teams' poor results.

Wall of frustration can also be caused by:

1. An excessive importance placed on winning rather than the development of the player and having fun. Soccer in North America has evolved as a middle and upper class sport. Parents are generally well educated and successful in their business and professional lives and they seem to expect their children to be successful (win) at what they do, even youth soccer.

   These expectations increase the level of pressure and the natural reaction, the wall of frustration, occurs if the success expected does not occur quickly enough.

2. Excessive criticism from coaches or parents that doesn't allow the player to learn from mistakes.

3. General lack of communication between coach, player, and parent as to his or her expectations. Many times a coach will criticize a player's performance without offering any solution to the problem. An effective coach will spend time developing the necessary skills that a player is lacking, correct mistakes and always look for the solution as soon as possible. In order to correct the problem, it is necessary to share these problems with other coaches who have experienced these same issues or challenges. Be open to constructive input and helpful advice.

Finally, communicate your expectations very clearly. Be accepting of players' mistakes, offer solutions to their problems, and, if necessary, point out incorrect parental behavior.

THE PARENT COACH

A major challenge of the parent/coach is determining when to be the coach and when to be the father/mother. Many parents become coaches because of the lack of coaches in North America. The fast growing number of players outpaced the growth of coaches.

Vital psychological and technical development occurs in the younger ages. Normally the coaches at these ages will be dads and moms with a great deal of desire and dedication but with little education and experience in coaching youth soccer. These coaches educate themselves through books, videos and coaching courses. The parent/coaches' commitment is a big reason for the rapid growth of the sport in North America.

It is important that these parent/coaches receive an education exposing them to all kinds of soccer philosophies and coaching methodologies. The parent/coach spends more time educating himself and planning practice than many college or pro coaches. These coaches are learning the love and passion for soccer and passing this on to the young players who will be the next soccer generation. This love and passion must be based in fun. A North American soccer style is starting to be developed as these parent/coaches combine the European influences with the Brazilian philosophy and input.

Often a parent/coach will quit coaching after his son/daughter leaves the game or graduates. These coaches should continue coaching and begin the process with another younger team, applying their previous experience and allowing the young players to benefit from their commitment and knowledge.

IMPORTANCE OF EDUCATION

Not every one of the youth players will be well educated. Socio-economic factors influence a child's opportunity, capability and desire to do well in school. That's not to say that one has to spend time in school to be educated. A child can learn proper behavior from his parents: the so-called basic education based on the principles of respect and common courtesy for other human beings and nature. The culture in North America also values the classical (Cultural combined

Rai has been one of the most successful international players. His high cultural education facilitated his quality adaptation to the european customs, traditions and especially the tactical game variations.

with the environment) education - certain fundamentals are needed to facilitate human interaction such as reading, writing, and math. Most often a player acquires these needs at school. He learns to function in the modern world for his life after soccer.

In Brazil - as in many other countries of the world - many good players come from very poor backgrounds where they spend their early years working to help support their family. Any spare time is spent playing soccer and education goes by the wayside. The game is viewed as the player's way out of poverty, the road to wealth and to establishing identity, much as basketball is viewed in North America as a way out of the ghetto.

There is currently an effort in a few clubs in Brazil to establish mandatory schools inside the Clubs. A lack of schooling and consistent cultural learning affects a player's decision-making and can become a limiting factor to a player's performance, particularly tactical awareness and team play.

It is difficult for many skillful players in Brazil to develop their tactical intelligence. They have developed their technical skills in a natural environment playing on the streets or anywhere else a ball and other players were to be found. However, the tactical aspects were never presented. Their technical ability earned them a spot in the youth department of the professional club. Many clubs in Brazil do not see cultural education as an important ingredient to the eventual success of that player. Even as some of these players acquire an ability to make correct decisions individually these decisions are not always the best team decision based on tactical priorities.

Skillful players often have great expectation placed upon them. They frequently find it difficult to adjust to the coach's system and many players, having hit their wall of frustration, will quit the game without any other professional skill (leading too often to alcohol and substance abuse problems).

We have learned in our BRUSA educational programs that young North American players, with their developed mental capabilities, perform very impressively in their tours in Brazil, especially after just a short time of training, even those players without strong technical abilities. They tend to play well as a team, even if they have not played much together before. Part of this success is directly attributable to the educational system in North America, which has prepared these players to receive information, think and respond faster than a technically sound Brazilian player lacking this cultural educational background.

Even playing in the Brazilian environment, where the speed of reaction and decision-making is much faster than their previous experience in

North America, the results are very positive. Educated players tend to be much better tactical players than the merely skillful players. It is important to build a team with a combination of skillful players and players who are intelligent and good thinkers, even if their skill level is not as proficient.

It is important that we remember that the aggressive or abnormal conduct or behavior we see in our players on the field is likely a sign of frustration or a fear of failure. This behavior is a player's way to protect himself against his own technical or tactical weaknesses.

It is a coach's responsibility to support the educational opportunities of his young players, helping to prepare them for life after soccer.

Psychological Principles

"The clean mind is always able to think faster, increasing the players speed of reaction. This fast reaction will generate quick decision making. The faster the decision making, the more time that player has to analyze the best decision to make, becoming unpredictable in the direction of that play, promoting the effectiveness of the attack."

A clean and healthy mind results from control of the emotions and balance of each individual personality, and this achievement belongs to the field of Sports Psychology.

Sports psychology is the science responsible for observing, analyzing, and educating coaches and athletes about the factors that could interfere with their success or failure inside the environment of competition. Sports psychology has been one of the most improved areas in sports over the last decade and has been so helpful in the development of the game of soccer.

This field is so fascinating and complex, it would take us a new book to deeply cover this principle. We will, therefore, focus on the daily common routine of the team and some obstacles which may prevent the team from accomplishing the edge of the performance individually and as a group.

We will briefly describe the factors which could interfere in the coach/player relationship and could positively or negatively affect the player and team performance. These factors will change the athletic balance. This balance is composed of the physical, intellectual and spiritual state of each individual. A good balance will promote good feelings of liberty of action, improve self esteem, and originate the confidence to perform under high pressure and be able to respond positively to any unexpected situation.

1. **Physical:** The ability to perform the movement of the body in a speed requested by the intellect.

2. **Spiritual:** The development of personal beliefs and principles and the ability to identify right and wrong. This is the basis for any human development.

3. **Intellectual:** The way to approach any challenging situation with full control of the actions, knowing that physical mistakes will occur many times.

The major goals of the applicability of the psychological principle are;

1. Avoiding over excitement, which may promote extra spending of energy, or have the opposite effect of total lack of motivation. Both can interfere in the physical balance, decreasing the technical quality of that performance or motivation to produce during the game.

2. Understanding the factors which could interfere in the psychological process of developing high performance conditions, combined with the relations of coach - player - management and fans.

3. Understanding the importance of adjusting the system to the player and not the player to the system.

4. Accepting situations of failure and success as part of the competitive environment and taking the positive points in any of those.

5. Applying common sense in any situation during the game and accepting normal mistakes as part of the development process.

In this chapter we will discuss the importance of understanding the psychological factors that could interfere between yourself and your players, and relay the appropriate approach in all the different phases of coach - player relationship in preparation for high performance in any level of competition, under any level of pressure and in any environment. These psychological factors were observed, analyzed and applied in previous experiences with youth and pro Brazilian clubs, and with youth programs and universities in North America.

These factors must be mentioned to give you a better understanding of the obstacles that could occur during your daily coaching activities, and enable you to avoid many mistakes in the coach-player relationship because of the lack of necessary analogy.

1. The coach's personality
2. Establishing the goals to be achieved by your team.
3. The player's personality.
4. The role of the captain.
5. The weekly preparation.
6. The pre-competition preparation.

7. Pre-game meeting.
8. The half time conversation.
9. The post game evaluation.

1. THE COACH'S PERSONALITY

The new season is coming. You have organized your tryouts. The players have been chosen by technical skills, analogy in tactical/positioning aspects, and speed, but not by personality. You have prepared a good season plan. It is time for your first practice. BUT wait! Before you approach your players, you must be prepared to identify who **you** are, and what is the real reason that you want to coach that group of players.
We have identified three basic coach personalities in soccer.
Verify which one fits your personality:

a. The COMMAND COACH:

He is always right in his decisions, never shares opinions with the players, and constantly prefers to criticize rather than encourage the players. His command is a must, and consequently it becomes unpleasant to be coached by somebody with this personality. In many cases, he becomes so commanding because of the lack of the analogy of the game, promoting a lack of motivation to participate on his team. With the constant commands, this kind of coach tries to intimidate the player, forcing an unrealistic relationship.

b. THE SUBMISSIVE COACH:

He is the opposite of the command coach. He is simply there in practice to baby-sit the players. He does not spend any time preparing his practices, is constantly complaining about players behavior, and does not show much control of the players' attitudes.

   He is very lacking of soccer analogy, and primarily he accepts the job because of the financial interest or his children are part of a team without a coach.

Two major problems normally occur with teams with submissive coaches:
1. No quality in the information given by this kind of coach.

2. Excessive number of players will drop from the team and consequently drop out of soccer, because of the lack of motivation to keep playing.

3. Excessive lack of discipline.

c. THE COOPERATIVE COACH:

Soccer is a team sport, and the only way to achieve any kind of success is through the consistency of the unity, where each member of the coaching staff and any one of the players have the same importance and their participation will consolidate a high performance of the team. The cooperative coach will be the leader of this achievement.

Each important decision to be made is exposed to the full group to analyze and identify the best decision for the team. The cooperative will explain the general planning for the season, establishing goals and evaluate together with the group the realistic options and expectations.

Communication among everybody will be strongly recommended, and he will have the discipline of the team without force or need to punish anybody to establish the team rules.

The cooperative coach will try to assist the players in their personal problems, guide them to positive attitudes and have a very important role in the athletes' individual development.

Coaches Carlos Alberto Parreir and Zagallo: Cooperative coaches with emphasis on discipline and hard work. 1994 World Champions.

2. ESTABLISHING THE GOALS TO BE ACHIEVED BY YOUR TEAM

As was mentioned before in the Comportment chapter, team expectations could become an important factor in establishing team goals. You now understand your coach personality, and you agree that being cooperative with your coaching staff, players and, of course, with the people behind the organization, such as parents (youth soccer in North America) or the directors (professional soccer) will create a very friendly and positive work environment. Your next step as the head coach or the coaching director is to establish the goals for your team.

Fun, player improvement, and winning are the three major goals to be accomplished for any successful team, but it is very dangerous when the order of these three goals changes. Even in high level professional clubs, the constant emphasis on the financial points normally do not reflect in final team accomplishment.

I believe you must do things that you want to do, and the real fun comes when you love what you are doing. The North American Soccer community must change the direction of the way players are treated. They do not have the freedom to express themselves on the field because creativity is not allowed. No freedom to enjoy what you are doing means routine and mind limitations; these limitations will promote slow motivation to think and concentrate, decreasing the thinking process. When a player does not think, the consequent technical/tactical development is not going to happen. Without excitement or development the players start to lose interest for the sport and finally they will quit. To change this process coaches must focus on creating an environment where the enjoyment is available to the players. The practices are intense, but the more they enjoy what they are doing, the more they develop themselves. They now start the process of loving it. With love in their attitudes, the commitment and concentration in practices will increase and the final reward is the constant success in their games.

IMPORTANT: Everybody begins to play because it is fun. When you are having fun your self-esteem and self confidence will improve, helping you to achieve your individual technical/tactical development, which will consequently give the opportunity to find the success of winning. We have identified that in any competitive environment the extreme emphasis is in winning, especially at the youth development level in North America.

The major role to identify a good pace in developing the team goals is in the hands of the head coach, and some considerations should be mentioned:
   • The team must have a positive environment where each one of the

calling his name during the game. Introverts are not the best leaders during the game, and it is unusual to have them as the captain because of their lack of communication skills.

b. Extrovert: The opposite of introvert. This type of player is outspoken, always needs to share his opinion, and many times is extremely critical of himself or his teammates.

An extrovert often complains about his life and what the future can provide (can become very negative, and this is extremely dangerous for the group unity). He is very happy in social situations and normally takes the leadership role. He is suspect of other peoples' attitudes and has a very high level of perception.

Constant group meetings and sincere conversation always help to control this kind of personality. They do not mind being criticized in front of the group, but be careful of overdoing it. You can use them in practice to demonstrate your coaching points, without hurting their feelings.

Always establish goals for them in each game, and challenge them to perform their best, they will respond favorably, but analyze their mood before you approach them.

Remember - they can lose their composure in moments of difficulty or under excessive pressure.

4. THE CAPTAIN'S ROLE

It is common to see, especially in North America, the captain merely identify which side of the field his side will be taking before the game starts or if they have the kickoff. It is time to understand that your captain is your coach on the field, and he is responsible for keeping the system, remembering the strategies and maintaining the team unity until half time, where the coach can review and correct the problems. I have a special admiration toward the coaches in American football, and their ability to educate their quarterbacks so well. Your captain in soccer

One of the most extroverted personalities in the world of Soccer (Romario).

has the same leadership function, and it is very important to prepare him for this role. One of the major problems we see in many clubs is that the coaches normally elect two or three captains to lead the team, and when you have two leaders, sometimes no one takes control, creating confusion and generating arguments among the group.

We strongly recommend to establish one captain, and when this one has to leave the field you will pass the function to the one, at that time, who is really heading the performance of the group. To elect your captain we recommend a democratic election, where everyone involved in the group must write on a piece of paper the three options they recommend as captain. After the election, the final decision will be yours if two or more players had the same number of votes. It is important that we explain to all the members of the team what will be the captain's role:

- Represent his club with pride, respect and leadership when requested.

- Establish the game plan with the coach, before the team meeting.

- Coordinate the final team meeting before the game. Lead the prayer or pep talk or identify someone who would like to.

- Make sure all the players are on time for practices, trips and games.

- Be the link between the players and the coach, when a player does not feel comfortable in coming directly to the coach for some specific reason.

- Lead the group for meals, meetings, rest time during the trips and in competition days.

- When on the field, take responsibility of leading the group to their best performance.

- Communicate when necessary, and be the role model in terms of friendship, leadership and. . .

- . . .especially provide the necessary patience and confidence to all the other teammates.

- Keep in constant contact with the coach during the game, requesting and offering suggestions.

The captain will be responsible, together with his board of directors, to identify the fines to be applied to players who break the team rules (See in Comportment chapter the concept of Caixinha).

Just to show how important the role of the captain is during the 1994 World Cup, Coach Carlos Alberto Parreira had Dunga sharing a room with Romario, and the effect of Dunga on Romario's performance was very clear during the tournament. Romario worked hard, helped to keep the unity and most importantly, helped Dunga to lead the team to the Championship final and win; but Dunga was the perfect fighter, running everywhere, winning loose balls, covering everyone's back, etc.. Dunga definitely took on his task as the captain and all the responsibilities.

5. THE WEEK PREPARATION.

Your week should start with a brief meeting reviewing your last competition, if you already are in season. Spend time talking about the major problems of the team (focus on a maximum of three points) and explain to the group what is going to be the goal for that 1st practice, i.e. correction of the old problems, before you move onto the preparation of the next competition. Individual technical concerns and/or small group tactical problems must receive individual attention and should be in private. Try to address those concerns before your team meeting in your first practice of the week. The most effective way to accomplish the players' understanding of your concerns is to show a video of the last game and point out the common mistakes that happened and concern you.

The most important points to remember and reinforce are:

The good performances by some players, make sure everybody knows you are very happy that those players have achieved a much better level of development. Avoid criticizing in front of the group, only call the attention to your concerns without calling specific names (as we said before). Do it in private. You have your individual meetings and you and your captain are comfortable about that.

The next step will be the team meeting before the first practice of the week. I would like to stress that you do not describe all the problems of your team. You will be wasting time and the players will not focus on the real problems you will try to correct in that practice.

Remember: The first thing to do with your team is correct the problems you had during your last game. Establish a good practice plan and make sure that everybody understands all the points and is able to apply them in the next scrimmaging situation. You can always complete your first practice with physical or technical training, but only after you have control of the previous problems.

During the rest of the week you will be focusing on the individual player personalities and the necessary approaches to keeping the balance.

Have fun, make jokes, create an environment where everybody wants to be and stay. Be a friend, be a father, be a brother to your players.

Organize social events where all your players and families can come and share some quality time. Provide your players an opportunity to get involved in community work, helping inner city kids learn how to play the game, or even assist any youth program. Make your players get involved.

6. THE PRE-COMPETITION PREPARATION

The pre-competition preparation is the cycle of the 48 hours that precede the competition. One of the most important aspects in anticipating the competition is the fear of losing. You have to understand that many of your players will be thinking about what could happen if they make a mistake and the team loses on that mistake. Your first effort to avoid this situation is to avoid the use of negative words such as: Lose, unsuccessful, failure, etc.. The positive approach works much better and your players will carry this positive energy through the rest of the week.

Some important points to be addressed during this period.

• **Faith** - We strongly recommend our players understand the importance of God in our lives.

We believe that He will protect the players against injuries and promote a positive and happy environment among the group.

• **Rest** - Make sure your players sleep at least eight hours per night in the last two nights before the competition. The lack of rest can interfere in the relationship between their intellectual and physical speed of decisions. **Example:** The player believes that mentally the correct position is taking control of the ball, but the physical movement does not follow with the same speed, promoting mistakes. The lack of rest is obviously a negative point, especially during the last part of the game when a lack of endurance will promote fatigue. The fatigue is followed by hurried decisions (lack of thinking) instead of fast decisions, increasing the number of mistakes, and exposing the players to injury situations because of excessive time of holding the ball for lack decision making.

• **Nutrition** - The players should be on a positive diet based on carbohydrates, proteins and some vitamins. This important point deserves a full book of explanation, but our major concern is warning about the relationship of what your players will eat and what exactly their body will need. The lack of adequate nutritional components will promote the production of lactic acid in their system, decreasing the quantity of oxygen, and promoting fatigue. Again fatigue will bring frustration, and could generate improper behavior on the field, jeopardizing the team unity and the quality of performance.

- **Injuries:** If any player is injured, an intensive treatment must be provided. Never allow your players to participate in any level of competition until they are totally recuperated. An injured player will likely perform below your expectations, and you will minimize the confidence of the other players in better physical condition, besides jeopardizing the team unity.

During a trip with the group, make sure you spend time learning about what is new in their lives; how is their family, the school, etc.. Always travel early enough to provide your players time to rest and time to do the psychological preparation. Avoid doing things in a hurry. You can put at risk a full week of hard work.

7. PRE-GAME MEETING
This should be done at least 60 minutes before the competition starts. Make sure you establish your routine of concerns to be addressed:
1. Individual concerns require private meetings.

2. Problems with a sector of the field - make sure you have a group meeting.

3. Finally, you hold the team meeting where the major goals will be to re-evaluate the problems of the last game and make sure everybody is comfortable, and address the system and the plan for this competition. When talking with your players, verify if any of them are showing different attitudes towards the competition or to the pressure he is going to be exposed to. To have a successful meeting you must have all the players sit-down in front of you. Talk slowly, be calm, be clear and objective in your points. You should conduct the meeting focusing on your three major game plan priorities. Do not talk too much, and finish your meeting with a quick review of what you said and what you expect. After the team meeting the players will start their game warm-up (see the chapter Physical Conditioning (page 63). During this warm-up you must observe if any player is not concentrating or motivated for the game. You must approach the player with a necessary intensity to bring him back to the competition preparation, and if no response is achieved the best suggestion is to replace the player and identify what is bothering him. As soon as you feel that player is back in his concentration and motivation to play, it is recommended to give him a new opportunity.

During the last part of the warm-up (6 v 4 and keeper) you should observe the team intensity and make sure the players will be prepared for the game condition. The next step will be the final team meeting without the participation of the coaching staff. The players, under the leadership of the captain, must have the last conversation about the performance to be achieved and bring the unity together. The last pre-game step is the team prayer, where all the players and the coaching staff hold hands and put their feet together and, led by any one of the group, thank God for the opportunity to be among such good friends and ask for protection for both teams to finish the game without injury. **It is time to play.**

8. THE HALF TIME TALK

The half time of the game is one of the most important periods to identify the correct way to approach the group. It is the time to consolidate the victory or explore the options available to reorganize the problems observed during that half.

Normal reactions of the players after an unsuccessful first half:
- Some players will blame the lack of team unity.
- Some players will point to their teammates, blaming them for the bad team performance.
- Some players will stay quiet expecting direction from the coach or someone else.

Normal reactions of the players after a successful first half:
- Some players will be too excited, creating an overconfidence situation, which could be dangerous.
- Some players will be quiet, because even though the team is having success, they are not performing their best.
- Sometimes a player will come out making comments about his first half. Make sure you approach this player very carefully requesting the same concentration during the second half.

As the coach, your first decision when the first half is over is to request that everybody stay calm, quiet and just relax. Players should sit down, dropping the socks and loosening the shinguards, making sure to drink enough water (do not allow any other fluid, because the sugar could increase the blood in the digestive system, taking away from the brain and the muscles). The players must sit facing the coach and prepare to organize the second half plan. Many times it is very common to see the coach talking with a group separate and apart and not concentrating as a team. The coach should be prepared to correct the problems in a short time. Here is a very effective way to approach the team, making sure to keep or bring back the spirit of that competition.

The first observation with the group is to verify if anyone is injured. Secondly verify if somebody is not of the physical capacity to restart the second half. The next step will be to approach the individuals with personality or discipline problems. Separate them from the group and identify the problem. If a solution is not found and the player's behavior could jeopardize the team unit, a replacement should be provided for that athlete. Individual technical problems should be solved in private meetings also.

The last approach will be to the total group. The coach always must be prepared to target the two (maximum three) major team tactical problems, more than that will be wasting time, the players will try to focus on too many points, naturally losing their concentration.

Do not allow anyone other than yourself to direct the information to the players, unless you feel that your assistant coach could bring a positive approach to the meeting. Many times we see two or three coaches bring their game points and the players will totally lose their focus and nothing will be accomplished. One voice, with consistency, is the adequate way to approach the players you work so hard with during the week, the players who learn from you, as you walk around the field giving advice, stopping at the right time for necessary adjustments, being patient with the players with less skills, and always giving the same attention as you give to the stars of the team. This is the person the players want to hear, the voice of their teacher, friend, brother and father, their Soccer coach.

It is time to go back and give the best performance possible in the 2nd half.

8. POST GAME OBSERVATIONS

In this sub-chapter we would like to mention many of the points that you, the coach, must observe which could affect the players and consequently the team's performance.

a. Each game is different. Be prepared to adjust the situation as soon as possible. Do not let the team lose their psychological control due to your lack of awareness.

b. Avoid mentioning a player's name when he does something wrong. Find the appropriate time to do that privately.

c. Be positive and realistic in your criticism when substituting a player or during half time. Players know when they are not performing well.

d. When approaching a player with problems in his performance make sure you know what the problem is, and especially the solution for it.

e. Celebrate the great plays and be calm and analytic when the bad plays occur.

f. Make sure your players are physically healthy. Injuries can generate frustration and the results will reflect on the group.

g. Request your captain to introduce himself to the referees and learn his name. Everybody should address the referee by name. This will create a good relationship and the feeling of respect will promote the referee's self-confidence. This referee will be much more concentrated on the game, and this will help the quality of the competition, decreasing the unfair play and the chance no injuries. No injuries means less psychological pressure on the team.

h. Motivation is the key. You are the best motivator. Coach each game as if it were your biggest game: Be prepared, be relaxed, be a joker, smile. **THIS IS FUN!**

IT IS TIME TO MOVE TO THE PHYSICAL CONDITIONING PRINCIPLE.

Principles
of the Physical
Conditioning

I believe that everybody involved in soccer will remember the game between Brazil and Holland during the 1994 World Cup. It was a game played in 110 degrees and conditioning became the most important factor in favor of the Brazilian team. Brazil was winning 2-0 and Holland took advantage of a few Brazilian defense mistakes to equalize the score. Imagine how depressing it can be for a team with full control of the game to come to a situation of losing control and finally the game, but the psychological factors come normally after the physical capacity of thought and reaction to the command no longer exist. Fortunately Brazil was very well prepared physically and did overcome that pressure situation and ended up winning the game. The same did not happen during the semi-final of the Olympic games in July 1996, when Brazil was winning the game by 3-1 with twenty five minutes to go and lost the game 4-3 to Nigeria, who really was very well prepared.

In this Chapter we will be discussing some of the physical conditioning capacities and some types of training developed and applied in Brazil. It is not our intention to cover each one of these physical conditioning capacities in deep detail, because this could generate a whole new book about this principle alone.

We will be focusing on the concepts we believe must be developed in the North American soccer community to produce players to compete with real success in international level competition.

The history of physical conditioning as an important factor in the development of a successful team began in 1966, during the World Cup in England. England was the host and didn't want to lose the opportunity to win the tournament and bring back the tradition of the best soccer in the world to the country that invented the game. The only obstacle they had was the Brazilian National team, world champions in 1958 in Sweden and 1962 in Chile, who played with high level technical skills and unstoppable speed with the ball.

England was creating the man on man marking system, and the

physical condition of the players was the big factor to make this tactical plan work. They could not allow any space to the Brazilian team, especially to Péle. England totally dominated the 1966 World Cup and the ability to neutralize the opponent's space was the initial step for the development of this very important principle in soccer.

All soccer schools around the world became very interested in different methods of training for soccer players, especially in Germany and Spain.

Brazilian physical trainers spent years together with the European schools studying the best way to prepare correctly and carefully a very effective program, and it was recognized around the world as the Total Training Method.

Total soccer method has become the base of the planning in any soccer club or National team.

Soccer in North America is going through a period of very fast development in the area of specific physical conditioning. Some MLS coaches are hiring professional physical trainers to be their assistant coaches. We believe that it is time to really understand the importance of having someone with the necessary knowledge to develop the body condition of the player, especially at young ages.

Physical conditioning principle is the development of the necessary physical capacities to allow the players to achieve high performance.

The major factors to consider when preparing your physical conditioning program are:

1. Increase the capacity of the respiratory system (aerobic and anaerobic)

2. Increase the volume of blood pumped by the heart to the circulatory system.

3. Hypertrophy of the necessary group of muscles.

4. Strengthen the necessary group of muscles and their relation to tendons and ligaments.

5. Decrease the presence of the lactic acid in the muscles during and after the soccer activity.

To guarantee the necessary understanding and supervision of these factors, the North American soccer community must understand the importance of having someone specialized in this field.

We call this person a physical trainer.

These are the responsibilities of the Physical Trainer recommended by Prof. Julio Mazzei:

1. Planning, educating, directing and supervising the physical conditioning program (athletic and physiologic) of the players related to the general training schedule of the week, month and year.

2. Planning, educating, directing and supervising the warm up during the training sessions (technical or tactical) and before each match.

3. Assisting the Technical director when requested during the technical and tactical sessions.

4. Establishing and orienting special physical training programs for the injured or players in physical rehabilitation, in conjunction with the medical and the physical therapy department.

5. Providing a summary of the activities weekly, establishing better supervision in each player's development.

6. Giving opinions about the importance, or not, of the quantity and quality of friendship games at regional, national or international level.

7. Keeping a control record (see planning) with all the data and information that could be important to the development of the activities and the next year's planning.

8. Organizing and directing physical evaluations of the players.

9. Attending seminars, courses, symposiums and secure licenses that could introduce new techniques, systems and methods of training.

10. Providing the players with their results in physical evaluations and game performances and always warning about the problems with their off of the field behavior that could interfere in their general physical condition.

11. Always analyzing with your players the phrase from the French physiologist M.Baquet:
'You walk with your legs, gallop with your lungs, run with your heart, but only achieve your destination with your mind'.

DEVELOPING THE PHYSICAL CONDITIONING PROGRAM.

Soccer power today has its success based on the results of the applicability of the Total Training Program: The Total Training Program is the combination of all the components needed to develop the high performance of the player without jeopardizing his health.

The components are: Planning and management, medical control, health habits, nutrition, adaptation to the training programs, psychological, technical, tactical and finally the physical conditioning principle.

The five important factors which must be analyzed when preparing the physical conditioning principle programs of the Total soccer philosophy:

1. The interaction of the physical conditioning program with the technical - tactical player development supported by the psychological aspects.

2. Evaluate the year planning constantly to make sure the final goal or the different objectives are still the focus of each member and especially the group.

3. Evaluate the comportment principles of each player and make sure the priorities of the group (fun, development and/or success) are still in order.

4. Organize the program and the specific training for each capacity based on frequency, intensity and volume of the activity.

5. Always have in consideration the motivation factor. The variants to analyze are:
   a. The physical capacities for each player.

   b. The health of each player and the conditioning to stay free of medical problems or injury (Training must always be safe. Never take risks with the health of your players If not 100% healthy - no intense practices).

   c. The possibility of receiving the appropriate training related to the weather (cold-no outdoor practice). Location - always switch the players to different environments to avoid the routine.

Before we explain the most important physical capacities and illustrate those with some specific training programs we must mention the importance of supervising the other aspects of a good physical condition program. **They are:**

1. **Rest:** Players must allow themselves a period of recuperation. This period is divided into three different situations. A minimum of eight hours sleep is strongly recommended. If practicing two times a day the player must have a short break to allow him to recuperate from the physical effort and strain on the mental/emotional system. Lack of rest can interfere in the quality of the play because of the increasing level of stress and emotional pressure.

2. **Nutrition:** Players must have a balanced diet based on nutrients important to the daily balance the body requests in order to perform necessary activities. The necessary nutrients are vitamins, proteins, salt minerals, carbohydrates, and fat. Pre-competition carbohydrates are very important because of the high percentage of energy that can be produced from each gram of this nutritional component.

3. **Weather:** Avoid work on excessively hot (dehydration) or cold days (probability of illness).

THE MOST IMPORTANT PHYSICAL CONDITIONING METHODS TO DEVELOP THE BRAZILIAN SOCCER STYLE.

Our goal is to explain to our coaches the types of training applied in Brazil and in many other countries to specifically develop the physical capacities of the soccer player.

The methods of training have been adjusted to the North American player's needs.

1. **BRAZILIAN WARM-UP** - Capacities developed with this training are flexibility, agility, body coordination and balance.

    a. **Warm-up without the Ball:** The following program should be performed before practice as part of general/specific warm-up. The exercises are done while running at a slow to moderate pace and to the commands of a coach. The coach leads the exercises in quick succession and the athletes are always in motion. Athletes can do this program as a warm-up prior to any specialized training on their own. This versatile program works all parts of the body and when coupled with increased running intensity can be part of an aerobic training workout.

Performance of each exercise should be as follows:
U8-U10: 6-8 times
U12-U14: 10-12 times
U16 and above: 13-15 times

Exercise #1 • Start in a soccer ready position and begin running. At the command put hands overhead, then down to shoulders.

Exercise #2 • At the command, while running lift both arms to the left and then to the right.

Exercise #3 • At the command, while running, extend arm straight out, alternating between left and right.

Exercise #4 • At the command, while in motion, pull both arms toward the front, touch fingertips, stretch both arms open. Run.

Exercise #5 • At the command, while in motion, twist at the trunk to the left then to the right. Try to keep hips forward.

Exercise #6 • At the command, while in motion, stop. With legs apart, place right arm overhead, bend at waist, repeat to the other side.

Exercise #7 • At the command, while in motion, stop. Face to the left, jump using ankles only; spin 180 degrees to the right. Run. Repeat in opposite direction.

Exercise #8 • At the command, while in motion, kick right leg up, stretch both arms out over leg, repeat with left leg.

Exercise #9 • At the command, while in motion, kick right leg to the left, twist trunk in opposite direction. Repeat in opposite direction.

Exercise #10 • At the command, while in motion, lift right leg up bending at the knee and swing leg to the left. Repeat with opposite leg.

Exercise #11 • At the command, while in motion, lift right then left leg up in front, knees bent. Perform a quick jump.

Exercise #12 • At the command, while in motion, kick legs back, touch feet with hands. Perform a quick jump.

b. **Warm-up with the Ball:** The Brazilian warm-up with the ball is based on four different speeds of reaction (as in game situations). These exercises must be performed with intensity, uninterrupted movement and body positioning with progression from simple to complex.

The four speeds of reaction are:

- In place, executing an exercise at full speed but with no forward or backward movement. This develops speed of reaction in situations without pressure.

- In place, executing coordination exercises in addition to ball handling. These include somersaults, diving forward, sit-down and stand-up, etc. This develops speed of reaction to unexpected situations or directions of the ball.

- Exercises with short sprints. After passing the ball 15 yards, sprint and come back to the starting point, sprint again.

- Exercises with movement forward and back on the soccer field.

We recommend that for U14 players and below a rubber ball be used in place of a normal soccer ball. This requires the young players to have a greater degree of concentration, the softness of the ball requires more precision when receiving and demands greater movement of the feet because the added "bounce" creates more improvisation when controlling the ball.

Progress of each exercise is as follows: U8-U10/30 seconds
U12-U14/45 seconds
U16 and above/60 seconds

Warm-up routine with a partner: (4 common heights of the ball).

a. Ball on the ground

1. Movement in place switching feet right/left, always trapping with the inside of the foot. U8-U10: 2 touches U12-U18: 1 touch.

2. Movement in place as in #1 with the addition of coordination exercises: somersaults, diving forward, sit-down and stand-up, etc.

3. Movement around the field, partners 5 to 6 feet apart with progression to coordination exercises moving back and forward for 25 to 30 yards. One player doing the drill, the other one passing the ball.

4. Movement with short sprints.

b. Ball at waist

These exercises are done with the ball through the air received in the area between the lower leg and waist. The player passes the ball back to the partner on the ground. Exercise progresses the same as in A. Player should focus on being on toes with good balance. Pass must be on the ground.

c. Trapping on the Chest

The player will pass the ball with the hands to his partner. The player tries to focus on passing as soon as the ball touches the ground. The exercise helps prepare the player for high-pressure situations. Exercise progresses the same as in A.

d. Heading

Player will pass the ball with the hands to his partner. Partner will head the ball back, alternating offensive heading (hitting down) and defensive heading (hitting up) for 10 to 15 repetitions. Players then switch roles. Exercise progresses the same as in A. U-8 to U-10 players may lack the skill to perform the progression effectively. Be sure to modify the coordination exercises with this in mind.

2. STRETCHING:

Must be done every day during all the phases of your year planning. Stretching can be done individually or with partners:

a. **Individual:** Helps to increase flexibility, giving better elasticity and generally amplifying the range of motion. Stretching is a part of the warm-up procedure leading to more strenuous activity. It is important that it is done correctly to obtain maximum results. It is not advisable to start the warm-up with stretching. Individual stretching is also known as static exercise and should be done slowly as far as the muscle can go without hurting it. The duration of the exercise is between 15 and 25 sec. The most important stretching is that done after the activity.

Important groups of muscles must be stretched in soccer:

Lower body: Groin, quadriceps, hamstrings, hip flexor, illio-tibial band and calf.

Upper body: Shoulder, back, pectoral.

b. **Partners stretching:** It is applicable to increase the level of the flexibility and help to decrease the contraction of the muscles after the soccer activity. The danger is that it can be injurious when used without caution. When another person applies external force on the muscles of a partner, he should take care to apply the correct intensity without causing damage. This part of the program should be used after competition or before competitions played on the same day or with a very short rest time for the players.

Aspects to be observed to achieve good stretching:
1. Be prepared mentally to spend the necessary time to stretch correctly.
2. Warm-up the muscles gradually when stretching before the games.
3. Do not stretch to the point of pain.
4. Always do both sides (right/left).
5. Daily stretching results in better flexibility.

3. SIT-UPS PROGRAM

A major factor which can interfere in a player's optimal performance and general health is the lack of natural alignment or balance in his posture. Having a good posture is fundamental and the best exercise to keep the back strong is sit-ups. The abdomen has the recto and transversal groups of muscles, and both must be worked daily. They can be worked in different intensity, quantity and frequency. The hip must always stay on the ground. Do not promote pressure on the spinal column.

Series between 20 to 30 repetitions. Do not forget to work the back muscles.

4. POWER TRAINING

Capacity that allows the muscle or group of muscles to beat the resistance and maintain the continuity of the action.

One of the biggest concerns with power training in North America for soccer players is the excessive emphasis in body building which can decrease the flexibility and agility which is so important for soccer. In Brazil the power training is divided in two phases:

a. **Development:** When working with young players - The hyper-trophy of the muscles is very important with low intensity and constant frequency and no more than 50% of the body weight of the player. Age recommended is after 15/16 years, to avoid interfering with the young players growing process.

b. **Maintenance**: This is the process of keeping the players in good neuromuscular condition. They are adjusted to the phase of the planning and divided in three cycles.

1. **Muscle endurance:** During the pre and middle season - Low intensity (maximum 40% of body weight during the pre-sea son going to 65% during the middle of the season) series of 15 repetitions and with 5 to 6 series. Working with medium speed. This capacity will allow the player to keep the same intensity during all the games in terms of the response of the muscles, decreasing the production of lactic acid and the feeling of fatigue.
It also helps to avoid injuries and provide the necessary support to guarantee quality of performance of the technical skills such as shooting and long passing. Other good muscle resistance programs are:
Running up and down hill at different speeds (forward, backwards, sideways, etc,), swimming and riding bikes. Avoid running up/down stairs, this can damage some of the joints.

2. **Power:** Between the middle of the season and before the play-offs of the season, the players must move to the 2nd cycle of the muscle development. Power training is based on decreasing the quantity of repetitions and increasing the weight to 80% of the player's body weight (some exceptions can apply due to the resistance of the exercise and the weight to be pushed). This second cycle should be done once a week in a maximum of 3 series of 10 repetitions with maximum 80% of the body weight. This cycle will make the muscles strong and can not last more than 1/4 of the season. Flexibility and elasticity exercises must be done before and after these sessions.

3. **Potency:** This is the execution of exercises with weights at the maximum speed possible. The previous cycle made the muscles strong, but decreased the speed of reaction. With the inclusion of the potency training the muscles will maintain strength while improving reaction time. This, the 3rd and final cycle of the power training, must be applied during the last period of the season and in conjunction with speed training. It is anaerobic and with high intensity. The goal is to bring the player to the pinnacle of his physical condition. The players can not stay in

this kind of intensity longer than 4 to 6 weeks. There is a high risk of injuries if not followed by a very intense program of elasticity and flexibility exercises. The potency training is done against time instead of repetitions. The players will keep a record of repetitions only to observe their development.

Example of potency training:
- 8 to 10 stations, each station working an important group of muscles.

- Lower body: Quadriceps - Hamstrings - Calf - abductor and abductors. Upper body: Pectoral - Back deltoids - Biceps - Triceps. The stations should alternate lower body with upper body muscles.

- Do two series of 45 seconds at each of the 8 - 10 stations with a 60 second rest between stations using 70% of the body weight of the player or a weight that is adequate based on a previous evaluation.
  This should be done once a week and the day after resting is normally the most recommended.

5. CIRCUIT TRAINING

One of the most important characteristics of Brazilian soccer players is their ability to move quickly from situation to situation, normally in the first touch. Their great foot speed requires that their movement be determined before the ball is received. This decision is often made with eye contact. This rapid decision making dictates the rhythm of play, forcing opponents to adjust to the Brazilian style of play.

The cultural influences of the rhythm of Samba and the Capoeria dances, learned by players at an early age, contribute to this style of play. Also influential as a training method are the physical conditioning and technical circuits. These circuits develop physical conditioning or work capacity relative to technical and improvisational situations, increase reaction time based on different game situations, and improve the player's ball skills and decision making. The following two circuits are part of the Brazilian system. Remember that this is only a part of a system, unique to Brazil and its way of life; soccer. Coaches and players must condition themselves to meet the requirements of their own national system. As you study these circuits, take from them what works for you.

The circuit can be adjusted to emphasize physical conditioning or technical abilities. Diagram (1) presents the circuit as modified to develop the conditioning aspect. Diagram (2) shows subsequent methods of training which will present the technical aspect.

These circuits should never be used as a teaching method. Skills will not be perfect. These activities work through repetition to improve technical skills in game conditions under stress and fatigue. Preseason is the time to do more strength, flexibility, agility and speed of reaction work. The circuits can be performed twice a week during the season, the physical circuit and the technical circuit once each. Do the more demanding physical circuit further from competition. Progress during the season by increasing the work time and/or by reducing the rest phase. Taper before a major competition to keep the legs fresh.

Table 1				
Age	Work Per Week	Rest	Frequency	Work Intensity (Speed of Exercise)
Low intensity				
8-9 Green	30 Sec	60 Sec	1	60%
10-11 Green	45 Sec	60 Sec	1	65%
Medium intensity				
12-13 Blue	50 Sec	60 Sec	1	70%
14-15 Blue	50 Sec	60 Sec	2	80%
16-17 Blue	60 Sec	60 Sec	2	80%
High intensity				
18-19 Black	90 Sec	60 Sec	2	90%
Over 20 Black	120 Sec	60 Sec	2	95%

The Physical Conditioning Circuit • Table 1 is the result of three years' work with a professional soccer club in Brazil. Observation of performance rather than scientific data collection forms its basis. Heart rate should be in the ranges of 170-180 beats per minute for the green level, 180-190 for the blue level, 190-200 for the black level. For a low heart rate, increase the work intensity. If it is above the target range, decrease the work intensity. A good conditioning base should be established before starting this program with young athletes. This program can also be used with highly skilled six to seven year olds at 50 percent intensity once a week and only under close and expert supervision.

Circuit Considerations
- Perform the 12-station circuit twice.
- Be sure the player is always 'on his toes' when performing each station.

- Flag distance should be: Green C = 5 yards, Blue C = 7 yards, Black C = 9 yards, unless otherwise indicated.

- Rope height should be knee level.

- Dribbling should be done on the outside of the foot unless otherwise indicated.

- Players should perform the circuit by rotating from station to station. Coaches, parents and non-performing players should help out at the stations as needed.

- The physical circuit should be done at the end of practice. The technical circuit is used at the first part of practice after warm-up.

- Work intensity increases as the players' skills improve.

Station Procedures:

Station #1: Sprint diagonally with the ball using the outside of the foot when running, and the inside of the foot when changing direction around the flag. Jog back to the start and repeat for the allowed time. The player should sprint to the ball at the start.

Station #2: Do a sit-up. The coach tosses the ball so the player can head it back to the coach.

Station #3: Pass the ball between flags and jump over the flag. Control the ball with the outside of the foot and accelerate around the cones. Repeat in opposite direction.

Station #4: Head the ball back to a partner. Jump over the rope in each direction and repeat the heading activity.

Station #5: Sprint with a ball, dribbling around the flag. Pass the ball to a partner. The partner passes the ball in front of the goal; player performs a diving header into the goal, jumps up, jogs back and repeats.

Station #6: Kick, and then sprint to the ball using long strides. Place the flag to mark the distance covered with each stride. This distance changes for each player. Players must be challenged to improve this quality. (**Note:** this exercise is designed to increase the player's stride length while controlling the ball.) This important aspect of speed is often overlooked in soccer.

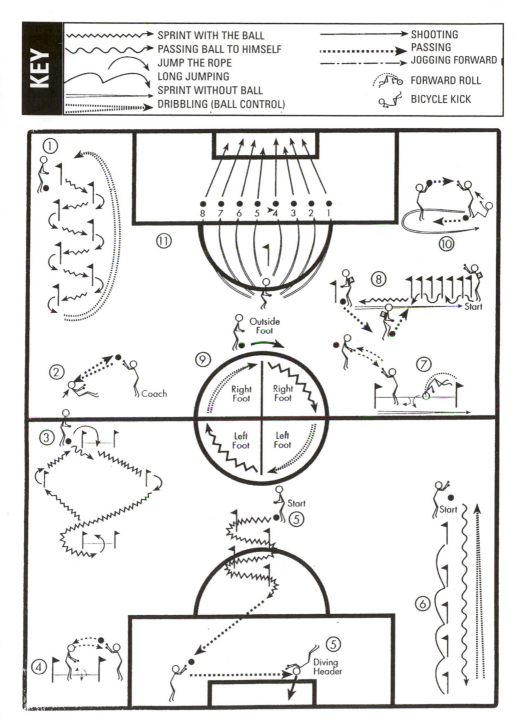

Diagram 1: *The physical conditioning circuit.*

Station #7: Jump over a rope, go below the rope and trap a ball passed by your partner, control with your chest and pass back. Run backwards and repeat.

Station #8: Set flags 18 inches apart. Sprint around 7 flags. Player B passes the ball as player A reaches the last flag, A then sprints with the ball to a separate flag 15 yards away and passes it back to player B. A Sprints back to start and repeats.

Station #9: Alternate sprinting and jogging, dribbling with the out side of the foot as you go around the circle. (**Note:** by varying pace this exercise can increase joint stability around the knee).

Station #10: Begin in a seated position. Stand as the ball is passed. Control the ball and pass back. Sprint around the partner and repeat.

Station #11: Place eight balls on the penalty kick line. The player starts on the top of the 18-yard box, back to the goal. On signal, the player turns and runs to the first ball, kicks with the left foot, returns to the 18 yard box, runs to the eighth ball and kicks with the right foot. Return and kick the second ball with the left foot and so on until all eight are kicked. To add intensity, increase to 10 balls.

Station #12: Begin in a seated position. Stand quickly and sprint 35 yards with the ball, controlling with the outside of the foot. Return dribbling the ball.

The Technical Circuit • Table 1 is the result of three year's work with a professional soccer club in Brazil. It is based upon observation of performance rather than scientific data. Heart rate should be between 140-150 beats per minute for the green level, 150-170 for the blue level and 170-190 for the black level. Notice that the heart rates are less for the technical circuit than for the conditioning circuit presented previously. This circuit emphasizes technical accomplishment using the ball. For a low heart rate, increase the work intensity. If it is above the target range, decrease the work intensity. A good conditioning base should be established before young athletes start this program. This program also can be used with more skilled players under eight to ten years old to help develop basic coordination between the soccer ball and the body. Train at 50 percent

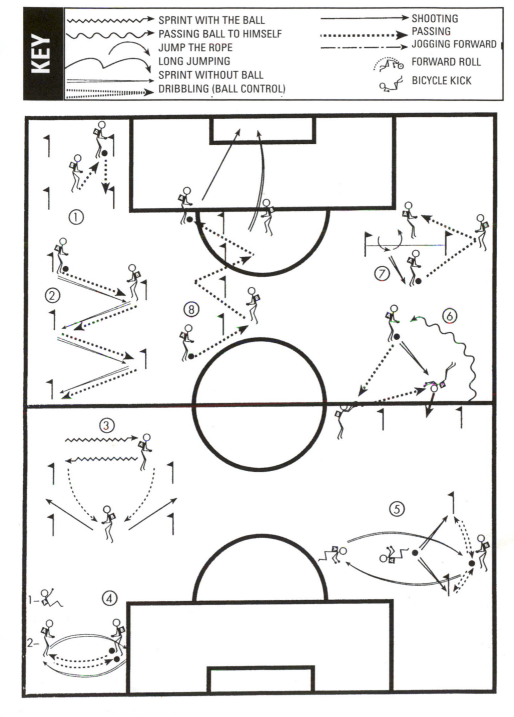

Diagram 2: *The Technical Circuit.*

intensity once a week, only under close and expert supervision.

Circuit Considerations

* Perform the 8-station circuit twice.

* Be sure the player is always "on his toes" when performing each station.

* Flag distance should be: Green C = 5 yards, Blue C = 7 yards, Black C = 9 yards, unless otherwise indicated.

* Rope height should be knee level for all players.

* Dribbling should be done with the outside of the foot unless other wise indicated.

* Players should perform the circuit by rotating from station to station working in pairs. Coaches, parents and non-performing players should help out at the stations as needed.

* The technical circuit is used at the last part of practice.

* Work intensity increases as the players' skills improve.

Table 1

Age	Work Per Week	Rest	Frequency	Work Intensity (Speed of Exercise)
Low intensity				
8-9 Green	60 Sec	60 Sec	1	60%
10-11 Green	90 Sec	60 Sec	1	65%
Medium intensity				
12-13 Blue	90 Sec	60 Sec	1	65%
14-15 Blue	120 Sec	60 Sec	1	70%
16-17 Blue	150 Sec	60 Sec	1	75%
High intensity				
18-19 Black	180 Sec	60 Sec	1	80%
Over 20 Black	180 Sec	60 Sec	1	80-90%

Station Procedures

Station #1: Player B is in the center of four flags. Player A makes quick passes to different open spaces in the square.

Player B should react as fast as possible and pass the ball back to player A with just one touch. Switch and repeat.

Station #2: Player A passes the ball to player B who controls the pass. Player A accelerates to the ball while player B continues to the next flag. The exercise is repeated until all flags are touched. Players jog back and repeat.

Station #3: Two small goals are set up 15 yards apart. Player A crosses balls back and forth to player B. Player B follows player A in both goal directions and finishes crosses of player A into the goal. Switch and repeat.

Station #4: Player A, in a sit up position, does three sit ups, jumps up and receives a pass, returning it to player B. Player A then sprints around player B and repeats the exercise.

Station #5: Flags should be 10 yards apart. Player A does a forward roll and quickly gets up. Player B passes the ball to the right flag, player A runs to the flag, controls and returns the ball and then runs to the left flag and repeats. Player A then sprints around player B, returning to starting position.

Station #6: Player A passes the ball to player B. Player A sprints to open space, receives a pass in the air and performs a volley.

Station #7: Player A jumps over the rope and quickly goes under, then sprints to the ball, passes it back to player B and repeats.

Station #8: Players A and B pass to each other with one touch between flags using the outside of the foot. The last player to receive a pass takes a shot on goal. Repeat, switching the player who takes the shots. Players should switch sides.

Note: Circuit training is one of the most exciting and intensive methods of training you can give to your players. Use your creativity and remember the goal of the circuit you are going to offer to your players. Establish if it will be physical or technical. If physical, what capacities do you want to develop? If technical, identify and educate the players. The most important thing is to make the training fun and for each player to devote his best intensity and concentration.

INTERVAL TRAINING

Interval training fundamentals are based on the system created by Pinkala from Finland and Waitzer from Germany. The big step in developing this system of training happened when Waldemar Gerschler and Herbert Keindell had the opportunity to prepare three great athletes: Harbib, Zapotek and Pirie, and with facts and results established a new direction for the training development.

The basic principle of interval training is based on the execution of short distance running (D), with the time close to the best possible of the player (T), with a number of repetitions (R), with intervals of resting (I) in constant action (A).

The important factors of this method or system of training are:
- D • Distance of the running (intensity)
- T • Time necessary to cover that distance
- R • Number of Repetitions.
- I • Interval to resting
- A • Action (activity) during the interval.

Upon the relation of the formula DTRIA, the physical trainer will be able to establish the best option for each player. The process of the training will create standards to apply those formulas. These standards can be constants (C) or variables (V).

The most common player formulas are:

C (DTIA) • V (Repetition) Results: Resistance Endurance.

C (DRIA) • V (Time) Results: Resistance Speed

The control of intermediate distances can be applied constantly with your specific or chosen formula. You can keep or alternate the formulas, but it is not recommended.

Simultaneously change two factors. Important information about the factors of training.

a. **The most common distances are:**
- 100m • Development of the muscle potency
- 200m • Physiologic adaptation
- 400m • Physiologic adaptation

These short and intense distances are inserted in the long distances, which are applicable to identify the rhythm and act as a physiologic factor of motivation. The long distances can alternate from 500 to 2000m, and the most common are 600, 1200 and 2000m. The Fartlek (running with constantly changing speeds, distance and intensity) is a good example of the long distance training, but without the rhythm. Interval training to develop speed uses distances from 60 to 80m.

b. Time to cover the distance (effort):
During the pre-season and at the beginning of the season the intensity of running should not be over 70% of the player capacity.
Some tables of control can facilitate and help the development of this method of training during the different phases of the season.
The most common intensity for distance expressed in seconds are:
- 100 m - 14 to 16 sec. 200m - 30 to 33 sec.

- 300m - 46 to 49 sec. 400 m - 64 to 70 sec.

- These times of execution will change depending on the weather and the improvement of the players' physical condition.

c. Repetition and Intensity:
The improvement of the players should help to accomplish the goal of reaching the level of the performance necessary during the game.

d. Interval:
One minute of light activity during the resting break. For this reason many physical trainers applied 45 to 60 seconds. Long distances require a longer break.

e. Activity during the break:
- Jogging, slow running or both. Jogging is the most common.
- Work with the ball (technical activity).

The Important factors of this method of training:
a. Technical development, improvement of coordination.

b. Psychological adaptation and stabilization accomplished by:
1. Development of the cardiac and respiratory function hypertrophies of the heart and better blood circulation.

2. Improvement of the body - psycho coordination.

3. Improvement of the protective body system against the promotion of stress.

4. Development of self motivation and challenge, because of the intensity of the activity.

5. Improvement of the physical capacities: Speed, power, endurance and flexibility.

c. Development of the anaerobic phase, increasing the potency (power with speed) of the muscles and the muscle tone.

Summary of the steps when undertaking Interval training.
1. Study of the player:
    a. Returning players: Previous tests and results. Analyze the reports.

    b. New players: Medical and physical evaluation. Evaluate the physical condition. Identify the weak and strong points of the player.

2. Choose the formula of the training for each player

3. Establish the Plan of training:
    a. Macro plan - 1 year.
    b. During the year identify goals, schedules and competitions as evaluation of the team (peak condition).
    c. Medical control: Basic (2 x year) monthly and nutrition evaluation (4 times a year).

4. Establish the medium cycle (1-month planning)
    a. Number of days of training
    b. Days of rest
    c. Cycle of control of the team (15 to 20 days)
    d. Percentage of work
        1. Endurance - Rhythm
        2. Endurance - Speed
        3. Control of the intermediate distances or Fartlek
    e. Measure of the areas of work: forests, fields, tracks, etc.

Let's look at the SANTOS F.C. training cycle during the period of April 1965 to April 1972.

During this period the Physical trainer was Prof. Julio Mazzei. Santos F.C. was unique in terms of the quantity of competition to be played per year. (Base year 1968 - 84 games). Santos won the following titles in seven years:

1. Twice Sao Paulo State champion
2. Champion of the tournament of Chile
3. Champion of the tournament of Buenos Aires
4. National Champion - (Robertao)
5. South America Champion
6. World Club Champion
7. Champion of the tournament of the Amazonas.

To accomplish this goal, Professor Mazzei had interval training as one of the most useful methods of training. Some important considerations of his work:

- Modern soccer requires players with exceptional physical capacities, especially potency, power, endurance, speed and flexibility. Interval training achieves in highly scientific ways all of these physical capacities.

- The coach must study the role of each player with intelligence and expertise, applying the concepts carefully.

- Characteristics of each sector of the field in terms of distances and intensity:
  a. Midfielders - the marathon players - endurance is very important.
  b. Outside full-backs, Outside midfielders and Forwards - speed is key.
  c. Inside defenders and forwards - Jumping and speed - Potency and muscle endurance.

A typical Brazilian training session for physical preparation during this period.

    Part 1 - Circuit Training
    Station 1 - Long jumps over obstacles, (12 obstacles 3 meters apart.)
    Station 2 - Push ups
    Station 3 - Sit-ups
    Station 4 - Burpee (flexion and extension of the legs)
    Station 5 - Different kinds of sit-ups
    Station 6 - Heading (forward role and heading)
Each station two to three repetitions. Interval - 5 min.

Sprints - 5 x 30 meters
Interval - 10 minutes playing with the ball
Long running - 6 minutes
Exercises of relaxation.

Conclusion.

The coaching director and the physical trainer must establish a specific program for each player, respecting each one individually. In today's soccer all the players need all the capacities.

The physical program is based on intensive activities and necessary resting periods.

Interval training is not the only method of training. The muscular, respiratory and circulatory systems can be developed in other manners, but it is very important that you adapt your planning to your group. Some training for Brazilian players may not work for American players, and vice - versa. Be flexible and improvise as and when necessary.

Someone once said: 'A human being, and especially a champion, can not be compared to a machine and reduced to an amount of numbers.' That is why it is so important that you, as a coach, remember the individuality of each one of your players and your assistant coaches.

Promote the TEAM UNITY, combining all the personalities and have FUN. Success will come.

These circuits develop physical conditioning or work capacity relative to technical and improvisational situations, increase reaction time based on different game situations, and improve the player's ball skills and decision making. The preceding two circuits are part of the Brazilian system. Remember that this is only a part of a system, unique to Brazil and its way of life; soccer. Coaches and players must condition themselves to meet the requirements of their own nation's playing style.

Technical Skills Principles

On watching any Brazilian team play, the first thing one notices is their level of individual technical skill; the second might be their ability to get numbers of players around the ball, both defensively and offensively; and the third probably some aspect of their tactical play, like the frequency of offensive runs being made by their outside defenders. Technical skill, fitness, and innovative tactics in combination with a natural creativity and surprise of play are all aspects of the game that make the modern Brazilian team special to watch but almost impossible to play against.

In Brazil's past, as in many other countries, coaches spent little time developing the technical skills of their players. Players developed on their own through unsupervised play wherever open areas could be found, much like basketball players today in the United States. That is probably why many people feel that the Brazilian player is just naturally skillful. Today in Brazil, however, this is no longer the case. Years ago, when large areas of the country were open to play, maybe so, but unfortunately today in Brazil space is limited in the populated areas, and technical skills must be purposely developed in players.

In fact, most of Brazil's good players over the past seven years have come through the youth systems of major clubs like Sao Paulo, Vasco, Flamengo, Santos, and

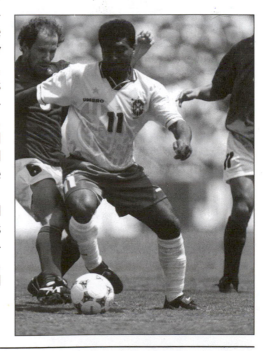

Romario - Incredible skills in a small space and under pressure.

Vitoria, where increased emphasis has been placed on developing a player's technical skills. These clubs find it both easier and cheaper to develop younger players rather than buy older ones with ingrained poor playing habits due to poor technical development.

Another factor important to the development of good technical play in Brazil's youth is the emphasis placed on playing a small-sided (5v5) game called futesal. Through age 12, when a player can enter the professional club system if good enough, Brazil's youth play on a basketball-sized court in organized leagues with parent coaches. Skills develop quickly by playing with the futesal ball (a size three but with twice the weight). The heavier ball helps a player's touch and, more importantly, forces play to the ground. Today, futesal is a sport played professionally in more than 70 countries across the globe.

In this chapter we develop training progressions for several technical skills that are critical to Brazilian play. A common theme stresses the importance of keeping the ball on the ground when the defensive pressure allows it. Attacking through a series of short ground passes keeps the speed of the ball fast, while at the same time insuring some degree of security of play until an opening to goal presents itself and leads to penetration, most times in a quick, creative strike at goal.

A player's technical development is one the most important pieces of the soccer-playing puzzle; it's a necessity for developing quality play in the game of soccer. Technical skills are the tools that a player has available to him to connect the triangulation process of passing and support and thus to apply correctly the team's tactical system and the various strategies within the context of that system during the course of the game.

Coaches and players alike need patience mixed with a good source of technical skill description and demonstration during the evolutionary phase of skill building. The emphasis here on information without adequate correction of the skill being taught too often generates bad habits in the player, habits unfortunately that often are never corrected.

The role of the coach educator is especially important at the younger ages. These coaches need to be good educators, able to show the step-by-step progression for each technical skill. They must develop in players both the habit of thinking about what they are doing and, within the context of game play, an understanding for the reasons they made mistakes.

One note here though: The good coach need not be a former great or even good player. As long as he has a player to demonstrate, understands the progressive steps in the skill's development, and can make corrections where needed, the non-playing coach can function well. Frequently, in this sport as in many others, the best players often make poor coaches. The game came naturally to them; they can't explain it; they just do it, and worse, they often have little patience with players who can't yet perform skills at their level. Some of Brazil's best coaches, like Carlos Alberto Parreira, coach of the 1994 World Champions, and Carlos Alberto Silva, another top Brazilian coach, were not great players themselves.

PHASES OF THE DEVELOPMENT OF A TECHNICAL SKILL

These three distinct phases of development are not unique to Brazilian soccer. Many countries, through their soccer federations, apply similar educational progressions in their development of technical skill. Remember though, in any system the key to good technical development is knowledgeable instruction, skill repetition, and skill correction at all levels from the very young to the most advanced players.

The progression used here to develop technical skill is first to break the skill down into its fundamental steps and develop each skill via a step-by-step approach before bringing it to game situations, and then finally exposing the player to the pressures of game conditions.

PHASE I: DEVELOPMENT OF SKILL FUNDAMENTALS

The following general observations address the development of technical skill in individual players regardless of which skill is being developed:

- advance from the simple to the more complex drills;

- first, establish the need for the particular skill's development, then start that skill's development from its very basics; this process identifies which stage of development your group is in and establishes the beginning point;

- always work both feet equally;

- use a variety of balls (small rubber balls, futesal balls, regulation balls);

- set time limitations for a set number of repetitions of a particular drill;

- repetitions can require speed, but remember, speed is often misinterpreted for hurry, and when a player hurries, he often doesn't think; as a result, the quality of play suffers; build speed but don't sacrifice quality;

- move on to another step, another phase, or a different technical skill only when players fully understand the necessary steps for performing the particular skill, and their execution has improved. Do, however, change the drill or the step in the skill development process when players begin to lose interest. When interest suffers move to a game situation to regenerate the excitement, one emphasizing the particular skill, then restart the development process in the next session.

- players must feel that they learn something from every practice and from every game;

- your job as coach is to provide the education and the environment necessary to make this learning process happen;

- be consistent in your coaching approach, but remember too, that planning on paper doesn't guarantee success on the field;

- be flexible and most importantly keep your player's interest and enjoyment in every minute of your practice;

- emphasize the skill being developed during the week in practice in the next match;

- for example, if the week's focus has been on the technical aspects of shooting, you must focus your observations on that during the next match.

- introduce the skill by playing with rubber balls; many times young players are afraid to touch the ball, especially when it comes high, but with a softer, lighter ball, they feel more comfortable and more confident to try the drill; further, this allows the player to get a better feel for the right part of the foot necessary to touch the ball; it increases foot quickness because of better traction on the ground and keeps play on the ground;

- follow with ball sizes appropriate to the age group: U8s #3, U12s and below #4, and above to pro #5; never allow players to train with flat balls because the ball, as a consequence, will be both lighter and softer than during regular game play and that, in turn, will decrease the player's quality of touch; when necessary, increase a player's number of touches on the ball by either diminishing the playing area and number of players (via small-size games) or keeping the game condition area and the number of players constant, but increasing the number of balls in play.

Don't rush the transition from technique development to game situation until you are sure that players are comfortable with the higher level of pressure. A good way to determine whether players have mastered the basics of a particular technique is through technical-physical circuit training - see chapter on physical conditioning - where players must execute the technique at game speed under a variety of conditions. Another method to determine their comfort level is to play a match against a weaker team where your team focuses on quality of execution of the technical skill under development. When your players demonstrate a level of comfort trying the particular skill, even though they still make the normal mistakes in trying, it is time to bring that skill forward to the game situation phase in your next practice.

PHASE II: SKILL DEVELOPMENT IN GAME SITUATIONS

After your players have had an opportunity to apply the technique under a low level game condition, and they feel comfortable trying the particular technique, the next step in a player's development is to make him understand when to apply the new skill and, as importantly, why to apply it. We do this by exposing the player to a progression of increasingly complex game situations: 2 v 1, 3 v 2, and 5 v 4 (**Note**: In the situational play described, the first number refers to the number of attackers and the second the number of defenders: for example: 2 (attackers) v 1 (defender).

Game situational play is the phase of training where technique deficiencies are exposed by the pressure of the game. Each small-sided game provides a game-like learning environment through which to teach various aspects of utilizing the skill: the proper execution of the particular skill under specific pressure, the where's and whys for executing the particular technique in combination with the proper body part to be used, and the time-space relationship's influence on our decision making.

Examples of technical skills to be developed under game conditions might be (1) shooting from outside the 18 yard box, (2) long crossing, or (3) defensive and offensive heading. The first stage of instruction works at developing the correct mechanics needed for the particular skill without pressure. The second phase, the game-situational phase, further develops the skill in terms of its use under the pressures of game conditions.

Though the subject here is technique, the tactical aspects of play need to be addressed as well. Technique and tactics go hand in hand. Technically, we move the ball, while tactically we move the players. The two can't be separated from one another; they must be developed together. Tactically, the perfect game condition is the one that leads to a 2 v 1 situation offensively or a 1 v 2 situation defensively. In a 5 v 4 game, for example, a team uses ball movement and off-the-ball running to create a 2 v 1 situation around the ball. We concentrate here on technique development in the game situational play.

Many decisions must be made when a player receives a ball, and these decisions are influenced greatly by the way the ball is received. A poor first touch (the ability to control the ball in the "first touch", inside or outside of the penalty box, is the trade mark of Brazilian soccer) costs the player time that he might have used for the decision making process. It can easily result in a goal or start a dangerous counterattack against your team. Consequently, the earlier a proper decision can be identified by the player, the more time he has to analyze options and play the best one available.

These three points are important during this phase of technical development:
- develop the technique from the simple to the complex in terms of number of players and intensity of pressure;

- develop the proper tactical aspects of play in each game situation;

- concentrate on the quality of the technical skills used in these game situations;

We recommend this general progression in the game situational phase:
1. **2 v 1 play where we analyze:**
   a. offensively:
   • the quality of the skill being developed,

   • the speed and height of the ball movement,

   • the positions of players on and off the ball,

   • the speed of penetration into open space by the off-the-ball attacker,

   • the quality of finishing under various levels of pressure.

Note: The best tactical mode of attack (or attacking player circulation) in 2 v 1 play is overlapping the player in possession.

   b. defensively:
   • the proper delaying position necessary to apply pressure on the ball,

   • the positional balance between players defending on- and off-the-ball,

   • the proper interplay with the keeper, when necessary, as he acts as second defender.

2. **3 v 2 play where we analyze:**
   a. offensively:
   • the quality of the technique,

   • the movement of the players on and off-the-ball where one off-the ball attacker takes the second defender away from the ball while the remaining two attackers create a 2 v 1 situation.

   b. defensively:
   • the balance of play between 1st and 2nd defenders,

3. **5 v 4 play where we analyze:**
   a. offensively:
   • again, the quality of the technical skill,

   • the speed of the ball movement and the speed and effectiveness of the off-the-ball runs made to gain outside penetration,

   • the speed of the ball and of the players without the ball made to build an attack with inside penetration,

   • the speed of switching the point of attack,

   • the correct supporting positions in defensive and offensive diagonals as related to the ball.

Note: To increase the pressure on the attackers, 4 v 4 or 5 v 5 situations can be applied instead. Or, if the technical skills of the attackers are well developed, a 4 v 5 (with extra defender) might be applied, thus increasing the pressure on the attackers. Another way to increase the pressure on the player's speed of decision making and the quality of the skill being developed is to establish restrictions: minimize the number of touches (3, 2 and finally only 1 touch), force the player to execute the skill with his or her weaker leg, or increase the number of balls in play at any one time.

   b. defensively:
   • identify the correct time to contain and the correct time to pressure,

   • the team shape in relationship to ball position and the speed of change of that shape with the ball's movement.

PHASE III: SKILL DEVELOPMENT UNDER GAME CONDITIONS
In this phase of training, players are exposed to game-like conditions, in terms of defensive and offensive pressure, of space, and of the decision making process necessary to properly apply the particular technical skill.

The space utilized depends on the number of players: half a field fits 11 to 12 players nicely while more players require more space (8 v 8 should use 3/4 of a field, for example). Remember too, the size of the field is age-group dependent as well.

This point needs to be made concerning the amount of space used to practice and the excessive use of small-sided games to develop player touch and the short passing game: excessive use of small-sided games in small spaces interferes with the development of a player's peripheral vision, i.e., limits the area that players visualize in the game. That, in turn, develops players who constantly play with their head down, players who look exclusively for the short passing options (and frequently miss the longer, more dangerous options). Unlike the Dutch who develop their player's technical play through extensive 4 v 4 play, Brazilians prefer larger spaces with more players. In phase II (game situation) we used smaller-sized games to increase a player's number of chances to perform the technical skill, not as a tool to develop short passing play. While the Dutch ability to hold possession through a short passing game is unmatched in the world, their ability to find dangerous, creative attacking options is not so well developed.

In this phase too, players should focus on playing in the areas of the field that they occupy in the full-sided game, using small-sided play within the context of actual game situations: in 3 v 2 play for example, two forwards and an attacking midfielder might play against two defenders in the attacking third, or three defenders against two strikers in the defending third, or three midfielders against two midfielders in the middle third.

Further along in the progression, the space and number of players can be combined in two or more thirds of the field. The game condition advances from six players attacking (four defenders and two midfielders or four midfielders and two forwards) versus five defenders to a full 11 v 11 scrimmage. One point though: Defensive and offensive pressure must be at a game level of intensity to maximize results.

The coach moves around the field during this phase of the technical development and corrects anyone who needs correcting without stopping play too often. Sometimes he can stop the practice to point out a mistake or make a point to the group, but these interruptions should be kept to a minimum.

In terms of building the playing progression, always start without pressure and concentrate on the quality of the technique over the speed of its performance. Before adding pressure be sure that the players can perform at the necessary speeds. Coaches frequently jump from one step to the next before achieving the necessary skills. If a general lack of concentration is observed during development, move the drill to a game condition that places restrictions to emphasize the skill.

For example: You are working on offensive heading, and during the 2 v 1 situational play, the players have limited success. They lose their motivation and concentration. Stop the 2 v 1 play, divide the group into two teams, and play a crossing game where two balls are in play against two goals. Stop play infrequently to make coaching points and corrections. Then in your next practice, add players (3 v 2 or 5 v 4) to the drill and revisit the game situation. Again, finish the practice under game conditions but now with added crossers or added balls. Multiple balls in play with multiple crossers leads to more offensive and defensive heading chances.

Start the game condition progression without a keeper. Add the keeper when players show confidence, understanding, and control of the game condition. Train keepers separately to ensure that they understand and can make the right decision in the appropriate game condition, then put the groups together and try to work as closely as possible to actual game conditions.

Each of the technical skills utilizes this progression: play progresses from small rubber balls, to futesal balls, and finally on to regulation balls, all to increase player concentration and help the players learn to utilize the correct part of the foot and to lock their foot correctly when passing the ball. Futesal (mini soccer) is excellent for developing technical skills generally, but in particular, the fast movement with and without the ball, the aggressiveness on the ball, and especially the ability to hold and protect the ball. Many popular Brazilian players, such as Rivellino, Tostao,

Defensive Heading

Offensive Heading

Ronaldinho, and Zico, to name a few, began their soccer careers playing futesal.

The skill development sessions emphasized here are meant to proceed over many seasons. The coach emphasizes different aspects at different sessions as the players progress, not trying to cover the entire progression with all its variations in a single session.

As I said earlier, we will cover the technical skills most important to the Brazilian soccer philosophy. While realizing that many authors in North America have done a great job in educating North America about the game, we review these techniques to emphasize the Brazilian approach. For instance, the need to have the ball in control on the ground as much as possible, and the need to play one or two touches as much as possible. The technical skills covered are passing, receiving (trapping), protecting the ball, heading, crossing, finishing, and shooting.

As we proceed, we do not wish to imply that particular skills are unique to a given position, just more critical to that position in terms of the Brazilian soccer philosophy. For example, while every player on the field needs to be skilled at trapping the ball, for midfielders especially the ability to trap well is a must. The speed of play, the ball movement so characteristic of Brazilian play, starts with them being able to take a ball out of the air, put it on the ground, then move it along quickly with a minimum number of touches. Players must be skilled enough to use the body surface that not only brings the ball under immediate control but also requires the fewest number of touches to move the ball along with maximum safety and speed.

The Brazilian approach to the following technical skills will be developed in the remainder of this Chapter:

I.   Defensive/Offensive Heading
II.   Reception (Trapping) - Protecting the ball.
III.   Passing
IV.   Shooting
V.   Crossing and Finishing

I. DEFENSIVE AND OFFENSIVE HEADING

The image of the Brazilian team is that it doesn't often put the ball in the air. While that's generally true, the emphasis on attacking down the flank through its wing defenders results in many air-born crosses; therefore, skill is needed, particularly by inside defenders, in defending the ball in the air and by forwards in trying to score on those situations, i.e., skill at both defensive and offensive heading.

Heading, moreover, is one of the more important skills to teach because the risk of injury to the neck or face or to the knees when landing, is always a concern. The player should clearly understand that in heading a ball it is important that he go to the ball and head through it as opposed to reacting passively by waiting and letting the ball strike his forehead. When a player uses correct body positioning and has his neck locked on contact, as he will when heading through the ball, injury is far less likely.

A. GENERAL POINTS OF EMPHASIS: DEFENSIVE AND OFFENSIVE HEADING.

Keep the following six points in mind during the heading progression:

1. The header should contact the ball as high as possible, lock the neck, eyes open, mouth closed, and keep his or her arms up to minimize any challenge from opposing players, increase the power of the jump, improve his balance; and finally to protect his face.

2. The player should move to meet the ball, defensively striking the top of the forehead against the bottom of the ball, and offensively striking the top of the ball with the lower part of the forehead;

3. When heading without pressure, the defender should jump from both legs so as to minimize the injury potential of landing as opposed to jumping off and landing on just the front foot;

4a. The defender clearing a ball in the air always tries to switch the direction of the incoming ball, sending it far and high enough to go over the pressure and away from the danger zone in front of goal. To better do so, the player's feet should be positioned slightly off parallel to the flight of the ball with the player's back to goal so the defender can easily see the space to his opposite side, the direction he wants to clear the ball to;

4b. An attacker, on the other hand, meets the ball as high as possible, then, bending his neck toward the ground, uses the lower part of the forehead to send the ball to ground, bouncing in front of the keeper. Further, he faces the goal and tries to position himself to see both the flight of the ball and the opposite side of goal. Finally, jumping from one leg gives better mobility to any body rotation needed as the ball is met.

5. With the attacker fronting the defender and a cross coming in, the defender positions one foot in front of the other and initiates the jump off the forward foot, the one closest to the attacker, while at the same time, he keeps his front arm up to protect against a collision with the back of the attacker's head;

6a. For balls coming in from the center, the defender should position himself between the ball and the center of the goal; for balls from the flank, coming from outside the 18 yard box the defender should position himself between the center of the goal and the crosser but next to the attacker; and from crosses coming in from nearer the end line, the defender should be able to get position inside between the ball and the attacker so he can intercept the cross.

6b. A single attacker positions himself inside the box, somewhere between the far post and the opposite corner of the 18 yard box. He reads the speed of the flighted ball so as to penetrate the danger zone around the penalty spot and receives the ball just as it arrives at that spot. Ideally, he arrives just as the ball does with a good combination of power and balance.

Heading.

B. SKILL PROGRESSION FOR DEVELOPING DEFENSIVE AND OFFENSIVE HEADING

Let's now look at the particulars of the progression needed to develop the technical skill of defensive and offensive heading. First, it's important that just before the ball arrives, the player has bent his head backwards and locked the back in a straight, upright position as heading the ball with bent back lessens the power generated by the head as it snaps forward through the ball.

The locked back follows the neck, thus adding forward momentum and generating even more power. The back often bends forward slightly because of the motion of the neck, but excessive bending of the back destroys the cooperative effect between neck and back, thus lessening the power of the header.

STEP ONE in the progression isolates the proper head and neck movement: In this first step we concentrate on the full movement of the neck while practicing the head-to-ball contact in a safe environment. The player lays on his stomach while raising up on arms extended directly underneath at a shoulder's width. The player's weight is supported by the extended arms and the player's upper legs lying flat on the ground.

The player's partner, on his knees about four feet away, throws a ball underhanded to the receiving player lying down. The receiving player bends his neck back, looking skyward for the moment, then uses the top of his forehead to power through the lower portion of the ball, for offensive heading the lower part of the forehead hits the top of ball. The neck's range of motion ends with the player looking down at the ground.

The exercise is continuous for 45 seconds for U-10s and younger, 60 seconds for U15s and younger, and 75 seconds for older players, after which the players switch positions. Again, a first round is conducted with rubber balls then the second uses regulation balls.

STEP TWO increases power by adding the movement of the locked back. This time the player receives on his knees and tries to coordinate the movement of the locked back with the snap forward of the head. As before, contact is made with the top of the forehead to the bottom of the ball or the lower part of the forehead to the top of the ball; duration times are the same; and again both types of balls are used in succession before moving on.

STEP THREE brings the coordinated movement of the arms into the sequence, thus adding protection and even more power. The arms protect by establishing the header's space and increase power by adding more forward thrust to the head movement. Again on his knees, the receiver raises both arms up shoulder high and parallel to the ground to both establish the header's area of play and to hold off any defensive pressure. With arm movement in the opposite direction to the movement of the head and locked back (forward as the head moves back and snapping backward as the head snaps forward) the power of the contact is maximized.

The arms move forward while the head is drawn back, and the back remains locked, then the head snaps forward while the arms are thrust back. As always, the player ends with contact off the top of the forehead to the bottom of the ball for defensive heading and off the lower part of the forehead to the top of the ball for offensive heading. Arms are held up shoulder high for protection.

STEP FOUR in the progression incorporates leg movement: Now the player stands to receive the thrown ball from his partner. As the ball comes, the player moves to meet the ball, always coming to meet the ball rather than standing and waiting for it.

In the first stage of step four, the player doesn't actually jump from the ground, he merely raises up on his toes to meet the ball. Of course, the mechanics to this point are as before: head back, locked back, and arms up and forward, then thrust back as the head moves through its range. It doesn't matter whether the ball is played off the side or the front of the head so long as the top (defensive) of the forehead contacts the bottom of the ball, or the lower part of the forehead (offensive) touches the top of the ball.

The final step in the heading progression adds the jump to meet the ball. Here, the arm movement forward followed by their sudden thrust backwards is combined with the spring from the legs to gain height. **Note:** the player must jump as high as possible, not just bend the knees and bring his heels up behind the bottom, a common mistake.

Once in the air, the final important point to stress concerns the direction of play. The direction of the incoming ball should be changed if at all possible: If the ball comes in from the left, it should be headed out (defensively) of the box to the opposite side or (offensively) to the side of goal opposite the keeper's movement. To change direction effectively, the player must be able to see both the incoming flight of the ball and the opposite side. To do so, he should position both feet approximately parallel to the flight of the ball (or just off the parallel) with his back to goal (defensively) or front to goal (offensively), as opposed to placing the feet perpendicular to the ball's path and facing the incoming ball.

Defensive and offensive heading with directional change is practiced in groups of three or more. From a triangle configuration with player-to-player distances of five yards or so, one player throws an arced ball that a receiving player must come to, jump for, and redirect with a headed ball to a third player who, in turn, catches the ball and restarts the sequence.

The thrown ball should be high, arcing, and aimed to land a few feet in front of the receiving player to force the header to come to the ball. Again, power is generated through the coordinated movements of the motion forward to meet the ball, the neck snap, the locked back, and the arm movement; protection is provided by the raised arms; the probability of success in any challenge is increased by being first to the ball, i.e, by jumping to meet the ball; and the success of the clearance from the danger area in front of the goal is better insured with the ball redirected high and away (defensive), or to the ground (offensive) redirected away from the keeper to the opposite side from which the ball has come.

STEP FIVE in the progression brings different aspects of the technique together in a series of heading exercises where the time involvement versus age group is as before. First, we improve player coordination by requiring players to do a forward roll, stand then receive a high ball from a partner.

The receiving player must complete the roll, jump and properly head the ball back defensively or offensively (depending on the technical approach of the coach). **Note:** Here, don't worry about changing the direction of the incoming ball. The action improves coordination and quickness by forcing the player to be more reactive to each new heading opportunity; the skill becomes instinctive with practice.

Next, we differentiate the passing header from the clearing or finishing header. Here two players stand about 10 yards apart. The receiving player runs at the other player and receives a thrown ball at about 5 to 10 yards between the two (depending on the age group). This first ball is passed back to the thrower by striking the lower part of the forehead against the upper part of the ball and heading the ball low to the ground, with much less range of motion from the neck and with far less power, more finesse and touch (passing the ball). The technique for offensive heading is similar to the passing heading, except power is demanded in offensive heading.

The first player moves backwards and sprints away 10 yards to receive a second ball, this one to be cleared with power, both far and high (clearing the ball defensively). Again, a change of direction is not stressed.

Finally, we develop the technique of lateral running for the defensive clearance or offensive finishing. Frequently in a match the defenders and attackers are called on to react laterally to high balls: crosses, corners and free kick are examples.

In groups of three: two players are positioned about 10 yards apart with balls while a third, the receiver, is positioned in the middle. The latter player slides or shuffles from one side to the other with feet parallel to the two outside players and receives, in turn, a high ball from each.

The inside player returns the throws by executing the proper technique for a defensive or offensive header, though with no attempt at changing the direction of the ball. The throwers then move 20 yards away from the receiver and now deliver long crosses from both sides. Do a number of repetitions until the inside, receiving player becomes comfortable receiving the long cross.

STEP SIX is the last step before moving to game situations. At this point the player should be able to execute the technique correctly without real pressure. Here, we add light pressure to see if the players can execute the skill properly in more game-like situations. The defender should be on the penalty spot with the keeper behind communicating and an attacker putting light pressure on the defender's reception of the flighted ball. Six players with balls outside the box, at a distance related to age group and skill level, cross long balls from different angles and directions. Common positions for the crossers are at the four corners of the penalty box, each corner kick area, and the area directly in front of goal. When emphasizing attacking play, the defensive pressure is light; conversely, when emphasizing defensive play, the attacking pressure is light.

For an offensive header, the attacker should be positioned six yards behind the penalty spot in line with the ball. This player should move sideways, parallel to the flighted ball, positioned facing the ball, and observing the goalkeeper until making a final run to meet the ball, then finish it. Players outside the box provide a variety of crosses as before. **Diagram 1** shows the position of the balls to be crossed and the common target for these crosses.

The defender will move to clear ball one or the attacker will move to finish ball one. As soon as the first ball is touched, ball two will be crossed from the opposite side, slightly behind the defender or forward who must now react as quickly as possible to head the new ball away to the opposite side (defender) or to try to score (attacker). This constant movement should be kept up until six balls have been crossed. When adding light pressure, the function of the forward will be to move to the ball and try to occupy the space where the ball is arriving, thus forcing the defender to learn how to react quickly, to judge the momentum of the incoming ball, and to communicate with the keeper. The keeper and defender must work on making the correct decision as a team.

The same is done when emphasizing play by the attackers, but now we ask the defenders to apply light pressure. When working with young or less skilled players, we also recommend that crossers throw the balls instead of kick them to insure the quality of the high balls.

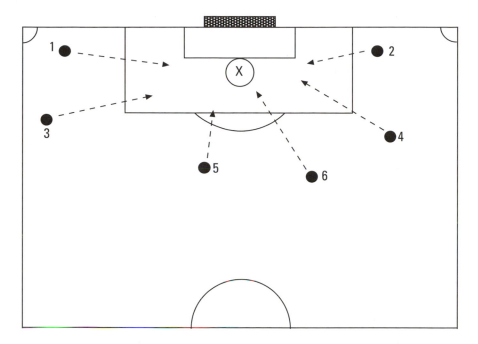

Diagram 1: *Development of defensive/offensive heading without pressure. Attackers or defenders receive crosses from different angles.*

C. EXTRA ACTIVITIES FOR DEFENSIVE AND OFFENSIVE HEADING

- **Circuit Training:** We apply technical circuit training after the steps of technical development are complete. Circuit training improves the speed of execution of the drill. Such training, which is appropriate to offensive and defensive heading, is covered in the Chapter on physical conditioning.

- Before moving to the game-situational phase of the defensive and offensive heading techniques, apply the technique in fun games that are similar to actual game conditions but have an emphasis on heading.

  We recommend the rugby game for heading: two teams with an equal number of players play on half a field; the game keeps two balls in play simultaneously, adding a third when players are capable of handling the increased pressure; players in possession cannot move more than three steps before passing to a teammate; the game is played with hands to facilitate the number of high balls; goals are scored by heading a ball into goal; no tackling is allowed; defenders must intercept the ball in the air with their hands; a ball hitting the ground causes loss of possession; attackers can only score with their heads, and keepers play conventionally. Game duration is 20 minutes. Younger ages play first with the rubber ball, then add the regular ball later.

D. SECOND PHASE: GAME SITUATION FOR DEFENSIVE AND OFFENSIVE HEADING

From applying the technical skill under light, token pressure, we bring the skill to the second phase of instruction, the game situational phase. This phase should be entered when players show enough confidence and consistency of execution to perform the skill well under light pressure. Remember though, it is important that we not be in a hurry when developing skills; sometimes players need several practices to achieve quality, and if you move too fast through the phases of instruction for that particular skill, the player's comprehension of the skill's proper execution often remains poor and that leads to developing bad habits that have a way of showing up in the game.

We start the progression playing 1 v 1 by using two goals placed about 30 yards apart or 1/3 of the field related to the age group. Each goal is manned by a keeper; two crossers roam outside the width of the penalty box up and down the field; and two attackers and two defenders play inside the width of the penalty box, a defender and attacker being constrained to play in their respective halves of the field with the variation of switching sides of the field after a cross is made. This option will increase the physical condition and develop the ability to intercept or finish crosses at speed. The crossers, playing with the team in possession, deliver crosses to both goals both right and left-footed from anywhere along their line within the offensive half of the field, sometimes from the endline, sometimes from the top of the box. Diagram 2.

Note: The heading confrontation is 1 v 1, an attacker at goal (offensive heading) and a defender away from goal (defensive heading), though other players are involved as well. The attacker tries to score, heading the ball low and away from the keeper, while the defender tries to clear the ball to the opposite side high and away, either to the opposite-side crosser or his teammate attacker, and should the keeper intercept a ball, he plays it out to the opposite side crosser. The players switch functions after many repetitions, but not until some consistency of quality is seen in the heading. Strive for quality, don't let players become lazy and develop bad habits! But be quick to stop the session when fatigue sets in and affects quality. Move on to a game condition, with additional players involved and less emphasis on instruction.

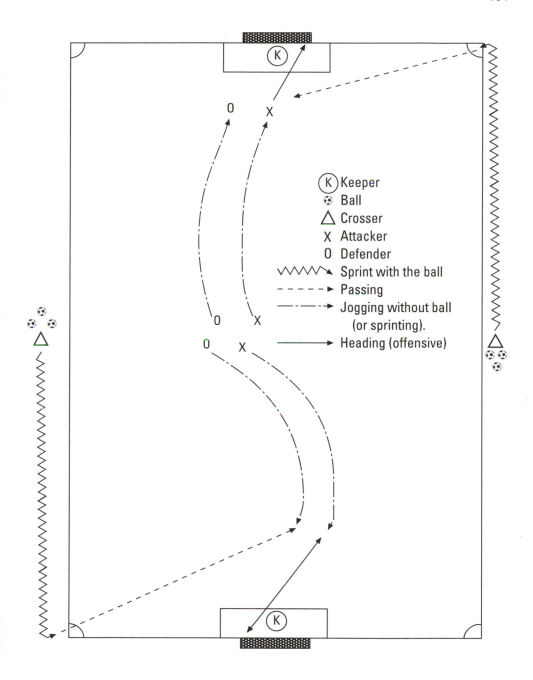

Diagram 2: *Progression of 1 x 1 (defensive/offensive heading) with pressure. Played on a third of the field.*

As soon as the players demonstrate the quality expected in their 1 v 1 defensive and offensive heading, add a player to each team and move on to a 2 v 1 situation (emphasizing the attack) or a 1 v 2 situation (emphasizing the defense), but note that it is extremely important that all players receive both defensive and offensive heading practice because both techniques can be used in any part of the field. Two attackers increase the pressure on the defender and that, in turn, helps to increase the defender's fast reaction to the ball; conversely, the lone attacker against two defenders does the same thing for the attacker. Use the same field organization as used in the 1 v 1 play.

An important point to stress in this play is the need for communication between the keeper and the defender(s). The keeper should tell the defender to cover either the near or far post, while the keeper takes the other, or to just leave the ball. This type of communication is necessary in the real game all over the field, not just inside the penalty box, that's one reason why everyone (even forwards) need to take a turn at defending. Communication lays a foundation for good defensive organization.

With field space, not to mention regulation goals, at a premium and practice time limited, it is necessary to use these sessions efficiently. So divide the team in half; let your assistant coach handle one of the groups; and set up another field with flags for goals and flat cones for boundaries. If necessary, let field players be keepers. Half way through the session switch groups between fields and between coaches.

After the players consistently can identify the correct positioning and the correct momentum of the ball, and their fast-reaction speed, the level of concentration, and the communication skills with the keeper have improved, the next step is to add another player (attacker or defender) and create the 3 v 2 and 2 v 3 situations. Again, the field organization remains the same. In these situations the most important point to evaluate, and further develop if need be, will be the communication between the keeper and defenders. Further, defensively observe the positioning in relation to where the pressure is coming, and offensively the positioning for goal coverage and coordinated running at goal.

Finally, the last game situations are 5 v 4 and 4 v 5. Both create actual game conditions and demonstrate the applicability of the technique to the real game. The organization in terms of number of goals and the use of keepers and crossers remains the same, while the distance between goals increases to 60-70 yards or 3/4 of the field. You must add more time between crosses, by forcing the attacking team to take 10 touches or only cross from the endline to give both sides time to position properly. More than before, communication among the players and in particular between the keeper and his defense is a major factor in applying technical and

tactical development.
Communication must be emphasized here.

E. THIRD PHASE: GAME CONDITION FOR DEFENSIVE AND OFFENSIVE HEADING

The final phase of instruction brings the heading technique to actual game conditions where the player is exposed, as closely as possible to the game itself. To this point, you as coach have been analyzing technique, correcting mistakes, and improving play. The major goal of this phase is to improve these specific aspects of play: speed of ball movement, less predictability in the choice of the point from which the cross originates, the entire team's defensive marking and covering in anticipation of the flighted ball into the box, and again the level of communication between defensive players.

Game condition - Defensive heading.

Game conditional play should always involve two teams playing 11 v 11 or the specific full team related to the age group. One of the biggest problems in North America, especially at the club level, is the lack of players available to scrimmage with two full teams. In this phase, the coach should plan ahead and invite additional players to form the second team or invite another team to a friendly scrimmage. If you're inviting additional players to play with substitutes against your starting 11, it would be helpful if the invited players were experienced, perhaps older and better skilled, so as to increase the pressure against the starting team and help the substitutes play at a higher level.

Two teams play a regular game with certain restrictions: at least 60 minutes for U-14 and above, 40 minutes for U-13 and U-12, and 25 minutes below that. As coach, our goal is to focus on the quality of the heading, both defensive and offensive. In your comments concentrate on heading, don't try to fix tactical, positioning, or correct any other technical skill problems. Excess stoppage for a host of corrections becomes boring. If you need to make an observation to an individual player, just walk

Game condition - Diving heading.

on the field and make your comment to just that player; don't stop the flow of the match.

Before play begins two balls are placed in each corner of the field. The game starts with the following general restriction which is made to improve the possession characteristics of the team with the ball: the ball must be passed on the ground; it can be played in the air only when shooting or crossing. Every time a team takes a shot or header at goal and the keeper saves or the ball continues out of play, that team follows with four crosses from the two corners (two from each corner). The crosser is the player closest to each corner when the last ball is played out.

As soon as the additional crossed ball is cleared from the penalty box, that ball is no longer in the game and a new cross is played in from the opposite side. The two teams should re-organize themselves for the next ball with the attackers moving out of the penalty box to restart their penetrating runs and the defenders again identifying their marks. It's important that the situation inside the penalty box remain dynamic as the cross comes in; the attackers should try to meet the ball with as much forward momentum as possible rather than just standing and waiting. The latter is just too easily defended. The keeper should call for his defense to push out when the ball is either cleared by the defense or held by the keeper.

The second and third extra balls will be played similarly to the first, but the fourth becomes the game ball with which the defense can now counter-attack.

These points should be analyzed:

- the positioning of the attackers and defenders: each defender must face the player he is marking at a distance close enough to touch him so they can bring immediate pressure; attackers should move to open space, run to meet the flighted ball, and try to anticipate the defenders' reactions.

- the techniques used to clear and to finish and the players' use of arm and leg motion to protect themselves;

- the level and effectiveness of the communication.

As soon as quality play is demonstrated in these areas, increase the pressure by introducing another ball into play. Playing with two live balls, while decreasing the number of players fighting for each, increases the number of crosses. **Note:** with two live balls in play, the four cross condition is no longer applicable.

You should always use your imagination to increase the pressure on the players executing the heading, but be careful not to go through the phases too quickly. This progression could take half a season for U-12s and younger, one-fourth of the season for U-16 and below, and perhaps two practice sessions with U-17 and above through the professional level.

F. SUMMARY OF IMPORTANT POINTS FOR DEFENSIVE AND OFFENSIVE HEADING

These points are most important to defensive and offensive heading:

- The neck should be locked to allow the defensive player to send the ball as far away as possible from the danger zone switching the point of attack. Or offensively to allow the offensive player to send the ball as hard as possible to the ground away from the keeper;

- It is always important to try to switch the direction and the height of the ball. Defensively, the header should send it directly to a team-mate or at least create time for the defense to re-organize for the next offensive pressure by clearing the ball far and high; offensively, he should shoot low to the opposite side of goal from which the ball has come.

- The defender and attacker must go as high as possible to meet the ball, and a good player will read the momentum of the ball as it comes;

- Arms should always be held up to protect against unexpected pressure and from being hit in the face;

- Defensively, heading high balls under pressure, the attacker in front of defender, the feet should be positioned diagonally, with one forward and one back, to create a better platform for jumping into the ball; this creates more power for the clearance; the arm should be held up between the defender's face and the opponent's head so as to avoid injury;

- The top of the forehead should hit the bottom of the ball (defender), and the lower part of the forehead should hit the top of the ball (attacker);

- When heading under no pressure, we recommend jumping off both legs to avoid landing on just one knee and risking injury. Remember, the momentum of the jump must be correct, and both arms should be up for protection to the face, to help with balance, and to increase the power of the jump;

- Defensively and offensively, the body position should be held in diagonal to the ball, between the point where the ball is crossed and the point where the header wants to send the ball.

- Defensive positioning depends on where the cross is driven from:
  a. from near the center of the field, the defender must be in position, as explained before, but now between the ball and the center of his goal;
  b. from outside and at the top of the penalty box, the defender should be in a position that allows him to see both the ball and the opposite upfield corner of the penalty box;
  c. from the endline, the defender should be positioned between the ball and the penetrating opponent.

G. TRAPPING AND RECEIVING

One of the most important moments in Brazilian soccer came in group play in the 1970 World Cup held in Mexico: the goal Jairzinho scored against England. England at the time was perceived as the best team in the world having won the Cup in 1966. But this win by Brazil set the stage for their dominance in this Cup and in the ones yet to come. The final ball to Jairzinho was so perfectly placed by Péle that the best defense in the world at the time could do nothing to stop it. The key was Péle's preparation of the ball: he received it while turning to the opposite side and with one touch was able to read the situation and then identify the necessary power and proper direction to send the ball on to Jairzinho. That kind of ball reception is what makes the Brazilian player unique in his ball control and use of quick feet.

The ball should always be received while facing the opposite side of the field from where the ball comes. Péle gave Jairzinho a great pass, resulting in an important goal for Brazil, and later, in the final against Italy, he repeated the identical reception then provided Carlos Alberto Torres a great pass. The quality of these passes and the success of the subsequent finishing resulted directly from Péle's ability to receive the ball, and quickly bring the ball to the ground under control.

Ball reception is the most important technical skill to be taught. It is most responsible for a team's consistency of play, its quality of passing, its speed of play, and its degree of safeness of play (safety of play in terms of the degree of ball exposure to the other team). Even more importantly, a team with good receiving skills reduces its chances at injury because good receiving skills create fewer 50/50 challenges.

More than 50% of the body contact in soccer today comes from the defensive pressure applied as an offensive player receives the ball. The long-ball game, prevalent at the lower levels of the sport where the emphasis is on speed and athleticism rather than skill, is particularly susceptible to contact. Utilizing the long pass without first teaching the player how to prepare the body before and after the ball arrives invites violent collisions and serious injury. Just observe American football players who spend hours in practice learning how to position their bodies to protect against the hit expected following a pass reception, and they absorb the blow encased in an extensive array of safety equipment. In soccer a similar long ball sends an inexperienced attacker and defender racing into a potentially violent, uncontrolled collision, one that often generates injuries. This type of play is the major reason injuries occur in recreational soccer programs.

Not enough coaches spend enough time educating their players as to the injury ramifications of long-ball play. Probably most don't even understand the risks themselves; they think violent collisions without pads are just part of the game. Brazilians, on the other hand, play a style of soccer that, while being secure and at the same time unpredictable, is also safe, a style utilizing short diagonal passes played most times on the ground. The technical aspects of play that promote this style are the speed of the ball movement and the individual player's receiving skills, i.e., the utilization of the minimum number of touches necessary to score goals.

If the ball is received while facing the player making the pass, the pressure on the receiver will be greater because defensive pressure naturally follows the ball, and the receiver's first touch will always be toward that pressure. That type of reception, consequently, forces the receiver into a second touch aimed at better control and ball protection and a third touch to identify the best option available. When this last touch is taken, the defenders have had enough time to pressure all the available options and force the player in possession into a mistake. Rarely does a North American team take four or more touches without a resultant loss of possession. The major reason for these possession breakdowns is the lack of proper reception fundamentals.

Another equally important aspect of good reception is the height of the ball. Passing through the air forces receivers to waste at least two touches controlling the ball. After the receiver's third touch, defenders have had time enough to identify where the next ball is going and stop it. Even skillful players who are not tactically prepared receive poorly and that fact alone makes the movement of the ball and their resultant play far too predictable.

To improve play in this area, many national teams spend time in Brazil training and playing games where their sole purpose is to increase team speed of reaction on the reception so as to better control their possession: teams like Jamaica, Japan, China, and South Korea.

We think that receiving and trapping skills are fundamental to defensive players as well because the Brazilian philosophy starts by building out from the back. If your defenders do not have good trapping and receiving techniques, they will never be confident enough to try to control the ball and start to build. Instead, they most often will just kick it away without any thought of control and, in so doing, either create 50/50 balls or give possession outright to the other team. On the other hand, once the correct reception mechanics are taught and mastered at an early age, the defensive player will experience less pressure and develop more confidence in playing the game properly, playing under control. Understand though, this process is one of proper education and practice; mistakes are a natural part of learning so have patience as a coach.

A. GENERAL POINTS OF EMPHASIS FOR TRAPPING AND RECEIVING

Keep in mind the following six points during the trapping and receiving progression:

1. The receiver should always be in a position diagonal to the ball-either in the defensive or offensive diagonal relative to the ball-because square balls are dangerous: They decrease the speed of the attack and make play much more predictable to defenders;

2. The receiver should face the player with the ball, thus showing he is an option to receive the ball;

3. When the pass is made, the receiver should move to the ball so as to avoid the anticipation of the covering defender;

4. The first decision of the receiver should be to put the ball on the ground with the first touch if at all possible; if the receiver is in his defensive zone and under pressure, the reception with the head in the air is optimal, a clearing ball must be played;

5. The receiver should receive the ball while turning his body to the opposite side of the field from where the ball came and, also as important, change the direction of the ball, even if it comes in the air; the second touch on high balls should either be to pass it on to another player on the ground, or if that is not possible, should bring the ball to the ground under control;

6. The receiver should have his arms up to protect himself against the defensive pressure with knees bent enough to allow good balance; balls higher than the knee should be received with feet in the air so as to avoid injuries from collisions with the defensive player (receptions of high balls with feet planted firmly on the ground promote knee and ankle injuries).

Proper receiving utilizes a combination of body position relative to the height and power of the ball. The most common parts of the body used in trapping and receiving:

• **BALLS ON THE GROUND** (the easiest and fastest kind of ball to receive): the part of the foot used in receiving is related to the area of the foot closest to where the ball is being received, the intensity of the defensive pressure on the receiver, and the direction the receiver wants to then take the reception:

(a) **inside of the foot**: the most often used method to receive the ball; this reception is applicable in general when the receiver has pressure coming and must play safely; the ball should be

Inside foot trapping.

received at the ball's center by the middle of the foot with the inside sole of the foot tilted down to help prevent a subsequent bounce; heels are also down (toes raised) to help avoid the mistrap, and the receiving foot is held in front of the foot not receiving with that leg bent; at the point of reception, the receiving foot should come backwards with the ball so both feet are now in line with the ball in between; finally, arms are held up and knees bent to better define the receiver's space and help him to ward off defenders;

Inside foot reception - medium ball.

(b) outside of the foot: generally used when the defensive pressure comes from behind the receiver (Dunga of the Brazilian National Team is a master) or when the pressure is far enough away to allow a quick forward penetration (Ronaldinho of InterMilan and the Brazilian National Team excels here); its quick response helps create a fast counter-attack; the outside middle of the foot is tilted to the outside with the reception, and as before, the receiving foot begins in front but gathers the ball and returns to be in line with the other foot; the opposite arm should be held up to shoulder level so as to ward off defenders; often the outside foot reception arises out of desperation as a consequence of the extreme pressure placed on the pass reception coupled with the slow reaction of the receiver; a major problem with the outside foot trap is that poor reception mechanics (and body positioning) invite knee injury;

(c) sole of the foot: this reception should be attempted when the receiver is playing with his back to the goal, and he wants to generate time for defenders to get closer to midfielders or for forwards to gain time for midfielders to push up and close the gap between sectors (Romario of the Brazilian National Team used this technique many times in World Cup '94); three major situations arise where this technique is especially useful: the receiver wants (1) to generate time for his supporting players to close gaps forward, (2) to create time for an overlap, or (3) to establish balance for himself before making the decision to turn and shoot or wait and prepare the shot for someone coming from the back; remember these important points: the receiving foot should be away as far as possible from the pressure at the player's back; the receiver should, if possible, lean on the chest of the defender; the arms again should be held shoulder high to ward off the defender's anticipation of the ball; the non-receiving knee should be bent, and the body balanced but locked against the defender's pressure;

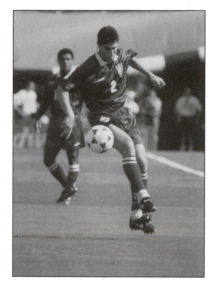

• **THIGH** (used when the ball comes higher than the knee but lower than the hip): The receiver's thigh should face the ball as it comes and move forward to meet the ball (in the air if possible); the receiving leg is raised and bent at a 60 degree angle, causing the quadriceps to relax and on the reception move the ball to the ground;

• **CHEST** (part of the body generally used when the ball comes higher than the hip but the leg is unable to reach it): The receiver holds air in his chest and releases it at the moment the ball is touched; the chest is positioned to face the sky so as to guarantee that even should the reception be poor the ball will pop up and thus help put the ball on the ground with the second touch;

• **HEAD:** though it's unusual to trap a ball with the head, we mention this technique and practice it because the head trap can provide an unexpected offensive weapon; the player uses the top of his forehead with a locked neck just before the ball is received; the ball will again pop up under a controlled power; the player follows the ball with his or her eyes and waits for the ball to reach the ground before finally bringing it under control or volleying.

B. PHASE I: SKILL PROGRESSION FOR DEVELOPING RECEPTION OF THE BALL

Now we will observe the step-by-step particulars of the progression needed to develop the technical skill of receiving.

In **PHASE ONE** we develop technical fundamentals, always working with partners, both right and left legs with the same intensity in this phase (especially true for U-12 and younger players). The technical progression is divided in four steps:

In **STEP ONE** the receiver should look up and make contact (eye, vocal, or signal) with the passer. The receiver, in turn, should move in the opposite direction away from the passer (check away). He takes the defender away before coming quickly back into the open space created by the first run away. In the open space created the receiver wants to gain possession. Remember two things: (1) these checking runs should be made into spaces located to the passer's defensive or offensive diagonals, and (2) the player with the ball is not the one who makes the good pass; the player moving into open space away from the pressure is the one who creates the safe quality pass.

STEP TWO has the receiver sprinting into open space on his toes as fast as possible, into a diagonal position relative to the passer, while at the same time identifying the easiest surface on the body to use for control of the incoming ball.

STEP THREE begins at the moment of reception. The receiver slows his speed to the ball and at the same time adjusts his body positioning relative to the ball. This step is perhaps the most important step in the progression; all four parts of the body, foot, thigh, chest, and head should be practiced until there is clear comprehension as to the relationship between height of the ball and what part of the body receives the ball.

STEP FOUR focuses finally on redirecting the ball, either preparing for a new pass, shooting, or dribbling. At this point it's important to remember that developing the concentration and the decision making process necessary to continue play after the reception is important before moving on to game situations.

C. ANTICIPATION IN RECEIVING AND TRAPPING

We have been developing techniques for receiving the ball from a teammate or sometimes from a mistake made by the other team, but one of the most important aspects of Brazilian soccer is the ability to win possession by anticipating the next pass to be made. This skill creates opportunities for initiating fast counterattacks.

Attention should be paid to teaching this phase of the reception technique so as to avoid injuries. These important points need to be

considered when teaching defensive anticipation of the offensive pass:
- The defender should follow the movement of the ball with the eyes;

- The defender trying to anticipate the ball should be able to touch the player he is marking;

- The defender should wait for contact (by mouth, eyes, or hand signals) to be made between passer and receiver before deciding if the anticipation will be possible.

This development is done in groups of three: one with the ball, a receiver 10 yards away in line and facing the passer, and the defensive player responsible for the anticipation behind the latter at a distance of one yard. As soon as the pass is made by the passer, the defender anticipating the interception moves quickly to front the receiving offensive player by using his inside leg to try to intercept the pass and then play it back to the original passer.

The four most common heights used for anticipating the ball:
1. On the ground: The defender sees the last contact the passer had was with the player he is marking. At this moment the defender must be on his toes awaiting the right moment to advance in front of the receiver, moving as quickly as possible to intercept the pass. The defender uses the inside leg and inside foot so as to avoid knee injuries. In our drill the defender moves quickly to the front of the receiver and touches the ball back to the passer. After returning the pass, the defender runs back-

Anticipation on the ground.

wards, going around the receiver while facing the ball and the passer, and then anticipating from the other side.

This drill should be done for 60 seconds for U-15s and older, 45 seconds for U-14s and younger and 30 seconds for U-10 players. The three players alternate functions. *Remember:* The receiver should keep arms up and the defender push the arm down with his elbow (never hands) to facilitate the penetration of the defender and subsequent anticipation of the ball.

2. Medium balls: The sequence is the same, but the passer now serves the ball at hip height, and the defender anticipates by sending it to the ground away from the attacker.

3. On the chest: balls higher than the hip, ones that cannot be anticipated with the feet, should be taken with the chest. Now the balls are intercepted in the air by the defender, and he anticipates by sending it to the ground first, then back to the passer.

Anticipating high balls.

4. High balls: Heading anticipation becomes necessary when the ball comes higher than shoulder level, and the chest is not an option. The defender should again force the receiver's arms down and anticipate the ball with his head.

Anticipation by the defender (and a subsequent interception) should be practiced at the same time that the reception is practiced during the game situation phase. Anticipation is a very important defensive aspect to teach young players.

D. PHASE TWO: GAME SITUATION FOR DEVELOPING RECEIVING AND TRAPPING SKILLS

As soon as some development of the reception techniques of players has been observed by the coach, he should expose this technical skill to pressure. The recommended progression is:

1. 2 v 1 play with two goals, two keepers on 1/3 of the field: Players break into four equal groups placed next to the four goal posts. Attackers and defenders are on opposite sides (Diagram 3). One player from one of the defensive groups passes the ball to an attacking player at the opposite

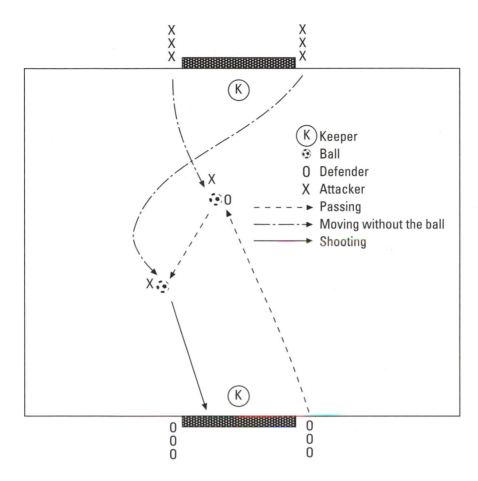

Diagram 3: *2 x 1 with long ball trapping and for passing technique.*

side. The receiving player makes decisions concerning the trapping and subsequent offensive play while the defender moves quickly to apply pressure. Most often the receiving attacker holds the reception as his teammate makes an overlapping run if the pressure is put on the attacker with the ball. If the pressure is put on the player overlapping, the attacker with the ball will do the penetration. Of course, the balls given by defenders are of varying heights. The attacking player not shooting retreats to the back of the opposite line of attackers while the defender moves to the other line of attackers, and the shooter moves to one of the lines of defenders. Continuous balls are played in this way by alternating the side from which the ball is played. At this point only one option to switch the point of attack is available: the pass to the overlapping attacker.

Points to observe from your players in this step:
- The correct movement on the diagonal into open space away from the defensive pressure;

- The quality of reception technique, confirming that it was the right decision based on the height and the power of the ball;

- The body position before and after the first touch.

2. 3 v 2 play with two keepers and two goals on a 1/3 sized field: with a keeper in goal, groups of two defenders send the ball to three attackers; the three attackers then have 15 seconds to score; taking more time to control the reception gives less time to score the goal. Players must train in these situations trying to limit their play to just two touches and, of course, using both feet.

Points to observe:
- The first attacker's reception and the movement of the other two attackers;

- The speed and correctness of technique of the trapping, observing if the best decision was made;

- To facilitate the decision of the receiver one player should move away from the ball while the other shows for the ball, both in diagonal directions;

- minimize the situation to 2 v 1.

3. 5 v 4 Situation play with five attackers, four defenders, two keepers and two goals on a 1/3 sized field: This is the best and the last situation to be developed before moving to game conditions. Here we observe the circulation of offensive and defensive players relative to the quality of the reception. Play is started by one of the outside midfielders. Attackers try to score while defenders try to intercept the ball and build a counter-attack using one of the outside parts of the field, trying to dribble through cones (five yards apart) placed to each side, thus defining the wing zones of play.

Important points to observe:
- The speed of movement of the ball related to the quality of the reception;

- The body position related to the pressure, direction, and power of the ball;

- The constant movement of the players to provide diagonal playing options;

- Observe the number of passes without losing possession, confidence and concentration could be factors limiting the success of this game situation.

Variations can be applied to increase players' speed of reaction: identify a part of the body to be emphasized during the session: using 3 touches, 2 balls; 2 touches, 2 balls; 2 touches, 1 ball; and limiting trapping to the weaker foot. Always remember to receive the ball facing the opposite side of the field from which the ball came.

E. THIRD PHASE - GAME CONDITION

Two important game conditions (8 v 7 and 8 v 8 with goals and keepers) are commonly used before graduating to 11 v 11 play (for over 12 age group). All aspects of play, concentrating on receiving decisions, are analyzed and corrected. The coach moves around the field identifying common mistakes and privately correcting them during the session. As the players improve in their quality of performance, it is important that the coach compliments the players' effort and decision making ability. Remember to isolate on the players' reception skills, especially those of outside defenders who find outside midfielders and strikers showing up wide at the flanks. A deep pass by them along this line is a very effective way to counter-attack.

The final game condition will be 11 v 11. We strongly recommend the 11 v 11 situation because it simulates real game play. Here, you will be able to identify any problem with the reception technique and its development. Each player will be covering, marking, or penetrating as the evolving game situation dictates. Further, the speed of ball movement and intensity of defensive pressure will be game-like. One major problem likely will show up: a slow speed of decision making, often because of incorrect positioning, affects the time available to the players for the correct receiving preparation. As they develop the receiving technique, their decision making comes quicker and that in turn leads to more time for the right decision.

To increase pressure you might add these conditions or restrictions:
- the team must link at least six passes before taking a shot, thus increasing its number of receptions;

- technical skills can be emphasized in the 11 v 11 game; forcing players to concentrate on techniques and the short passing game on the ground.

III. PASSING

Brazilian soccer is recognized throughout the world for its speed and security of passing, for creating unexpected opportunities and counterattacks. Here, we consider the technical principles of passing.

One of the most important aspects of passing to be developed is the ability of the passer to identify which player is in the best diagonal position and/or the best open space to send the ball safely. The passer must also understand that the pass need not always be made in an offensive direction; many times a defensive diagonal pass can create a quick switch in the point of attack and lead to a very dangerous counterattack through the other side of the field.

Mentioned earlier and especially appropriate to this technical skill is the use of small rubber balls. Each step in this progression utilizes the small ball. This helps increase the softness of the pass, and the players identify the correct body part to use in any kind of pass by feeling it.

A. GENERAL POINTS OF EMPHASIS: PASSING

Keep the following six points of emphasis in mind during the passing technique progression:

1. The quality of the pass is a result of a good reception;

Reviewing: For a good reception, the receiving player must be positioned diagonally, either defensively or offensively to the ball; the receiving player receives the ball while turning to the opposite side from where the ball came; and finally, the receiver makes decisions (what body part to receive with, where to play the next pass, etc.) before receiving;

2. Pass the ball on the ground to facilitate the reception;

3. If a long ball is the best option to be played, the passer should try to send it into an open space two to three yards in front of the receiver; this helps the receiver identify the next correct decision to make and the speed to apply to the next pass;

4. The pass should be made to any receiver in position to play quickly;

5. The passer should move in a direction opposite to where the ball was passed, except when an overlapping situation is available to create a 2 v 1 situation;

6. Always keep arms up and knees bent when executing the pass for better body protection and balance.

Body positioning for a good reception.

B. SKILL PROGRESSION FOR DEVELOPING PASSING TECHNIQUE

PHASE ONE: Fundamental Development
Because of the consistency obtained from playing the ball on the ground and the safeness of play with regard to holding possession with passes on the ground, we emphasize the development of the technical skill of passing.
The following seven steps are used here in the passing progression:

STEP ONE: In looking for the best decision, the passer must consider all the available options for playing the ball. The player with the ball is not the one most responsible for making the good pass: the one moving into open space for the reception is much more responsible for the good pass. Looking for the good passing option is very important, but when a good option is unavailable, the passer is forced to delay the pass too long, and that effectively neutralizes all options. If the receiver, on the other hand, looks around and decides where the ball has to be played before he receives it and then moves into that open space, the receiver can insure that an effective pass is made.

In **STEP TWO** we explain how the ball should be prepared to facilitate the pass. For the longer passes, touch the ball diagonally 2 to 3 yards away, use the outside of the foot for this diagonal preparation of the ball. For passes shorter than 15 yards, this preparation is not necessary because power is less important than accuracy. This diagonal preparation is necessary when the ball is to be sent long distances of 25 yards or more.

In **STEP THREE** the passing execution is considered: for short passes on the ground, the passer moves to the ball as fast as necessary but wants to produce accuracy rather than power. However, the longer the pass, the less the accuracy expected. When preparing to make a long pass the passer should run on his toes to the ball. Short steps are taken when moving to the ball to better enable last-second corrections should they be necessary. The steps are taken quickly to increase power.

In **STEP FOUR** we observe the correct placement of the non-passing foot. Short passes do not require proper placement of the opposite foot to ensure accuracy and power. Longer passes, however, require more power, allowing less attention to accuracy. For passes longer than 15 yards, the opposite foot should be placed on line with the ball, with toes pointing at the passing target. The distance from the opposite, non-passing foot to the ball should be equal to the distance between the foot and the knee.

It is important for the passer to know where the non-kicking foot was placed because this helps him make corrections in positioning when mistakes are made. The non-kicking foot provides balance, power, and accuracy. When the non-kicking foot is poorly placed, common mistakes are observed:

When a ball passed with the right leg moves too far to the right side of the receiver, the passer's non-kicking foot is too far from the ball. This forces the kicking foot to hit the ball too much to the inside. To correct that pass, move the non-kicking foot closer to the ball, verify the correct distance between foot and ball (foot to knee) and try again.

When the pass moves too far to the left of the receiver, the reason is the non-kicking foot is too close to the ball. This placement forces the kicking foot to hit the ball too much to the outside. To correct, move the non-kicking foot further away.

Many times the non-kicking foot is correctly placed distance wise, but problems occur when that foot is placed too far forward. The ball is hit on the top, which forces the ball to the ground and wastes power. This, in turn, causes the pass to be short. Correct by moving the non-kicking foot back on line with the ball. If, on the other hand, the ball goes constantly up into the air and over the receiving player, either the non-kicking foot is too far behind the ball or the knee is not bent enough. Correct this by moving the non-kicking foot forward in line with the ball or bending the opposite knee further.

In **STEP FIVE** we look at the kicking foot as it touches the ball. The foot must be locked; the kind of pass will dictate the correct part of the foot and correct part of the ball to be hit.

• **For short passes on the ground** (no more than 20 yards): the inside or outside of the foot hits the center of the ball. For longer passes on the ground, the opposite knee must be bent at about 60 degrees, and the ball hit with the instep of the foot.

• **Curved passes on the ground** (inside or outside of the foot): ball is hit on the outside edge, either to the inside or outside of the ball depending on the curvature desired.

• **Driven ball passing (medium distance balls 20 to 35 yards):** the instep of the foot hits the center of the ball, and the opposite knee is bent about 30 degrees.

• **Curved ball passing (medium distance balls):** the instep hits the ball on a wide edge at its
center height; it is not necessary to bend the opposite knee.

• **High ball passing (over 35 yards):** Kick under the ball, again with the instep part of the foot, but without bending the opposite knee.

• **Curved ball passing: (long distance balls):** Kick under the ball at its widest part with the instep and again not bending the opposite knee.

These important points need to be observed in passing:

• **Inside of the foot passing:** It is the most accurate way to pass the ball because of the size of the area of the foot used in hitting the ball; even when you lack precision in the strike, the ball still goes in the direction desired. This pass is ideal for short passes on the ground. The one drawback: Normally, the player using the inside foot pass will not be able to give the receiver much quicker attacking support.

• **Inside or outside foot curved balls:** It is very important to change points of attack, especially to a counter-attack behind the defense into the open space. The large bone above the big toe strikes the widest 1/8 of the ball and creates a curve that moves away from the defender to meet the attacker behind the defensive

Outside of the foot passing.

pressure.

To introduce the necessary coordination for producing curved balls with the inside of the foot, you place the players on the endline 18 yards from the post and ask players to approach the ball at 45 degrees for inside of the foot curving (30 degrees for outside of the foot passes). Ideally, the ball curves away from the line and into goal. Ask younger players to kick from 10 yards out. Use both sides of the goal (or flags) to practice inside and outside curve passing with both feet. age recommended to start is 10 years old.

• **Outside of the foot passing:** The most common way to pass the ball when a passer has pushed up to receive a ball played back. This type of pass can be used to create long, low passes, especially from the midfield into the attack. Further, it's useful for quickly changing the point of attack and when counter-attacking.

• **Passing with the instep of the foot:** This type is very effective for long ball passes, especially to switch the point of attack.

• **Passing with the heel of the foot:** A useful technique in pressure situations around the corners or in creating an unexpected offensive penetration in the attacking third.

• **Sole of the foot pass:** An effective option in attacking situations when playing with the passer's back to goal. He holds the ball and waits for midfielders or forwards to support, laying the ball off for a first time shot. This technique creates opportunities for long shots outside the penalty box.

In **STEP SIX** we observe how the direction of the ball passed is related not only to the placement of the non-kicking foot but also the body as it faces the target. The non-kicking foot, the knee, and the head must all face the target. Further, the shoulder's rotation plays an important part in the success of this pass: The shoulder moves the upper body in the direction of the non-kicking foot.

Finally, **STEP SEVEN** deals with the follow-through after the pass leaves the foot. The passer should move to place his weight on the non-kicking foot after the pass is made and move away from defensive pressure into open space - except if the situation calls for overlapping or avoiding offside situations or outside penetrations.

C. FOOT COMMUNICATION

We recommend that you develop in your players a fast decision making process as to their passing technique. There is no better way to do that than teaching foot communication. We have applied this technical development concept with great success. The reason for doing this is the general lack of speed in the decision making process of North American players. No decisions are usually made until the player receives the ball at his feet.

This decision making process is naturally developed in soccer countries where the game is played often in the streets without supervision and refereeing. There, if players do not make quick decisions to move the ball, they probably get hurt because of the defensive pressure. They come to understand naturally when it is time to hold, time to dribble, or time to use the give and go. They know that in playing that way the defenders do not have the time to pressure the ball. As a consequence, there is quickness in the movement of the ball, and necessary decisions are made before the player receives possession. This rapid decision making process develops out of necessity in unstructured free play.

Foot language skill is applicable to the three most common parts of the foot:

• **Instep passing:** The passer tells the receiver that he is not able to support the passed ball. Consequently, in this case the receiver must receive while turning to the opposite side and look there for an option to make the next pass. *Remember:* The passer could need at least two additional movements of the body before making the necessary penetration; the direction of the next pass becomes predictable to the defender; and finally, this type of passing does not allow the passer time enough to support the pass once made because of the extra time needed to accelerate and penetrate in the open space.

• **Outside of the foot passing:** This pass says to the receiver, the passer is already moving into the open space so he can become an option for a wall pass or double pass situation. This type of pass is executed when the defensive pressure is aggressive. *Remember:* Unlike the instep pass, the outside of the foot pass does not call for extra body movement; this allows the passer to make himself available in open space that the defender leaves to come and pressure the ball. The receiver should use the wall pass as a first option, except when the open area to play behind the defense is too small for a give and go pass.

• **Toe passing**: This pass is normally applicable to situations arising close to the penalty box, such as when the receiver has his back to goal. The passer with this pass is telling the receiver to prepare the ball back in a slight diagonal for a shot from the top of the box. The receiver can hold the ball if necessary or play it back with his first touch.

Note: Other parts of the body can be used for passing as well: for example, the thigh, chest, or head; but we will not spend time in this book explaining the technique of these types of passes because we believe in many cases that these balls should be trapped and passed with the instep on the ground.

D. PHASE II: GAME SITUATION

As soon as development of the various passing techniques is observed by the coach, he should expose this technical skill to defensive pressure.

The progression recommended is as follows:

1. 2 v 1 play on a 1/3 sized field with two goals and two keepers. Players break into four equal groups standing next to the outside posts of each goal, attackers at one and defenders at the other.

Play starts when a defender passes the ball to an attacker located at the diagonally opposite goal post. The receiver now must make a decision before receiving the ball: either take the ball to goal or pass to the other attacker. The defender makes passes of varying heights and with different parts of the foot, as required by the coach, and then moves quickly to pressure the ball. The receiver then executes a pass after seeing and understanding where the pressure is coming from and where the available open space is. Further, he should try to apply foot language as a non-verbal signal to the receiver. On completion of the pass the passer should move to support the ball.

The lone defender trys to intercept the pass, then once the play is complete, moves across to the back of the attacker's line. The attacker not making the pass and subsequent shot comes back to the end of the other attacking line. Continuous balls are played alternating the side from which the ball starts.

Points to be observed from your players in this step:

- The correct movement of the receiver is in the diagonal into open space away from the defensive pressure so as to help the passer quickly make a good decision;

- Observe the passing technique, confirming whether it was the right decision based upon the height and power of the ball;

- Notice the body position before and after the pass; in this situation the best option available is passing the ball and overlapping the receiver when the pressure comes directly against the passer, or if the defender anticipates the pass and moves to the receiver, the passer holds possession and penetrates himself; again, foot language is a key factor in facilitating the speed of penetration.

2. The next step is the 3 v 2 situation with keepers in goal and groups of two defenders who send the ball to three attackers placed again on a 1/3 sized field; three attackers have 15 seconds to score; the passes should be made quickly and the body positioning at the reception will help identify the correct decisions to be made concerning passing; the more time spent executing the pass, the less space and time available to the supporting players.

Points to observe:

- The first attacker's reception and passing decisions and the off-the-ball movement of the other two attackers;

- The speed, technique, and decisions made by the attacking team;

- To help the passer make a quick decision, one potential receiver must move away from the ball while the other shows for the ball, both moving into space diagonal to the passer, defensively or offensively.

Players should train in this situation using only two touches and using both feet.

3. The 5 v 4 situation follows before moving on to the game condition stage; We observe the circulation of the ball offensively and the defensive rotation of the players related to the quality of the passing; we use one goal and 1/3 of the field with the ball starting with one of the outside midfielders. Attackers try to score while defenders try to intercept and build a counter-attack using one of the outside flanks of the field and dribble through two cones placed on each side of the 1/3 field line, five yards apart.

Important points to observe:

- the speed of ball movement related to the quality of passing;

- the body position of the passer as it relates to the defensive pressure and direction and power of the ball;

- the constant movement of players into diagonal options;

- the number of passes without losing possession (Confidence and concentration are factors that interfere with a team's success in this situation.)

Variations can be applied to this situation to increase the speed of reaction of the player. Specify the kind of passing and the height of the ball to be emphasized in the session. Use three touches with two balls, two touches with two balls, and two touches with a single ball; pass with the weaker foot - and always use your imagination. Remember too: Receive the ball facing the opposite side from where the ball came.

E. PHASE THREE: GAME CONDITION

Two important game conditions are necessary to fully cover all the aspects of passing to be analyzed and corrected:

- 8 v 7 moving to 8 v 8 with two goals, keepers and playing under no restrictions or the number of players relative to the age group:

The coach moves around the field identifying common mistakes. In private during the drill, he instructs players and observes if their quality of performance improves. Players making good decisions should be recognized. Remember to strive for ideal passing, especially by the outside defenders finding outside midfielders and forwards showing up at the flank - a deep pass down the line is a very effective way to counterattack.

- The final game condition is the 11 v 11 play (full sided game):

We recommend this situation because it is as close as you can get to the real game. You identify problems with technique and its development. Each player will be playing in areas of the field where they find themselves in a match; they cover, mark, and penetrate into areas that they would in a real match. Further the speed of the ball is game speed, and the intensive defensive pressure is game-like. One major problem often shows up at this stage: the slow speed of the decision making as a result of poor positioning and a resultant limited time for the correct preparation of the next pass.

To increase the pressure on the teams, you might add these restrictions:

- The team must link at least six passes before shooting, thus increasing the number of receptions;

- Play the 11 v 11 game to isolate technical skills;

- First use rubber balls to improve the softness of touch; Second use the Futesal ball (heavy ball) to educate the player as to how to properly lock his foot and identify the correct part of the foot to be used; finally use the regulation ball related to the age group you are working with.

IV. SHOOTING

It is 30 minutes into the second half and Brazil is tied with Holland, playing one of the quarter-finals of the World Cup in Dallas. Branco is fouled and he has the opportunity to take a direct kick, and who could forget the curve and power of that shot that gave Brazil the victory in one of the best games of the tournament; or maybe the 45 yard shot from Roberto Carlos scoring a wonderful goal versus France during the Umbro Cup '97 in England. We will now be looking at the different kinds of shots related to:

Shooting.

- the various parts of the foot being used
- the power on the ball,
- and the area of the field from which the shot is taken.

We have divided this process of directing the ball at goal into two distinct technical skills:
- **Shooting:** When the ball is shot from outside the 18 yard box or around the box line.
- **Finishing:** When the ball is played inside of the 18 yard box.

The factors which establish the difference between the two are power and accuracy. Shots request more power and less accuracy, and finishing requires accurate placement of the ball with less power on it.

We will describe both as separate technical skills with their specific points, trying to facilitate the understanding of the coach in how to prepare the offensive penetrations based on the opponent's style, and intensity of the pressure on the ball and the open area for penetration.

You must teach the right technique and build the confidence to try shooting with both feet from any part of the field when the opportunity is available. Many times players hesitate to take shots because they are afraid to make a mistake and be punished by the coach or criticized by teammates. The technique should progress with understanding and persistence as a unique way to succeed.

A. GENERAL POINTS OF EMPHASIS FOR SHOOTING.
Remember the following three points to be emphasized during the shooting technique progression.
1. The quality of the shooting is a result of a good reception and or correctly penetrating the ball - **Reviewing:** For good reception the player must be in a defensive or offensive diagonal position to the ball.
    • Receive the ball turning to the opposite side that the ball comes from,
    • try to figure out your decision which must be made before you receive the ball.

2. Try to always keep the shot lower if possible and target the opposite side of the goal. The keepers reaction is always slower when they have to dive low to the ground.

3. If a shot is going to be taken after a penetrating run, the shooter must penetrate carrying the ball with the outside of his foot, opposite to the pressure.

B. SKILL PROGRESSION FOR DEVELOPING THE SHOOTING TECHNIQUE.
PHASE ONE • Fundamental development.
Shooting the ball on the ground with the instep part of the foot hitting the ball is the first type of shooting technique we will be teaching. This is because of the emphasis on keeping the ball on the ground in Brazilian soccer. They use this technique for better control, safety, and quality of the shot. We will be looking at all the particulars needed to develop this technique with the ball. We will identify the different kinds of shooting with the foot, where to hit it, how to hit it, and the height of the ball.
We will be analyzing the seven necessary steps in this progression.
Organization of the development session:
1. 2 goals with 2 keepers

2. Goals 1/3 of the field apart (related to the age group you are working with).

3. One ball per player - Players will be dribbling the ball with the outside of the foot opposite to the pressure.

4. Execute the shot against the keeper and after switching the goal repeat the drill. Both feet should be used.

STEP ONE • This step starts as soon as the player becomes the best option to receive the ball, prepare the body to receive it in position to penetrate and/or take a shot; the next action will be to look for the best kind of shot to take related to the position of the keeper and the pressure on the ball. The shooter has to have in his mind all the options available to play that ball. This decision comes after the shooter looks up and reinforces the confidence that he is making the best decision.

The shooter must have the ball always at the outside foot and outside leg, this will help him to penetrate with the ball much faster. The opposite side arm must be up to shoulder level to hold off the defensive pressure.

STEP TWO • This is the correct placement of the ball by the shooter. He should place it in an offensive diagonal position (45 degrees for driving balls and 30 degrees for curve balls) no more than 3 yards away to avoid the loss of control. It is recommended this touch on the ball should be done with the foot that is going to take the shot and that the shooter slow down a little before the start of the final sprint to the ball, allowing him to take a last look at the keeper and again identify the correct kind of shot to be taken.

STEP THREE • Here we focus on the correct approach to the ball. It should be short steps on the toes as fast as possible. The short steps will allow the player to attain the adequate balance and avoid placing the opposite foot too far forward or too behind the ball line. The fast sprint to the ball will help to increase the power of the shot.

STEP FOUR • We will be observing the correct technique of the placement of the opposite foot. It should be placed on the line to the ball, toe facing the target point of the shot. The distance of the opposite foot to the ball should be similar to the measure of the foot to the knee of the player's leg.

It is important that the coach understands the key for good balance and coordination for a good shot is established by the opposite leg and foot. Some common mistakes can be observed related to the inadequate placement of the opposite foot, such as we observed during the passing technique.

If the shot is taken with the right foot, and the ball moved too much to the right side of the goal, it is because the opposite foot is too close to the ball, forcing the kicking foot to hit the ball too much outside the ball. The way to correct this is by moving the opposite foot a little further away from the ball (verify the correct distance between foot and ball), and try again.

If the ball moved too much to the left side of the goal, the reason is because the opposite foot is too far away from the ball, forcing the kicking foot to hit the ball too much inside. The player should correct the position.

Many times the distance from the ball to the opposite foot could be correct, but other problems could occur if the foot is placed too far forward. In this case the ball will be hit on the top, pressuring the ball against the ground, wasting the power, and the shot will bounce along on the ground.

- To correct it, just ask the shooter to move the opposite foot back to the ball line.

If the ball goes constantly in the air, over the target player, the problem could be that the placement of the opposite foot is too much behind the line.

- To correct it, ask the player to move the opposite foot forward to the ball line and bend the opposite knee.

STEP FIVE will be the time when the kicking foot is touching the ball. It must be locked and the kind of shot will dictate the correct part of the foot and the part of the ball to be hit.

a. For shots on the ground: Shots from outside penetrations. The attacker must have the defender side arm up to hold off the pressure. The ball must be shot on the ground, to the opposite side of the goal. The instep (Tarsus - the top bone of the foot) hitting the center of the ball helps to increase the power.

To better identify the correct points we recommend that this progression be practiced with rubber balls, especially for young players.

The progression to this level should be done as follows:

• Player with the rubber ball in his hands 10 yards from the goal line. Walk four steps and kick the ball with the instep. The player must start the approach with the non-kicking foot. At the time the ball is going to be hit, the player should move the trunk forward and the ball should be on the ground in line with the knee when kicked.

The rubber ball is soft and builds the confidence to hit the ball hard and with the right technique.

b. On the ground curving shots: Used on inside penetration with the ball, with the keeper coming out to close the angle and stop a deeper penetration. The foot to be used is always the opposite from where the pressure from behind is coming. For both inside of the foot shots, hit with the inside metatarsus bone facing the ground, and outside of the foot shots, hit with the outside metatarsus bone facing the ground, the ball must be hit at the widest 1/8 of the ball, and the opposite leg should stay straight. The foot that is going to hit the ball must come straight in full extension as if it were going to kick with the toes, but only the part of the foot mentioned above will hit the ball. The longer the range of motion of the leg coming from the back, the stronger the curved shot will be.

The first steps to introduce the curve shots are similar to when you teach curve passing.

c. Medium balls - driving ball shooting: Used when the forward receives the ball with his back to the goal, needs a fast turn and has no time to let the ball rest on the ground. Very effective in diagonal shots from the corner of the 18 yard box. It is not too low to be intercepted by the defenders nor high enough to be read easily by the keeper. Hit through the center of the ball with the opposite knee bent about 30 degrees. The instep of the foot will hit the ball.

d. Medium balls in curve shooting: Recommended for balls received on the top of the 18 yard box. The outside foot is always better because the ball will be struck from the top to the bottom, keeping it low, instead of from the bottom to the top, when the ball will sail too high, wasting a good opportunity. It is applicable in situations when the keeper is in a poor position, leaving the opposite side of the goal wide open. With the inside or outside of the foot, hit the widest part of the ball and keep the opposite leg straight.

e. High balls shooting: It is applicable for balls from direct kicks or bounced balls from corner kicks or defensive clears from high crosses. In these cases the goal has an excessive number of players around it. To increase the accuracy, you have to decrease the power. Kick on the lower part of the ball - using the instep part of the foot. Do not bend the opposite leg.

f. High balls curve shooting: Direct kicks close to the 18 yard box. From the right side we recommend left leg and vice-versa. Kick on the lower part and at the widest part of the ball. Use the inside or outside foot and do not bend the opposite leg.

STEP SIX we will be observing the direction of the ball related not just to the placement of the opposite foot, but with the whole body facing the target. Opposite foot, knee, hip and the head must be pointing or facing the target point. The shoulder rotation will move the upper body towards the same direction of the opposite foot.

Finally, **STEP SEVEN** will be the following through with the body after hitting the ball. The player must apply all the necessary power to accomplish the kind of shot he is looking for. It is important to let the players make mistakes in applying the correct power and slowly correct the steps to improve the accuracy.
Diagram 4: Attacker working on reaction to the cross and finishing or shooting depending on where the ball is received.

IV. PHASE II: GAME SITUATION
As soon as the development phase of the shooting is done, it is time to see when and how to apply the shooting technique. The recommended progression will be:

a. 1 v 1 - 1 attacker v 1 defender - keeper and regular size goal.

In this situation you will be able to identify the correct position to receive the ball, how many extra touches before taking the shot, and what kind of shot depending upon the height of the ball and the position of the pressure. Most common situations for shooting:

1. Forward receives the ball with his back to the opposite goal and the defender is behind him in a delaying position. The attacker should receive the ball with the sole of the foot, move the body slightly (not the ball) to the opposite side of the intended turn, let the defender commit to that side, and quickly turn the body with the ball - arms up to hold the defender pressure, and take the shot.

Note: If the ball comes high, the necessary trapping should be done, turning as fast as possible to avoid the close pressure.

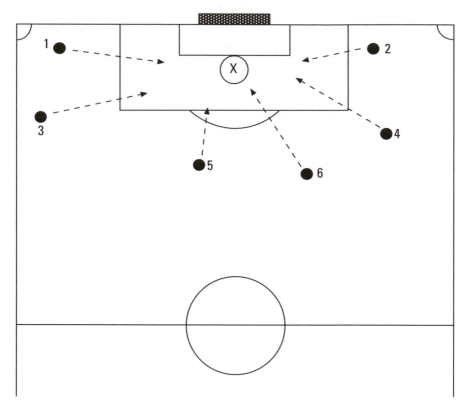

Diagram 4: *Players cross the ball from the most common areas.*
(X) *The target player must finish the play. The cross can be in the air or on the ground from a distance of 30 yards from the target.*

2. Rebound balls: Diagram 5
The ball comes from the back of the goal. The shooter will receive it preparing for the shot. The shot should be taken as soon as possible. It is not necessary to let the ball die on the ground. The shot should be a medium to high ball driven if at all possible. Do not allow time for the keeper or the defenders to react to the shot. The shots should be taken from the top of the 18 yard box and from the corners of the 18 yard box.

3. Penetration shooting: (1 x 1) Diagram 6
The ball is served by a long pass, the attacker will penetrate as soon as possible with the outside foot. The defender should come in at full speed, pressuring the attacker. The attacker will have his arms up for balance and protection against the pressure. The ball should be shot on the ground to the opposite corner of the goal. Players should practice with penetrations from both sides of the field, practicing with both feet.

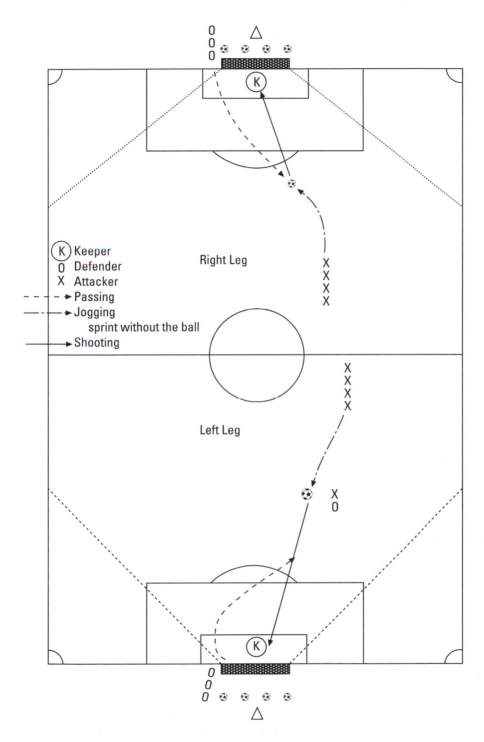

Diagram 5: *Shooting. Rebound balls under pressure.*

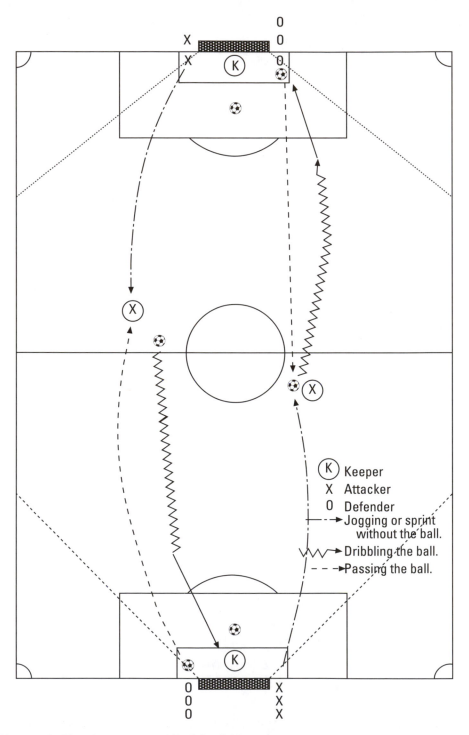

Diagram 6: *Shooting - 1 v 1 on 1/3 of the field.*

b. 2 v 1- two goals - two keepers - 1/3 of the field:
Players in four equal groups start next to the outside of the goal.

Explanation of the drill. Diagram 7
The attackers and the defender will always alternate sides. One player, a defender from one of the groups, will pass the ball to the opposite side. The ball will be passed to one of the attackers and he should make the decision before he receives it, to take the shot, hold it, or serve a short pass and overlap to take the shot. The defender should make the pass at different heights and parts of the foot upon the coach's request, and will move as fast as possible to put pressure on the ball. The receiver should execute the pass or the shot after identifying where the pressure is and/or where the open space is available.

The defender will try to intercept the pass. If the player did not take the shot he will come back to be an attacker together with the defender. Continuous balls will be played alternating the side from where the ball started.

Points to be observed from your players in this step:

- The correct movement in diagonal to the open space away from the pressure to help the passer make a fast and good decision to facilitate the shot.

- Technique of shooting, confirming if it was the right decision upon the height, type of shot and the power of the shot.

- The body position before and after shooting.

c. 3 v 2 situation • Keeper in the goal. Diagram 8
Groups of two defenders sending the ball to three attackers placed on 1/3 of the field. The three attackers will have 15 seconds to score the goal. The passes should be done with extreme speed, and the body coordination on the reception of this ball will identify the kind of shot. The more time spent on passing, the less space and time for the shooter.

Points to observe:
- The first forward reception and pass, and the movement of the other two attackers.

- Speed of the shot, correct technique, observing if the best decision was taken.

- To facilitate the decision of the passer one player must move away

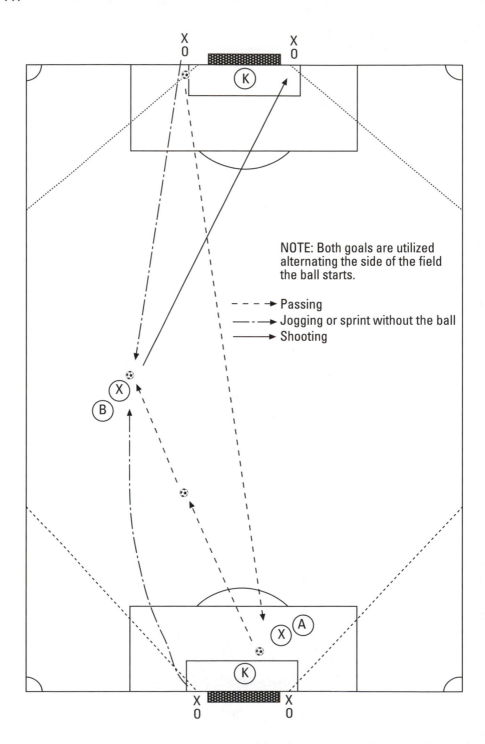

Diagram 7: *Shooting - 2 v 1, 1/3 of the field. X and O alternate defense and attack.*

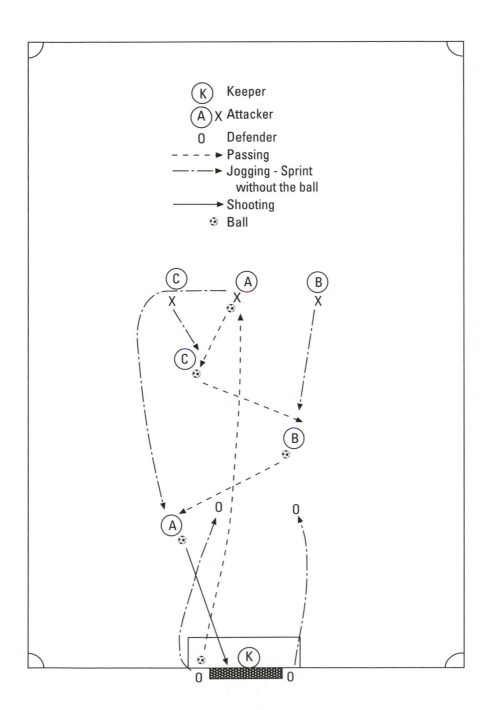

Diagram 8: *Shooting - 3 v 2. 1/3 of the field.*

from the ball and the other show to the ball, both moving diagonally. At this time the passer will establish who will take the shot.

To improve fast reaction the players will only use two touches and both feet.

d. 4 v 4. Diagram 9

In this situation you will be able to evaluate the quality of the technique and the speed of reaction to the ball while looking forward for good shooting positions:

1. 2 goals apart - 1/3 of the age group field size
2. 2 keepers
3. Field divided in the middle. Shots must be taken behind the midfield line.
4. Forwards can receive the ball in the attacking half, but cannot take the shot. They should hold the ball, passing back to a teammate who takes the shot. Every time a team scores 2 goals, a new team will replace the losing team.

You can establish restrictions to increase even more the speed of decision, such as:

- Play 2 touches.
- Introduce a second ball.
- Take shots only with the weak foot.
- Identify the specific kind of shot you want to see taken to count as a goal.

5 v 4 Situation - This is the last situation to be developed before moving to game conditions. We will be observing the offensive and defensive circulation of the players related to the quality of the ball to be shot.

One goal - 5 attackers v 4 defenders plus a keeper in 1/3 of the field.

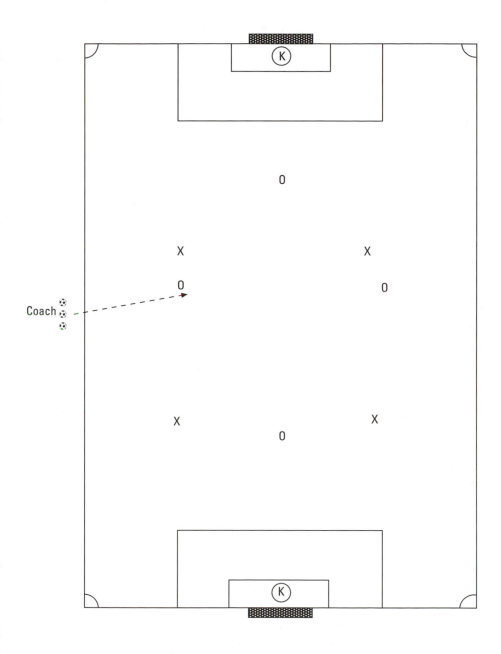

Diagram 9: *4 v 4 - shooting, 1/3 of the field.*

NOTE (1): Always apply the necessary restrictions to develop the technical skill of shooting.

NOTE (2): Shots must be taken from outside the 18 yard box.

Ball will start with one of the outside midfield players.

Attackers try to score - defenders try to intercept the ball and build a counter-attack using one of the outside parts of the field; trying to dribble through the goal (placed on each side of the 1/3 field line - 5 yards a part). **Important points to observe:**

- Speed of movement of the ball related to the quality of the shooting.

- Body position related to the pressure, direction and power of the ball.

- Constant movement of the players to attain the diagonal position to receive the ball and take the shot.

- Observe the number of correct and incorrect shots during a period of 15 minutes. Confidence and concentration could be factors which interfere in the success of this game situation.

Variations to be applied in this situation to increase the speed of reaction of the player. (Identify the type and height of passing to be requested):
- 3 touches - 2 balls.

- 2 touches - 2 balls.

- 2 touches - 1 ball - shooting with the weak foot
  Always use your imagination.

Note: Receive the ball facing the opposite side from where the ball comes.

C. THIRD PHASE - GAME CONDITION
Two important game conditions will be necessary to fully cover all the aspects to be analyzed and corrected:

- 8 v 7 moving to 8 v 8.

Two goals - two keepers - Playing with no restrictions. The coach will move around the field identifying the common mistakes, and in private during the drill will request a little more attention from the player, observing to see if his quality of performance has improved. The players who make good decisions must receive a compliment. Remember to correct the wrong shot.

The next step in the game condition will be to add extra balls to the game. We recommend the coach to allow a maximum of four balls at the same time. This will promote more concentration on the game and more repetitions of shooting. Establish which kind of shot should be taken Diagram 10.

The final game condition will be the 11 v 11 or the regular number of players related to the age group. We have strongly recommended the 11 v 11 situation because it is the closest you can get to the real game. You will be able to identify any problem with the technique and its development. Each player will be playing in the real zone to cover, mark or penetrate - with correct speed of the ball and the intensity of the opposition's pressure. One major problem will show up, and that is the slow speed of the decision making - This will be the result of wrong positioning minimizing the time for the correct preparation. Diagram 11.

To increase the pressure you should:
- Require the team to link at least 6 passes before taking the shot, increasing the number of receptions and improving the patience to identify the right time to shoot.

- Work the 11 v 11 game condition for these technical skills.

- Start with a rubber ball to improve the softness of the touch.

- Introduce the Futesal ball (heavy ball) to educate how to correctly lock the feet and identify the correct part of the foot to be used.

- Finally, use the regular ball related to the age group you are working with.

V. CROSSING AND FINISHING.

One of the most exciting aspects of American Basketball is the speed and the quick inside or outside penetration. The constant movement and quick passes keep the game exciting with large numbers of points. Brazilian soccer is based on the same concept of constant attack, with inside and especially outside penetration of the full-backs coming from the back. How many times do you hear the names of outside full-backs such as: Cafu, Jorginho or Leonardo moving to the attack and crossing the ball from the offensive endline.

A good cross and a good finisher is for sure one of the most important weapons to have on an offensive team. We will be discussing both as one technical skill, because they are directly related to each other.

We define finishing as the last touch done on the ball, inside the oppositions 18 yard box, by an offensive player with the intention of scoring.

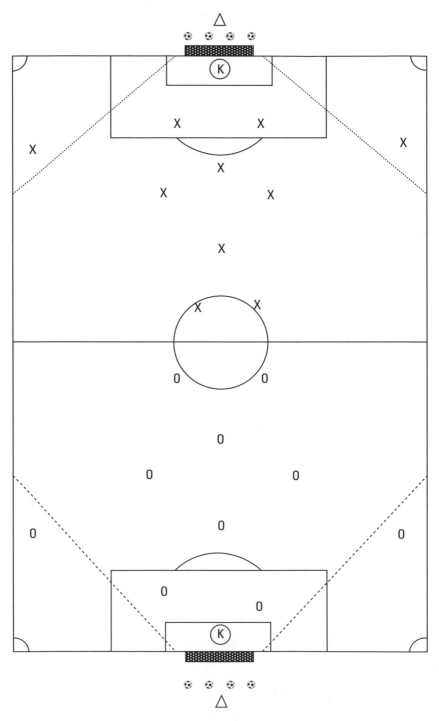

Diagram 10: *Shooting 11 v 11 - 4 balls.*
NOTE: Shots must be taken from outside the 18 yard box.

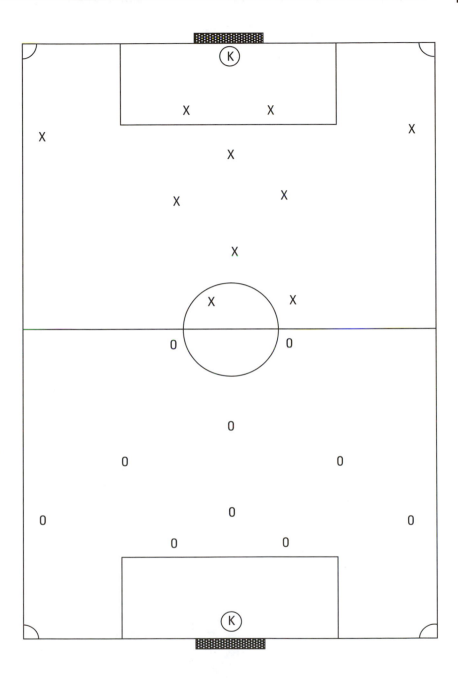

Diagram 11: *Shooting - Improving decision making.*
11 v 11 - 1 Ball. Observing a. Shooting with the weak foot. b. Shooting with outside foot.
c. Shooting with curve.

A. IMPORTANT POINTS TO EMPHASIZE IN CROSSING AND FINISHING

a. The crosser should always try to receive the ball in open space, allowing the time to observe the ideal ball placement related to the position of the keeper and speed of the penetration of the forward.

b. The crosser should always carry the ball with the opposite foot to the side of the pressure, and have his arms up to protect against the pressure and for better balance during the cross.

c. It is very important to try to go to the deepest point as possible (the endline) to make the cross; This forces the defenders to rotate their bodies so much that they will not be able to see the forward penetrating behind their backs to receive the cross.

B. SKILL PROGRESSION FOR THE DEVELOPMENT OF CROSSING AND FINISHING

The following five steps will help you to observe the points where your players are committing the mistakes related to the quality of performance in crossing and finishing.

The organization of this phase will be done with 2 goals in half a field with 2 keepers (one in each goal). Players divided into three lines separated 5 yards apart. Three players will each overlap. The ball will start with the player in the middle of the group of three. This player will make a decision to go right or left.

We will be using the following terminology:

1. Short crossing: Crossing is done with the ball inside the 18 yard box

2. Long Crossing: Crossing is done with the ball outside the 18 yard box.

STEP ONE • We will be analyzing the reception and penetration of the crosser.

The reception should be in an open space - in or outside of the box. The crosser must direct the ball with his first touch into the open space and should penetrate. The crosser should always have as a first option the deep penetration inside the box, cutting in front of the defender. If the space for that penetration is not available, the crosser should keep the ball straight to the endline and do a long cross.

STEP TWO is the preparation for the ball before it is hit by the crosser. For short crossing the player should direct the ball slightly diagonally to facilitate the rotation of the body and legs. For long crossing the ball should be directed in diagonally at least two yards before the endline. The cross-er needs more time to look up and read the finishers penetration and this distance from the ball will help to increase the power of the cross.

Opposite arm from the side of the ball must be up to hold off any pressure.

STEP THREE will be the correct placement of the ball related to the kind of cross, pressure on the finisher, and the open space available on that penetration.

Normally the defenders have the tendency to go to the goal line, expecting a straight cross. The short cross should always go to the back diagonally on the ground around the penalty spot.

The leg on the side the ball is crossed from should be used if the ball comes straight to the receiver of the cross - or the opposite leg if the ball comes in front and away from him. If the cross is along the ground, the shooter should use the inside of the foot, if the cross comes high, he should always try to hit the ball on the top. On medium height balls, the instep should be facing the ground on the shot. If higher than the foot can reach, the ball should be headed to the ground.

The long cross will always come from outside of the 18 yard box. If sent from the endline, it should target the open area between the penalty spot and the opposite corner of the 18 yard box. The ball should be high and always have the momentum to reach the open space created by the penetration of the attacker. A medium ball can be crossed when targeting the near post.

Note: Crossing curve balls from the top of the 18 yard box to the penetrating finisher without pressure is very effective.

STEP FOUR • We will analyze the time of penetration: Many times the finisher can miss a great opportunity to score because his penetration is either very early or late.

For short crosses the finisher should wait for the ball between the penalty spot and the 18 yard line almost in front of the goal.

For long crosses the forward should wait on the 18 yard line and the vertical line of the 6 yard box.

In the technical progression the middle player of the group of three will start the movement of the ball. He will pass and overlap the second player, then make a new pass and overlap the third player, who will pass the ball to the 1st player who is penetrating and will go for the cross.

The 2nd player will penetrate to the far post, and wait for a long cross and the third player will penetrate to the near post for the short cross. The crosser will make the decision upon the request of the coach. Diagram 12.

STEP FIVE will have the same organization as the drill in step four. The goal in this step is to establish the understanding of the correct body position to receive the ball and make the final touch in the direction of the goal, trying to score. If the ball comes on the ground from the crosser the ball should be hit with the inside foot to the opposite side from where the ball was crossed. If the ball comes moving away from the forward, the outside foot will be more applicable. The ball hit with the outside foot will stay low and it will have some curving effect.

Outside of the foot for fast penetration.

If the ball comes in at medium height the ball should be hit on the top with the instep or diving forward heading it to the ground and to the opposite side of the goal away from the keeper.

Short crossing - opposite foot on the ground is the correct technique.

If the ball is high the offensive heading technique must be applied.

Before we move to the game situation phase, circuit training with stations with different kinds of crosses at different heights should be done. This is a good way to verify the performance of crossing at speed. Do not make corrections during the circuit training.

C. SECOND PHASE: GAME SITUATION

The game situation phase should be used when the players show enough confidence and consistent quality during their performance under light pressure. It is very important not to hurry when developing skills, sometimes you need to spend at least 3 practices to really achieve quality, and if you go too fast, the players' comprehension will not be very clear and bad habits will show up during the game. The progression to be recommended will be:

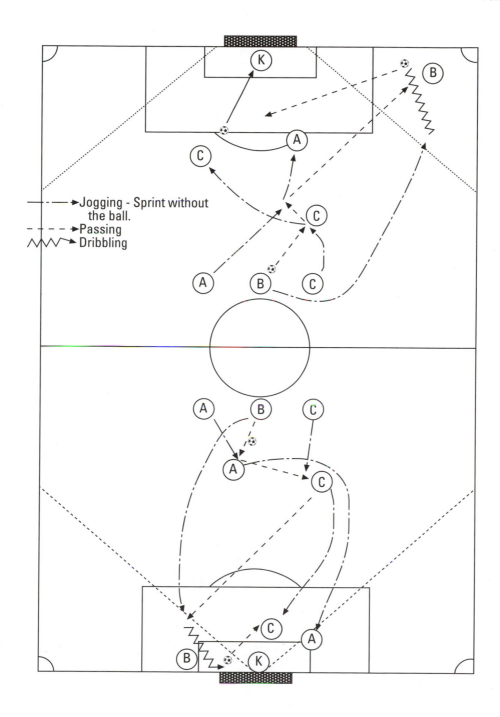

Diagram 12: *Short and long crossing.*

- 1 v 1 with constant movement:

- 2 goals - 2 keepers - 2 crossers - 2 defenders - 2 attackers

- 1/3 of the field from goal to goal (size of the field related to the age group you are coaching). Crossers will be running next to the side line of the field - and making the crosses sometimes from the middle of the field and sometimes from the endline next to the corner spot. The crossers will alternate goals, crossing to one with their right foot and the other with their left.

The defenders and attackers will run from goal to goal - the defenders will try to intercept the ball and the attackers will try to score, applying the correct finishing technique to each cross. The players switch functions after many repetitions. This drill must be done until a quality of performance is verified. You must stop the drill if fatigue is noticed, because the quality can be jeopardized. At this point move to the Game Condition phase.

As soon as the players show quality in their 1 v 1 situation, it is important for you as coach to make sure that all your players are capable of performing crosses and finishing, and if possible with both feet because these technical skills are very important to create goal scoring opportunities.

At this point you should move to 2 v 1. Two attackers will penetrate simultaneously. One moving to the near post and the other to the far post. The crosser will identify the best option for finishing and understand that the kind of cross is directly related to where the ball is before the cross happens.

At this point it is very important to correct the defenders' positioning relative to the ball and the penetration of the attacker.

The important point to be added in this situation is the communication between the keeper and the defender. The keeper should tell the defender to cover the near or far post, just leave the ball, or tell the defender that the ball is going out. The same communication that happens between the keeper and the defender should happen anywhere on the field, that is why it is so important to have everybody go through these drills as defender and attacker. Because of the number of keepers and, many times, lack of goals for training, we recommend the use of flags as goals and a field player playing as keeper.

- This way you can divide the team into two groups; your assistant coach will take care of one group and you get the other, switching groups after some time. The crossers must keep their intensity, crossing to one side, getting a new ball and going to the other goal for another cross.

If the keeper intercepts the ball he should pass it to the crosser on the opposite side.

After identifying the correct momentum of the ball, increase the fast reaction to the ball and concentration and the communication with the keeper. The next step will be the 3 v 2. The organization of the drill will be the same as before. The 3 attackers should identify the correct speed for penetrating and finishing. They will make their penetrating runs at different times, no more than 2 yards behind each other. They must be in a diagonal line to the ball - the near post man will penetrate first, followed by the penalty spot finisher and finally the far post player. This way the ball will always find a finisher to meet the ball.

The correct position and communication of the 2 defenders and keeper should be reviewed too.

Finally the last game situation to be applied will be 5 forwards v 4 defenders.

The 4 defenders and 5 attackers should be able to identify the application of the technique in this very common situation of the game. The organization in terms of space and number of goals, keepers and crossers is still the same. You must add more time between each cross to correct the positioning, technique, momentum to the ball and communication among the players. Communication among the players is a major factor to help in the technical and tactical principles. You must emphasize it.

D. GAME CONDITION PHASE.

The final phase of the technical development is the Game Condition Phase. As the term says, you will expose the players to the closest situation possible to the game. You have been analyzing and slowly correcting the normal mistakes which could occur, but now you must consider factors such as:

DEFENSIVE: Speed of the ball, unpredictable point of crossing, lack of constant marking and cover of some of the players, and insufficient communication.

OFFENSIVE: Correct position for crossing, time of penetration of the forwards, correct penetration in that open space related to the time of the finish, the body coordination before hitting the ball and finally the correct type of finishing.

NOTE: The Game Condition Phase should always be played between 2 teams and it is very important to have the regular number of players in this session. One of the biggest problems in North America is the lack of two full teams (related to the age group) to execute this phase.

The coach should include in his planning for this session the possibility to invite some players to fill the second team, and normally this will be better if these players could be older and more experienced than your group; this way you will increase the pressure against your starting team, and allow the sub players to feel comfortable in trying the skills, having an equal competition, promoting the fun, helping develop the techniques and finally making your team more successful.

The Game situation drill recommended is:

• Full field (specific to the age group) - 2 full teams - 2 keepers.

• The goal of the game is to identify the quality of the defenders' performance and the correct offensive crossing and finishing of all of the players.

Note: The major focus of this practice will be the technical aspect, do not try to fix the tactical or positioning or other technical skills with the group because this will promote excessive stoppages in the game and it will become boring. If an observation must be done to an individual player, just walk on the field and make the comment to the player and ask him to pay attention to that point.

Organization of the drill. Diagram 13.

- The 2 teams will play a regular game.

- This session should be done for at least 60 minutes for U14 and over, 40 minutes for U13 and below, and for 25 minutes for U10 and below.

- 4 balls will be placed in each corner of the field.

Outside foot finishing - very effective when inside the 18 yard box.

The game will start with the only restriction being that the ball must be passed on the ground. High balls will only be allowed for shooting, crossing or finishing. Every time a team takes a shot or finishes at the goal; that team has the right to cross four balls, 2 from the right and 2 from the left.

The crosser will be the closest player to each corner when the shot or finish was taken. The attackers and defenders should react to the 1st cross, defenders trying to clear the ball and forwards trying to score. As soon as the ball is out of the 18 yard box, it is no longer in the game. The 2 teams should reorganize themselves for the next ball, coming from the opposite corner. **Note:** We strongly recommend that the attackers move out of the 18 yard box to facilitate the next penetration and the defenders identify the player each one will be responsible for. The keeper should always call for the push out. The second ball will be played the same way as the 1st one, and as soon as the ball is out of bounds both defenders and attackers should prepare for the 3rd ball. The last ball to be crossed will be the 4th one, and this ball will not be stopped except for a goal or corner kick. The 4th ball becomes the game ball, and the defensive team can counterattack.

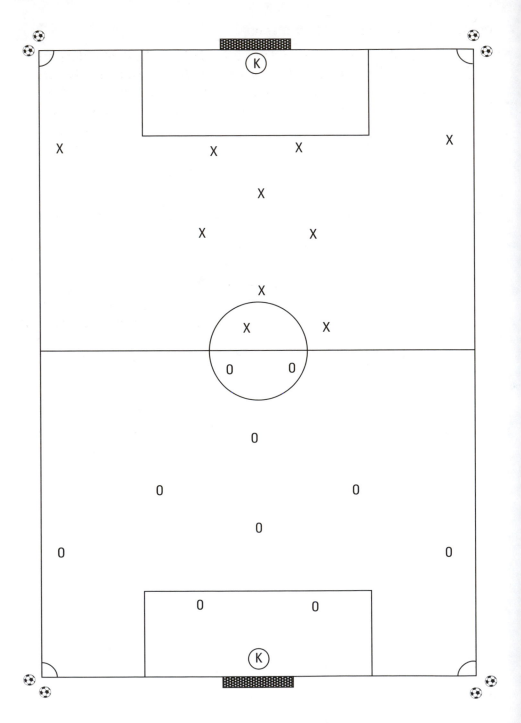

Diagram 13: *11 v 11. Crossing - finishing game - condition.*

Points to be analyzed in this phase:

a. Correct position of the defenders and attackers. The defenders must be facing the players they are marking, and the distance between them should be arms length, this way the pressure on the attacker to anticipate the ball can happen in just one step. The attacker should move to an open space, running to meet the ball, anticipating the defenders reaction.

b. Correct technique to clear the ball or finish, and protect against injuries.

c. Identify the quality of communication and finally the intensity and concentration on the ball.

As soon as you identify a quality performance from your defenders or attackers, you should increase the pressure, allowing the game to be played with 2 balls at the same time, decreasing the number of players fighting for the ball, but increasing the pressure with more constant crossing.

You should always use your perception to add more pressure, but be careful not to go too fast in each one of the phases of each skill. This progression could be your mid-season goal if you work with U12 and below. Or 1/4 of season if you work with U16 and below and you should be able to develop the necessary concepts in no more than two practices if working with U17 and above, including the pro-level.

Tactical Principles

In this chapter we will be talking about the secret key to Brazilian soccer success. Knowing that a player does not touch the ball more than three minutes in a ninety minute game, maybe we should ask the following question: What do the Brazilian players have that is special besides their technical ability? The answer is: Brazilians know how to play without the ball - utilizing very well the open space offensively and defensively.

The players will always be thinking how they can be more effective, instead of waiting for the ball in their feet. This chapter will help you to understand and teach a style of soccer that is attractive to those watching because of the speed of the game and the finesse of the players; with everybody moving simultaneously to create confusion among the defenders, the defenders must learn how to read that offensive decision early enough to anticipate the play and originate a counterattack. Brazil has been very successful playing against every country in the world because they have the ability to always force the opposite team to play their style, with their pace and especially forcing their tactical system, crafting counter-attacking opportunities, and turning the opposition's mistakes into goals. Brazilian soccer is a National philosophy. Every player of any age at any level will play with the same concept technically and tactically. The successful coaches in Brazil are the ones who spend more time educating players about the tactical principles.

It is very important we understand the definition of some terms we will be applying constantly in this chapter: **TACTICS** is the uniform and planned way to establish control on the ball as a unit, applying the tactical systems and the strategies defensively and offensively, taking advantage of the opposing teams' mistakes, controlling the game and consequently winning it. Tactics is the full picture of the team unit, and is composed by the **TACTICAL SYSTEM** and the **TACTICAL SCHEME**. The **TACTICAL SYSTEM** is positioning of the players on the field trying defensively to neutralize any opposite offensive maneuvers and offensively crafting the necessary confusion in their marking, allowing those game situations to become goals. The tactical system is pre-established during the week prior to the game and/or reorganized if necessary before the game starts. It is always specific to each game - the defensive system must be equal in numbers in each sector (third) of the field to the opposing team's organization.

Example: The opponent plays with five midfielders; in this case you need five players in the midfield to neutralize their maneuvers in that zone; offensive positioning must be organized to prey upon the opponent's tactical or technical weak points.

After identifying the adequate tactical system, the next important point will be the **TACTICAL SCHEME**: defensively, the strategies used to neutralize opponent's options during the game such as the pressure to be utilized, speed of the rotation of the players (synchronized movement of all the players in defensive position with the goal of stealing the ball) to neutralize any available option for pass, forcing the defenders to send long balls without good control.

Offensively, the scheme involves the applicability of the necessary circulation of the ball (constant movement of the ball from player to player in short and safe passes or sometimes a long pass in counterattack crafting the patterns and open areas of penetration to score goals). Set play strategy is also a major part of tactical principles. Pre-training for dead ball situations can transform these opportunities into goals.

We will be utilizing some specific terminology for Brazilian soccer, and this has as a major goal helping you better understand the tactical principles.
• We will mainly discuss the 4-4-2 tactical system.
   • 4 defenders
   • 4 midfields
   • 2 forwards.

The Brazilian vision of the 4-4-2 system had strong tactical development with the head Coach of the Brazilian National team during the 1978 World Cup, Claudio Coutinho. His concept of the counter-attack with the full-backs and the constant circulation in the middle was a tremendous step in the development of the Brazilian Soccer Philosophy played today. Brazil had won the World Cup in 1958 and 1962 without too much concentration on tactics. At that time the individual skill of the Brazilian players was enough to generate that success. It was during the 1966 World Cup in England that the 4-3-3 Brazilian tactical system proved uneffective against very organized man on man marking and against very strong and fit teams such as Germany, England, Portugal, etc. As the physical conditioning trainer of the Brazilian National team during the 1970 World Cup in Mexico, Claudio Coutinho saw coach Zagalo start a very effective way to confuse the opposite defense. Zagalo had too many good players in the middle, and the idea was to bring back left forward Rivelino, who was called "the false wing" to help to build the attack with short passes. He would drop to the midfield zone, creating an open space, allowing Tostao (Center forward) or any other player to penetrate in his back space. Zagalo had to find a way to organize so many good players without hurting their performance. Zagalo was creating the concept of play without the ball in open space. With players such as Péle, Gerson, Rivelino, and Tostao rotating in that open space, carrying their defenders with them, the space in the middle was open to Péle, who could penetrate as the center forward on the space left by Tostao. Péle could do the finishing or the penetration and had Jairzinho as the opposite point of attack always penetrating as right forward in fast counter-attacks. Zagalo was creating the first variation of the 4-4-2 system and it was very successful. Brazil won the 1970 World Cup playing very offensive soccer, with the first real tactical organization, coupled with the quality of technical skills and physical conditioning.

In 1974 Brazil went to Germany with some tactical adjustments, but the world was not prepared to see the most impressive tactical development in soccer during this World Cup. The Germans used the libero (Beckenbauer) coming from the back to the attack. Maybe Zagalo was tactically organized to play against the Germans, but he did not expect the tactical organization, especially defensively, from the Dutch.

They surprised the soccer world with the Famous Dutch Carousel, based on high pressure against the forwards always with double man on the ball, and very effective fast counter-attack through the middle, or quick counter-attack with long balls. The pressure on the ball forced the Brazilians to change their possession style to a tentative long ball counter-attack and the pushing up from the back of the Brazilian libero, Luis Pereira. Brazil lost 3-1 to Holland.

Brazil was out of the 1974 World Cup in the quarter finals. Something had to be done to bring Brazil back to be the soccer power it had always been. In 1978 Claudio Coutinho became the Brazilian National Team head coach just before the World Cup in Argentina. He had a great experience with Zagalo in 1970, and the problem found in 1974 could be fixed. Coutinho believed that the way to beat the excellent European defensive system was attacking using the outside penetrations of the field. He introduced the midfielders overlapping the forwards and the fullbacks overlapping the outside midfielders, penetrating the open space left by the two forwards. Coutinho applied the same system of Zagalo in 1970 with

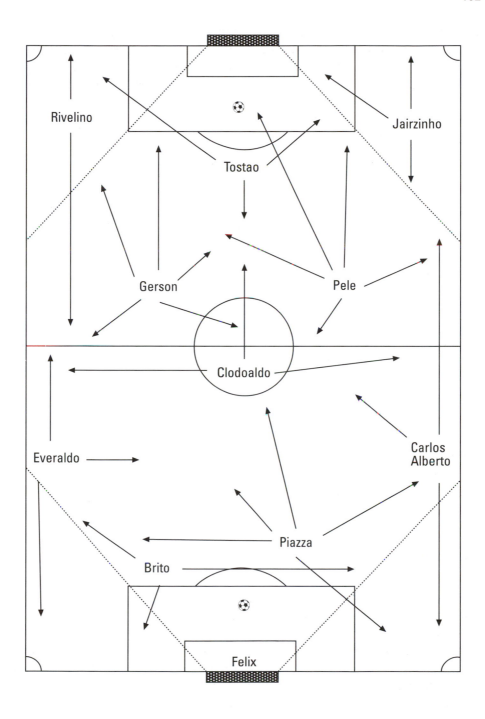

Diagram 1: *1970 World Cup.*

Eder coming back to the midfield, opening the space to Reinaldo or Roberto Dinamite who, taking the inside defenders, open a gap in their defense zone to Zico or Dirceu to finish. Coutinho had Roberto Dinamite doing with the right side the same function Eder had at the left side. Coutinho introduced the real 4-4-2 with an extra man in the middle and open space to be taken by one of the other midfielders. With this extra midfielder he could balance the number of midfielders against the Dutch. He requested the defenders to start from the back and the full-backs to push up to the attack, using the open space left by the forwards. The team was attacking with more numbers than before, but coming together from the back, especially through outside penetration.

Coutinho was establishing the new Brazilian soccer philosophy. Brazil left the world Cup in third place, without losing a game. Brazil showed a new exciting movement, with and without the ball. The 4-4-2 Brazilian vision was successful, and the only reason Brazil did not go to the final was one of politics. Coutinho was criticized by the Brazilian press, saying that he was concentrating too much on tactics, thus restricting the creativity and effectiveness of the best players in the world. But he changed totally the mentality of the country and established the new Brazilian system and a very effective game philosophy. Unfortunately Coutinho died in 1979 and the country and the world lost one of the best tactical coaches of all times.

The 4-4-2 became the official Brazilian system and the world was now going to see the third Tactical variation of the actual Brazilian philosophy.

In 1982 Tele Santana took the job as the Brazilian National head coach, and he did a great job playing the 4-4-2. The major variation from the 1978 system was the definition of two outside and two inside midfielders.

The two inside midfielders (Falcao and Toninho Cerezzo) played in line with the same defensive and offensive function, one moving to the attack and the other with the function to cover that midfield penetration and/or the penetration of the outside fullbacks. Tele Santana put together a very offensive minded team. Brazil played very exciting and aggressive soccer, but as Tele Santana said: "The team played the games to score goals, unfortunately accidents happen, and we lost, but the World soccer community knows that Brazil was the best team today". Unfortunately Brazil lost to Italy in the semi finals, with Italy winning the World Cup. However, it was proven that the 4-4-2 with two inside midfielders, two inside forwards and the freedom of the full-backs to attack was highly effective. This system became the national style of the game in Brazil after 1982 and it is still in place today.

It was in the 1994 World Cup that the 4-4-2 system with the outside penetration became a very attractive style to the rest of the world. At this

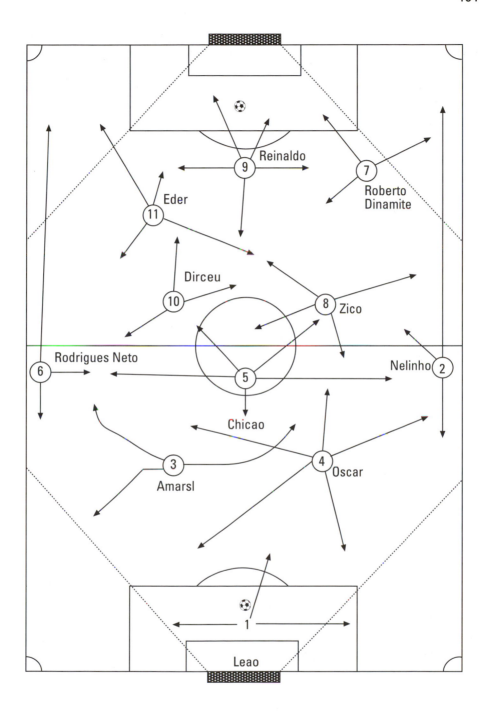

Diagram 2: *1978 World Cup.*

time the head coach was Carlos Alberto Parreira, who had assisted as the physical trainer and assistant coach with many of the Brazilian National teams in other World Cups, and was very well prepared to utilize the same 4-4-2 system. Zagalo was his assistant coach, and the idea at this time was to play very organized defensively and find the open space to counter-attack. Many countries employed a similar 4-4-2 system, but most countries just played with the ball at their feet. Brazil was exploring the open space created by applying only two attackers. Parreira established the midfielders functions very specifically with Mauro Silva playing mainly as the defensive midfielder, and Dunga with more freedom to support the two outside midfielders and the attackers. Maybe Brazil did not play the most offensive system, but played so organized tactically that after 24 years, won its fourth World Cup.

Probably the world will see a new small variation of the 4-4-2 Brazilian system in the next World Cup. The tactical system that coach Zagalo is tentatively preparing for the World Cup in France in 1998 is the 4-4-2 and should be very similar to that of Carlos Parreira used in 1994. The only possible variation will be that the center midfield offensive should become the third attacker, penetrating in the open space left by the two attackers. This midfielder will have more freedom to attack. The outside midfielder must slide inside to cover the gap that could be left for this inside offensive midfielder.

As you can observe, all the variations of the Brazilian system are results of the natural evolution of the game. You must understand that the system is a result of the strong and weak points of the opposition.

The importance behind the system is the philosophy of play. All the countries play the same philosophy based on keeping possession of the ball (play safe), waiting for a good pass in open space to a fast penetration. Players must learn how to play without the ball to be available to receive the ball without pressure, making quick decisions and surprising the defense.

The basic tactical system we will be focusing on in this book will be the actual Brazilian system and its variations, with the defensive center midfielder playing as a fifth defender (rarely pushing up to the attack) and the offensive center midfielder becoming the third attacker.

Before we move on to the tactical concepts in this chapter it is important to mention some aspects to be put in consideration for the success of your tactical development.

IMPORTANT ASPECTS TO BE CONSIDERED IN TACTICS.

The success of the team is based on how much you as the coach do to preview an analysis of both the positive and negative factors for your team

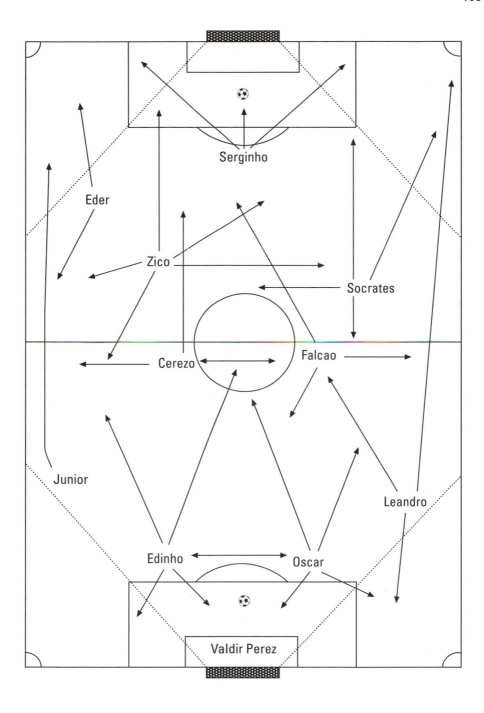

Diagram 3: *1982 Brazilian National Team.*

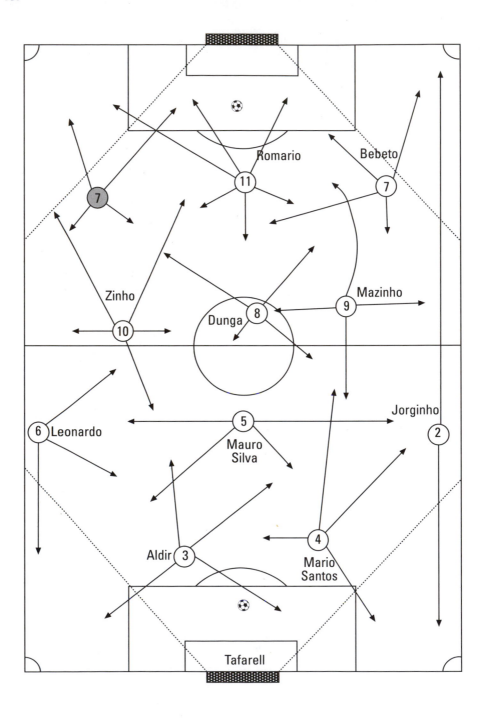

Diagram 4: *Brazil 1994 - USA World Cup.*

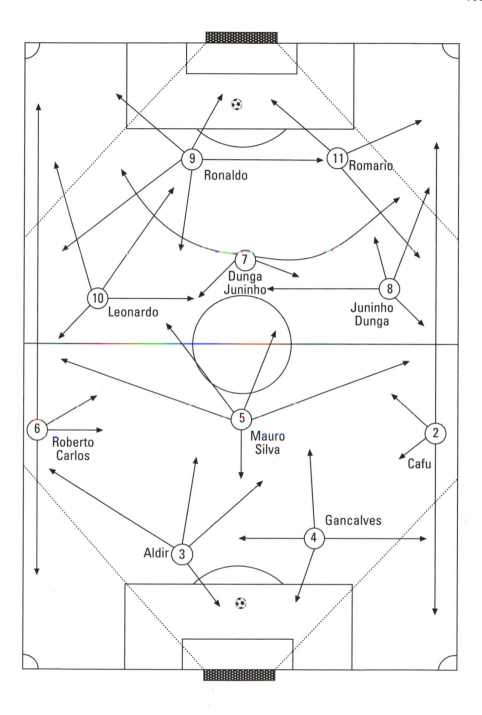

Diagram 5: *Tentative variation of the 4-4-2 to 4-3-1-2 of the Brazilian National Team in France 1998.*

before the game starts. We would like to put in consideration some factors which can interfere or help in your tactical principles.

You must always bring these factors to your team's meeting before the game, giving the necessary orientation to have all the factors working in a positive way.

1. Dimension of the field - as a coach you must always see the field where you will be playing your game, and analyze what is the best tactical scheme to be applied. Identify the advantages and disadvantages for your team and the adequate strategies.

2. Conditions of the field - Can alternate the way the team will be playing: An excessively dry pitch requires molded shoes, if it is raining at least the keeper and the defenders should wear cleats. Avoid the short passing game if the ground has too much water, especially in the back. Ask the keeper to deflect balls, instead of trying to catch. Forwards should take long shots as often as possible. Outside penetrations will work better than inside - (less people damaging the field). Always ask the keeper to check the position of the sun to avoid it bothering him, and the way the wind is blowing.

3. The weather factor - Too hot: quick movement of the ball (2 touches) avoids excessive running. Too cold: plastic bag on the feet and double socks, keep in constant movement.

4. The opposite team - It is important that the coach always try to see the opposite team play. If this is not possible, ask the assistant to do it. It is important to identify:
   a.   The technical level of the opposite team.
   b.   Their tactical system, scheme and strategies. The defensive tactical system is always related to the number of the players the other team has in any one of the sectors.
   c.   If the team is of an offensive or more defensive mind.
   d.   Players and sectors of the field to be of concern.
   e.   Weak spots to apply the counter-attacks.

5. The psychological aspect - is one of the most important factors to developing team tactics. If the players are not confident they can perform, they will try to clear the ball as soon as possible, making mistakes and keeping the pressure in their defensive sector. Motivation, leadership and communication will help to neutralize this factor.

6. Technical Skills - This is the most important factor to facilitate the accomplishment of the team tactics. The level of tactical information given to the team is directly related to the technical ability of the players. It will be difficult to link passes and establish the patterns without some quality technique. More skills means faster development of the tactics.

7. Laws of the Game - The tactics must respect the laws. The players and the coaches must always respect the laws and organize the tactical concepts related to them.

8. Physical Conditioning - The tactical aspects depend on the ability of the player to think and execute in the speed required by the tactical maneuvers.

You have organized planning. You know better the personality of each one of your players. You know how to bring them to the top of their physical condition. Technically you are able to observe the problem, analyze, correct and give the confidence to your players to execute, even in high level competition. Now is the time to develop the tactical concepts for your team.

Tactical development is the most complex principle to be accomplished. Many times it is very difficult to establish the adequate speed of teaching the steps when introducing the concepts. Experience has shown us that it is better for you to reinforce, repeat and consistently correct the same concept, before moving to a new one.

Too much information without a complete understanding can frustrate you and your team and create confusion and misunderstanding during the competition. Patience and analogy must always lead your explanations. To accomplish your goals, you as the head coach must be very sure of the progression and goals you want to accomplish in each session.

The concepts we will be sharing with you are a combination of the simplest way to teach tactics and we have observed many professional clubs in Brazil taking the direction to organize their youth soccer department with the same philosophy in terms of tactical/technical concepts carrying it to the pro-level, where the Coach Director becomes responsible for identifying the adequate curriculum for each one of the age group levels. These youth players will be much better prepared to play for the pro team than many very expensive quality pro players coming from outside this club.

Brazilian pro soccer Clubs are divided in 4 major levels of development.
- Infantiles: 14 and 15 years old.
- Juvenales: 16 and 17 years old.
- Juniores: 18 to 20 years old.
- Professional: Any age group.

We will provide the directions to organize the tactical planning for your team. It is up to you to identify how fast you can teach these concepts related to the players' age, technical skills, level of competition, and finally the team's commitment and dedication to accomplish the established goal.

Many soccer schools around the world divide tactics in three different situations:

INDIVIDUAL, GROUP and TEAM TACTICS.

These three situations are connected to facilitate the understanding of the players and for the adequate correction by the coaching staff during the progression.

PROGRESSIVE STEPS TO EDUCATE THE TACTICAL PRINCIPLE

1. Show the players the concept on a blackboard. The visual understanding always helps the execution on the field. Repeat as many times as is necessary until you are sure comprehension was accomplished.

2. Take the players to the field and start the progression with the most simple - many times no ball is involved (walk through the tactical concept) to the most complex (closest situation of the game) 11 v 11.

3. Introduce the concept without any pressure, adding later a keeper, defenders, midfielders and finally attackers, related to the concept or the sector of the field to be developed in that session.

4. Always follow the concept of: Individual tactics (the 1 v 1 concept defensive/offensive) - Group tactics (from the simple 2 v 1 up to 6 v 5 situation) and finally - Team tactics (in our philosophy we always try to apply the game condition in 11 v 11 situation - If the number of players is not enough, an invitation to other groups of players is always possible - The players must be exposed to the closest game condition as possible observing pressure, space and speed of the ball.)

When a team tactics (11 v 11) session is established the focus should be on increasing the level of pressure, fast reaction in the decision making, and helping to improve the performance of the tactical principles, by applying some technical or tactical restriction to the players, increasing their level of concentration and consequently the quality in their decisions.

Examples of some conditions and/or restrictions:
a. Increasing the number of balls - 2 balls (increase the players concentration)
b. Decreasing the number of touches on the ball (3, 2 touches and/or 1 touch)
c. Focus on a specific sector of the field (defense, midfield or attack) to play in a specific condition.
d. Develop the tactical concept with some technical restriction (Example: outside foot pass) and many other options using your coaching creativity.

1. INDIVIDUAL TACTICS: All the characteristics and concepts must be taught to each player in relation to the position of the ball on the field, level of the pressure, and the function of each player in a 1 v 1 situation.

Each player must understand the basic concepts offensively and defensively.

FIRST DEFENDER: Closest player to the ball and between the ball and the center point of his goal. His major functions are:
- Delaying the penetration of the first forward or the counterattack (giving time to the rest of the defense to get organized).
- Identifying the right momentum to pressure the ball.
- Correctly balancing between the player with and without the ball.
- Working together with the keeper when in a situation as the last defender. The keeper will become the second defender.
- Building the counter-attack as soon as possible after taking possession of the ball.
- Caution: when the attacker moves forward with the ball and the defender is delaying - Fast backwards steps can generate enough space to allow the attacker to take a shot. The defender must alternate the legs back and forward while marking a charging attacker.

FIRST ATTACKER: Player in possession of the ball. His major functions are:
- Maintaining constant speed of the ball.

- Receiving the ball facing away from the passer. Keeping or bringing the ball to the ground every time the situation calls for it.

- Penetrating with the ball as fast as possible when the situation calls for it.

- Holding the ball in the attack when playing in the offensive sector of the field with his back to the opposite goal.

We recommend the following decisions regarding the pressure of the defender:

- If the defender comes slow to the ball, giving space, the best decision, if close enough to the goal, will be shooting. If far from the goal, the best decision will be a give and go with an outside foot pass.

- If the defender comes too fast, without control, the best decision will be to fake the player with a body movement to the opposite side of the direction the attacker wants to take, and do the penetration, or again an outside foot pass in give and go situation.

- If the defender does the correct delaying, the correct decision will be to dribble the ball in diagonal to the opposite side he wants to take the shot. Wait until the defender is out of the front of the goal, and make a quick cut inside and take the shot as fast as possible, surprising the keeper.

Development of the Individual Tactics:
Warm-up: Two goals apart 1/3 of the field. Players in 1 v 1 situation around the field.
a. 5 minutes: the defender learns the concept of delay, the attacker develops quick decision making and the ability to protect the ball. Attacker dribbles the ball and the defender just contains, understanding the importance of delaying the attacker's decision, giving his team time to reorganize defensively.

Review the correct position of the defender - between the center of the goal and the ball line. Eyes on the ball, and waiting for it to move to tackle. Arms up for better balance.

Review the correct position of the attacker - both knees bent, legs in diagonal. Leg opposite the ball must be up, to force the defender to go wide and close his angle. The attacker must dribble the ball with the outside of the foot, opposite to the pressure side, arms up to help control the defensive pressure. Switch functions every 30 seconds. The attacker must try to score.

b. 5 minutes: the same as in (a), but the defender should delay first and as soon as the attacker moves the ball, the pressure should be put on, tackling if necessary and taking away the ball. Body positions are similar to (a).

Many times players move too aggressively or too early to apply the pressure. Early tackling facilitates the attacker's decision because of the predictability of the defender's decision, and normally the lack of covering of the defender will facilitate a counter-attack. Switch functions every 30 seconds. The attacker must try to score

c. 1 v 1 + Keeper: 1/3 of the field. Defender passes the ball to the attacker (placed at the opposite goal). Attacker controls the ball and does the penetration; Defender comes to pressure the ball. (Diagram 6(a)).

Use both goals, two groups working together at the same time. **Note:** Coach should correct the defensive and offensive aspects of the FIRST DEFENDER and FIRST ATTACKER.

d. 1 v 1 + Keeper: 1/3 of the field from goal to goal. Same number of players placed behind each goal. Players will be called by numbers. Each team will have the same number of players. Example: Coach will call players #1. Both players will sprint behind the opposite goals and come to the middle of the field trying to get the ball and score. The first to get to the ball becomes 1st attacker and consequently the other player will be the 1st defender. The attacker has 15 seconds to try to score. Defender becomes attacker if he steals the ball. Diagram 6b.

2. GROUP TACTICS: When the situation requires the involvement of more than one player defensively or/and offensively, they must understand their function related to the movement of the ball, zone of reception, pressure on the ball and the movement of the supporting player in open space. In group tactics development the players must be able to identify the situation, quickly evaluate the best solution, and perform successfully. The players must recognize the importance of:
- Communication during the play.
- The correct technical/tactical combination (wall pass, give and goes, overlapping, etc.)
- Accomplishing the result. If a mistake is made make sure that the evaluation and connection will be done through analysis of video tapes of the games.
- Looking for or becoming the supporting player in diagonal defensively or offensively.
- Establishing the more logical decision to each play for each one of the group tactics situations, leaving improvisation as the last option.

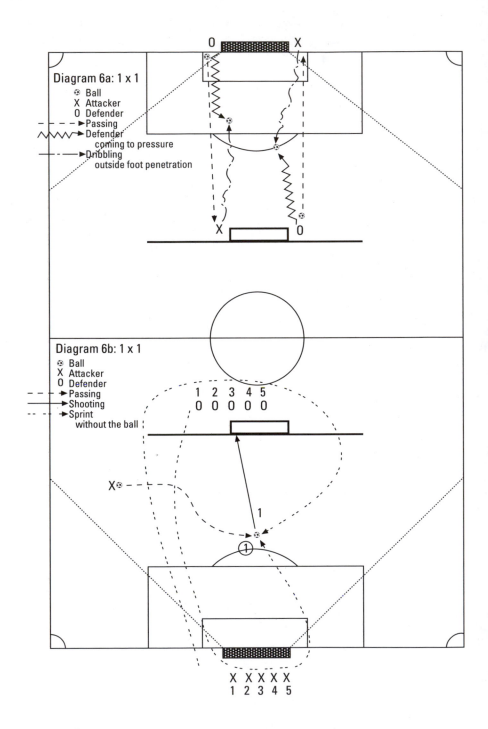

Diagram 6a: 1 x 1
- ⊕ Ball
- X Attacker
- O Defender
- – – –► Passing
- ∿∿∿► Defender
   coming to pressure
- —·—·—► Dribbling
   outside foot penetration

Diagram 6b: 1 x 1
- ⊕ Ball
- X Attacker
- O Defender
- – – ► Passing
- ——► Shooting
- – – ► Sprint
   without the ball

1 2 3 4 5
0 0 0 0 0

X ⊕

1

①

X X X X X
1 2 3 4 5

Diagram 6(a) and 6(b):

Example: Overlapping the ball must always be the first option for 2 v 1 with outside penetration in the attacking third, to avoid the off- side trap.
• Understand the role of the 2nd and 3rd defender
• Understand the role of the 2nd and 3rd attacker.

BASIC TACTICAL COMBINATIONS:

Before we explain the most common group tactics in soccer, we would like to explain some tactical combinations that will help to accomplish the tactical system, scheme or strategies in each game situation or condition. These combinations are common in many different soccer schools all over the world. We will explain those in the way we educate the players in Brazil:

a. WALL PASS: The 1st attacker serves the ball and penetrates in the open space to receive the ball back. The receiver will pass the ball back in his first touch.

Two common ways to establish the wall pass:
• Open space for inside penetration: The 1st attacker will pass the ball with the outside foot (faster acceleration and anatomically easier) and move to the open space behind the defender, continuing the attack. It is more applicable when in the defensive or midfield sector (third). See Diagram 7a.

• Open space for outside penetration (wall pass and overlapping). It is very common when in 2 v 1 situation in the attack. The 1st attacker will serve the ball, and the receiver (2nd attacker) will turn to the opposite side with or without his back to the opposite goal and will pass it back to the 1st attacker running behind the receiver (2nd attacker) overlapping him and building an outside penetration. See Diagram 7b.

This will help to avoid the off-side trapping. If the defender decides to pressure the 1st attacker moving without the ball, the receiver will do the inside penetration.

b. GIVE AND GO PASS: This is one of the most common tactical combinations.

This combination will involve a third player. The ball is passed to the 1st attacker (A), who will penetrate outside or inside depending on where the open space is. Player (B) (2nd attacker) will receive the ball turning to the

177

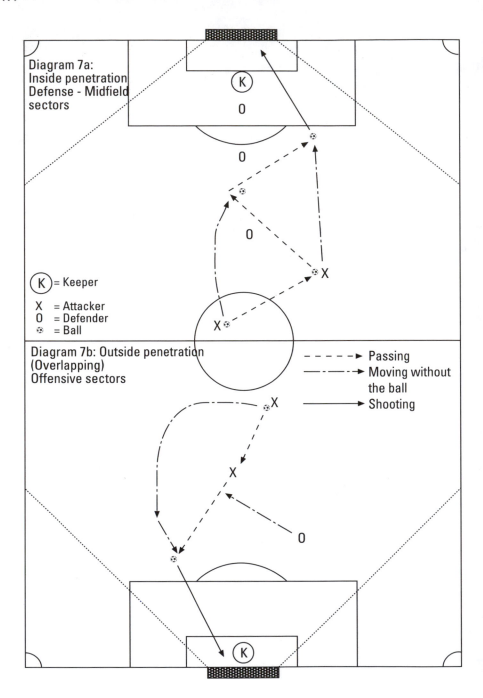

Diagram 7(a) and 7(b):

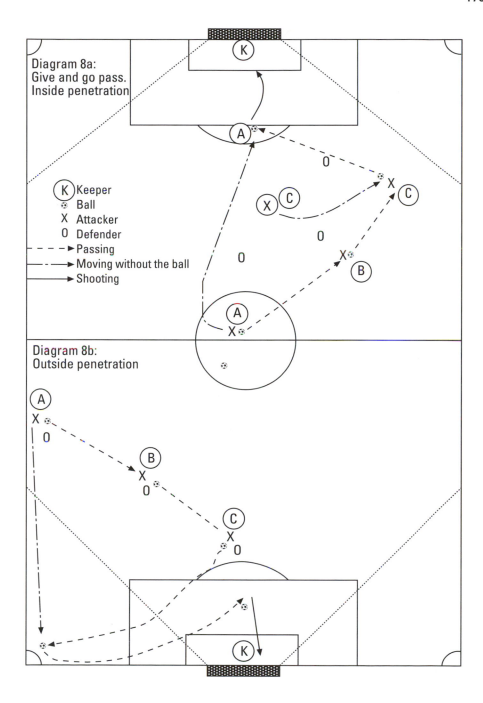

Diagram 8a:
Give and go pass.
Inside penetration

K Keeper
Ball
X Attacker
0 Defender
- - - - ► Passing
- · - · - ► Moving without the ball
────► Shooting

Diagram 8b:
Outside penetration

Diagram 8(a) and 8(b):

opposite side, looking for somebody to link the pass (C) (3rd attacker). (B) will pass the ball back to the 1st attacker (A), penetrating in the open space, who will be able to finish or continue the building up of the attack.

Give and goes can be applied to outside or inside penetrations.

c. In line Passing: This is a very effective way of quickly building up an attack. It is very common to apply when the ball is intercepted in the middle of the field and the opposing defense is disorganized. It is very applicable to outside penetration. Can be applicable from the defense to midfield and from midfield to the attack.

The passes in line should always be placed in the open space and not on the player. The receiver will be able to control the ball without excessive pressure. Diagram 9.

The most common **GROUP TACTICS** situations during the game are:
1. 2 v 1
1a. Offensively: We must understand the role of the 2nd attacker in this situation.

- The 2nd attacker is the closest positioned player to 1st attacker.

- Offensive function of the 2nd attacker: Move to an open space in a defensive or offensive diagonal to become a direct option for passing.

- Try to push the 1st defender away from marking the 1st attacker, facilitating his penetration.

- Show for the ball and come to meet it when the pass is made - Take the 2nd defender away from the function of supporting the 1st defender, creating a 1 v 1 situation for the 1st attacker.

1b. Defensive functions of the 1st defender V two attackers
- Be in correct delaying position.

- Identify the right moment to pressure the ball.

- Correctly balance between the player with the ball (1st attacker) and the one without the ball. (2nd attacker).

- Work together with the keeper as the second defender.

- Delay the penetration of the first attacker when in counter-attack (give time to the rest of the team to get organized defensively).

- Tackle the first attacker when possible.

- Build a counter-attack as soon as possible.

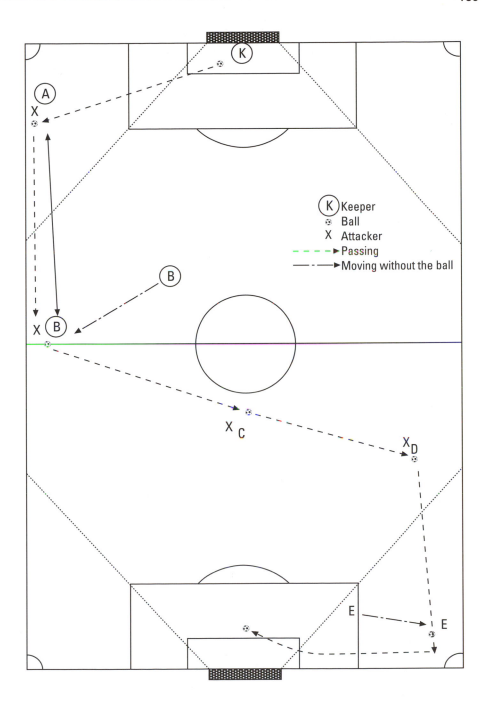

Diagram 9: *In line passing.*

Note: The 2 v 1 happens everywhere on the field and it is one of the most important tactical situations to be taught, even to young players such as U10 (development phase).

Progression 2 v 2: Two goals (1/3 of the field apart) - 2 keepers.
A group of players on each side of the goal. The defender will pass the ball to the opposite side, and one of the two attackers will trap the ball and make the decision if it will be outside or inside penetration (no offsides should be called).

This drill should be done first with passive defense to explain the movements of the players and the ball. Analyze the defenders' movement, and what kind of decisions are made by the receiver (2nd attacker) if the pressure comes on him or if the pressure is on the 1st attacker in penetration.

Bring the pressure after you make sure the players understand the options available.

2 v 2 should be done with one of the defenders sending the ball to the opposite goal and moving forward to pressure the 2 attackers.

Always expose your players to the most realistic pressure of the game as possible. The 2 v 2 is fundamental to develop the correct time of passing and penetration of the 1st and 2nd attacker.

The pressure put on the 2 attackers will increase their speed of reaction and the quality of decision making. You will be able in 2 v 2 to analyze better the level of communication and understand the functions of the 2 defenders.

2. 3 v 2 Situation.

This group tactic must be well explained to the players, because you as a coach will introduce the function of the 2nd defender and the 3rd attacker. Explain to them how both groups (defense and attack) must communicate to facilitate their task.

The 3 attackers will have specific functions: 1st attacker will look for the best way to penetrate (out or inside), upon the space and pressure from the 1st defender. The 2nd attacker will move in an offensive diagonal to create the option for that pass.

If the 2nd defender comes to pressure this 2nd attacker, he will pass the ball back to the 3rd attacker, moving in a defensive diagonal and will pass the ball in the open space behind the 1st defender to the 1st attacker, who will do the penetration in that open space. (Diagram 10a.) If the 2nd defender does not commit to the 2nd attacker, the ball should be passed back to the 1st attacker, and the 3rd attacker will move in a defensive diagonal trying to carry this 2nd defender who was covering the back of the 1st defender, and open that space for the 1st attacker's penetration. The 1st attacker can do an inside penetration or the overlapping with outside penetration. Diagram 10b.

Functions of the 3rd attacker:
- Support 2nd attacker.

- Move to an open space on a defensive or offensive diagonal related to the ball, trying to carry the defender, and open a space for the other attackers' penetration, finalizing in 2 v 1 situation.

Defensive functions of the 2nd defender:

- Establish a balance between himself and the1st defender (one will delay and the other will pressure the ball). The 2nd defender will stay behind the 1st defender, observing the offensive circulation.

- Become the 1st defender when the ball is passed to one of the other attackers.

Example: The 1st forward is the player in the middle - the 1st defender will move closer to him when the ball is passed to the left forward, the 2nd defender will step forward becoming 1st defender and the 1st defender will drop back becoming 2nd defender.

Educational progression of the 3 v 2.
- 3 v 0 - Area (1/3 of the field) - Two goals. One keeper in each goal. Players divided in four groups, waiting next to the goals. The keeper will pass the ball to the 3 attackers.
They will control the ball and will perform the inside or outside penetration, and the pass back to the 3rd attacker to feed the 1st attacker, penetrating in the open space.

- 3 v 1 - Add some pressure. Request the same intensity and quality in performing the options. The major points to analyze and educate the players will be:

  - The important function of the 1st defender delaying the extra number of attackers. Verify the correct position and procedure.

  - Identify the simultaneous time of the defensive and offensive diagonal moves of the 2nd and 3rd attacker.

  - Observe the adequate speed of the decision making of the 1st attacker.

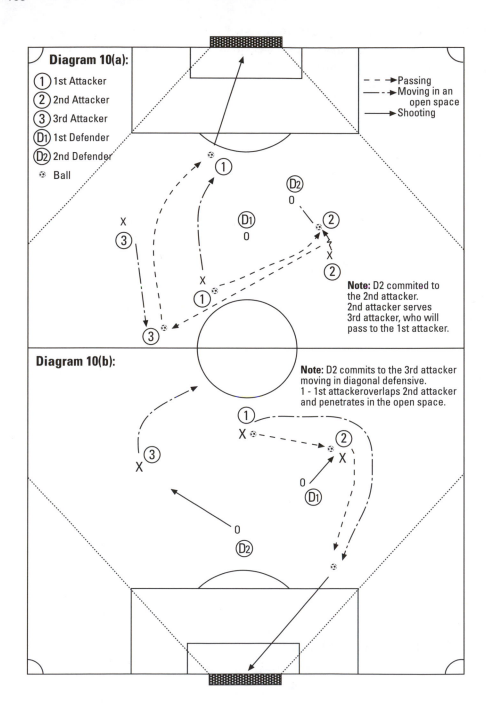

Diagram 10(a):

(1) 1st Attacker
(2) 2nd Attacker
(3) 3rd Attacker
(D1) 1st Defender
(D2) 2nd Defender
⊙ Ball

- - -→ Passing
---·-→ Moving in an
          open space
——→ Shooting

Note: D2 commited to
the 2nd attacker.
2nd attacker serves
3rd attacker, who will
pass to the 1st attacker.

Diagram 10(b):

Note: D2 commits to the 3rd attacker
moving in diagonal defensive.
1 - 1st attackeroverlaps 2nd attacker
and penetrates in the open space.

Diagram 10(a) and 10(b):

- 3 v 2 - Adding the 2nd defender the pressure will increase and the level of concentration and communication of the 3 attackers must increase too.

Points to analyze:

- Observe the adequate balance between 1st and 2nd defender.

- Analyze the speed of the decision making of the 2nd attacker serving the 1st attacker in penetration or serving the 3rd attacker in defensive diagonal.

- Analyze the speed of the pass of the 3rd attacker to the 1st attacker.

3. 3 v 3 situation.

It is important to explain and make sure the players will understand the 3 v 3 situation. You will be able to analyze the most common situation around the field and observe the speed at which your players will penetrate offensively or neutralize the options defensively.

We will introduce the 3rd defender whose basic functions are:

- Support the 1st or 2nd defender during the defensive rotation.

- Observe the penetration of the 3rd attacker, establishing the right moment to mark, cover or tackle.

- Minimize the space for penetration of the attackers, especially the 3rd one.

The build up of the attack in 3 v 3 is basically the same, with emphasis on the final penetration of the 1st attacker.
One of many variations of 3 v 3 with inside penetration - and 3 v 3 with outside penetration. Diagram 11b.

4. 5 v 4 - In this group tactic we will be analyzing the important points with the four defenders rotating trying to neutralize the extra attacker and offensively we will analyze the concept of circulation of the ball.

Rotation is a defensive term meaning the movement of the defenders to try to identify the best positioning to achieve the necessary balance to neutralize a successful offensive penetration.

The first defender is the closest man to the ball and the other defenders will move to a covering/supporting position.

185

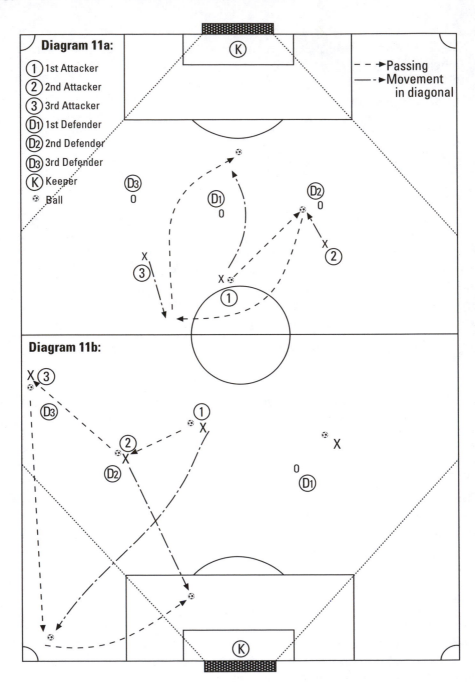

Diagram 11: *3 v 3.*

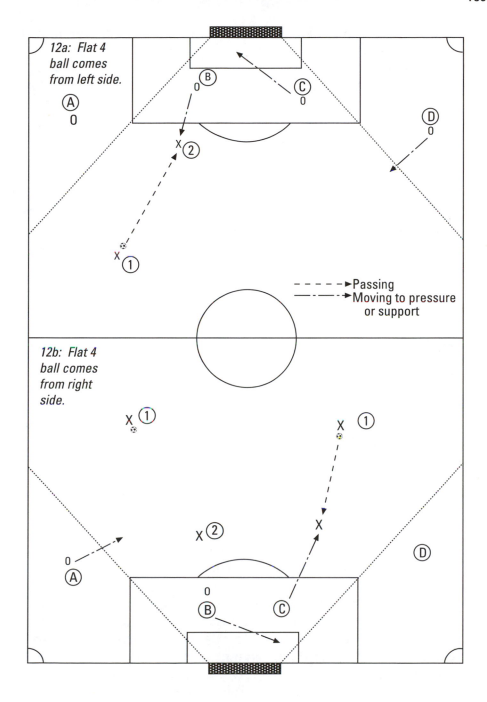

Diagram 12: *Defensive line - Flat 4 defensive.*

Important points to explain to your players during a 5 v 4 practice: (defensive aspects)

1. The positioning of the four back defenders:

1a. Flat four: When the two inside defenders have equal function of covering and/or marking, depending on where the ball is coming from and who is the closest inside defender to neutralize that attacker's penetration. (Diagram 12 - a. ball comes from the left - b. ball comes from the right).

In Diagram 13 - Playing with the Libero - Stopper. Attacker (1) has the ball. He passes to the attacker (2), at the same time the stopper - defender (C) (specific inside defender with the function of marking the inside attacker) pressures the attacker, forcing a mistake. The sweeper (libero) will have the function of covering and must always stay in or around the 18 yard box. He must only leave that zone when:

- The team is pushing up to the attack.
  (stopper or center defensive must cover)

- He has good heading skills to go for corner kicks or long crossing on indirect kicks to the far post.

- Coming outside to cover the fullback, who was beaten in counter attack.

The defensive rotation is the most important concept to be taught in this group tactics situation. To better understand, let's look at Diagram 14.

Attacker (5) has the ball. The 1st defender is (D), who will come to pressure the ball and try to steal. Defender (C) will slide to the left to mark the attacker (4). (A) will move to the left to try to mark attacker (2), and will keep his eyes on the attacker (1). Defender (B) will be prepared to double team the attacker, in case he starts a penetration.

Some important defensive concepts to be taught in 5 v 4 situation:
• **BALANCE** in soccer refers to the complete control of the open space, equalizing the number of defenders to attackers, and trying to utilize the gap left by mistake for the defenders, or neutralizing the possible open space for penetration by the forwards. Every defender will have his zone to COVER or MARK and establish in that zone which player must be his responsibility.

• **COVERING** - When the farthest outside defender moves inside to cover the gap left by the outside midfielder, leaving behind him the outside

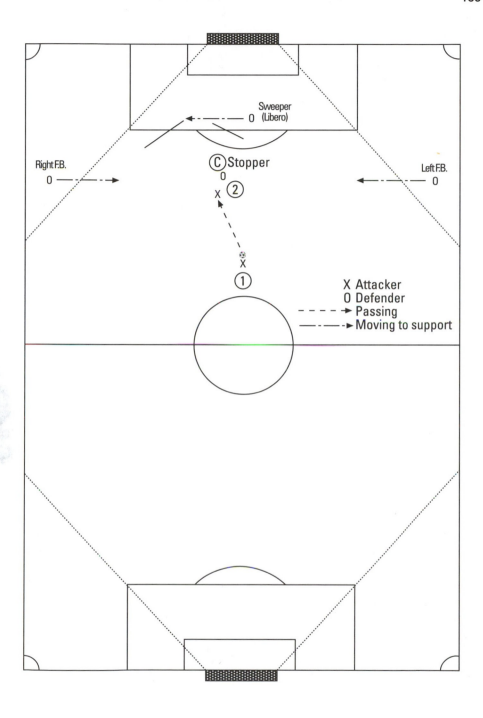

Diagram 13: *Defensive line with stopper - sweeper (Libero).*

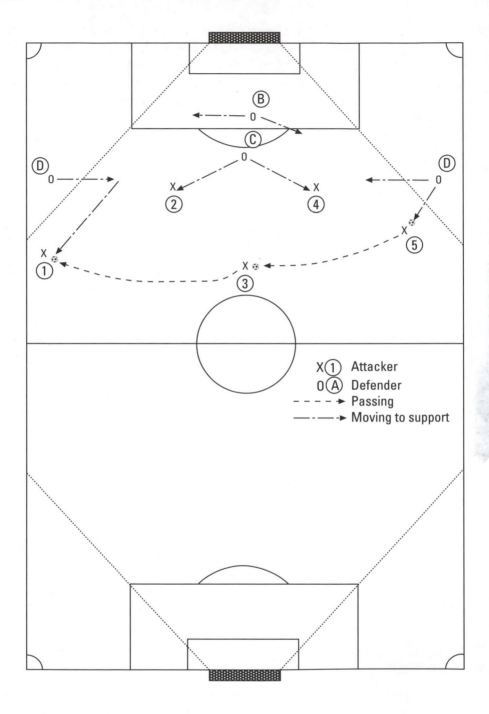

Diagram 14: *Defensive Rotation:* Defenders will move as a unit to the side of the ball putting pressure on the attacker, and organize the marking of the extra forwards.

midfielder or forward. This defender must tie the player he is marking inside, and observe the other forward or midfielder behind. When the ball starts to circulate to that zone, this defender will move back to the attacker he was just covering and start to mark. The distance between this defender and this attacker is related to the speed the defender can cover in that space.

• **MARKING** - When the defender keeps a distance that enables him to touch the attacker. In a marking situation the defender must be concentrating on the offensive circulation of the ball, and always be positioned between the attacker and the center of his own goal.

As soon as the defender identifies eye or verbal contact, he must be prepared to anticipate the ball, increasing the pressure on the attacker. If the attacker is very fast, but not so skillful, it is recommended to stay two yards behind that attacker to avoid the ball being sent behind (backdoor), and as soon as the attacker receives the ball with the back to the defender's goal, the defender can come fast and put the pressure on the attacker.

If the attacker is skillful, but no so fast, the defender must mark very closely and force the receiver to make a quick decision without being able to think to make the right decision, or try to anticipate the ball.

If the attacker is fast and has skills, we recommend to mark that attacker closely and request the libero (sweeper) to be prepared to cover his back.

After we identify the necessary cover on the defensive points in 5 v 4, we will be analyzing the progressive education to teach the offensive circulation of the ball.

CIRCULATION OF THE BALL: This is an offensive concept and means the capacity of the team to move the ball in consecutive short and sometimes long passes, always in a defensive or offensive diagonal, trying to identify the right moment to pass the ball in an open space to the starting player of that circulation, breaking the marking organization of the defenders and/or creating an opportunity for goal. Two major sectors to circulate the ball:

Defensive half circulation: major goal is to find a gap to link the pass to the midfielders.

Offensive half circulation: is done around the big central circle involving the four midfielders, the two forwards and many times one of the outside fullbacks. The ball should be moved with a maximum of two touches to avoid wasting time in organizing the attack, and at the same time not allowing the defense to get organized.

In the following progression we will be able to understand the offensive half circulation:

5 v 0 - Important to identify the correct movements of the players in penetration in single and double circulation.

a. Single circulation: When the first player to start the movement of the ball moves inside for the penetration and creates a situation for goal (single circulation). This pass must happen before the ball comes back for a new circulation of the ball. If the penetration is not available because of excessive marking, a new series of passes brings the ball back to the middle and the team tries to move back to the outside part of the field where the circulation started. (double circulation).

5 v 0 - Development of the concept: 1/2 field - keeper - 5 attackers. No defenders yet. Ball started with forwards playing with their back to the opposite goal, no more than 15 yards apart, waiting for a pass to be made to them. When the 1st attacker receives the ball the other four attackers must move into the open space to create the options for quick passes and build a very effective attack.

Example: Diagram 15 (single circulation). The first forward (attacker 1) will move to the left side in an open space. He receives the ball from the left full-back. Attacker (1) passes to left midfielder (attacker 2). The left midfielder will serve the offensive midfielder (attacker 3) moving to the open space in a defensive diagonal. The offensive midfielder will receive the ball, turning to serve the right midfielder moving in an offensive diagonal.

The right midfielder could keep switching the point of attack for one more outside pass, but in this diagram, the other forward (attacker 5), makes the move to the open space to bring the inside defender with him and open the space to the attacker 1, who penetrates and receives the ball to finish.

The progression of this group tactical situation will be adding the defenders:

5 v 2 and finally 5 v 4: The number of defenders will increase the pressure and consequently the speed of the decision making.

In 5 v 2 the two defenders must concentrate on their rotation inside the box, observing the role of each in the flat back four or with the libero. This situation is the correct one to educate these defenders when pressuring

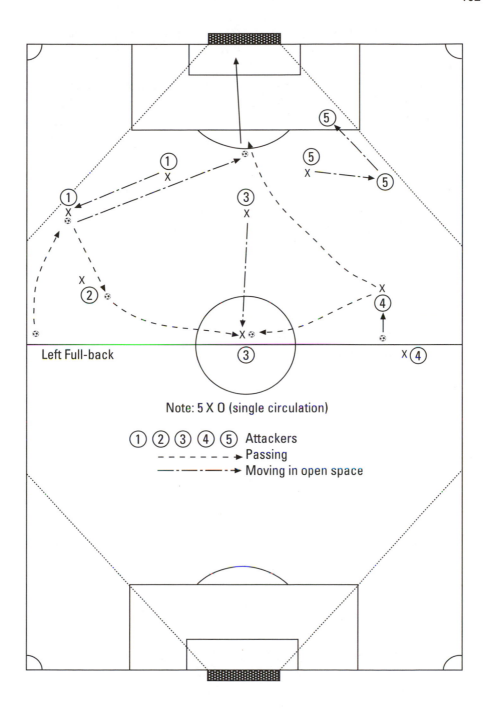

Left Full-back

Note: 5 X O (single circulation)

① ② ③ ④ ⑤ Attackers
– – – – – – – → Passing
——·—·—·—·→ Moving in open space

Diagram 15: *5 v O. Circulation (offensive half).*

(anticipating or tackling the ball), when covering and when marking.

Example: Diagram 16.
The same movement of the forwards. Inside defenders playing in flat 4 system. The defender (A) will follow the attacker (1) delaying his actions. Defender (B) will move to the defender (A) to cover his back. As soon as the ball starts to switch the point of attack the defender (B) starts to move to the opposite side to pressure the closest attacker to the goal (attacker 5). Now it is defender (B) applying the pressure and defender (A) covering his back and keeping his eyes on the attacker (1) penetration. It is important the defender (B) does not commit too much to that attacker, and observes where the ball is going to be passed during the attackers' circulation of the ball. As soon as the pass is done to the attacker (1), defender (A) comes to pressure and defender (B) quickly moves inside to cover defender (A)'s back. If you decide to play with the libero, the defender (A) will become the stopper and will pressure both sides of the field and the defender (B) - libero, will do the covering in both sides.

  5 v 4 • When you include the two outside defenders, you will be analyzing the understanding of putting the pressure on the attackers, marking the side of the ball and just covering the opposite side as we showed in diagram 14.

Note: If a long ball is sent behind the outside full-back, the libero or the closest inside defender (flat four) must come out and control the situation and the outside full-back will replace that inside defender position in the middle of the 18 yard box.

  You must finish this session playing 5 v 5, requesting concentration on the defensive and offensive aspects of this situation.

5. 6 v 5: In this group tactics situation we will focus on introducing the outside full-back to the attacking sector if the possible inside penetration was not available and a double circulation of the ball is necessary.
Double Circulation: The ball circulates from the starting point on one side of the field and through consecutive passes moves to the opposite side of the field. If no player in open space is found, the ball will finish the circulation with the widest offensive player available. This player could be the other forward moving wider to open the space to the forward moving inside, the outside midfielder moving very wide to receive the pass from the defensive midfielder or even the offensive midfielder overlapping the outside midfielder.
  This player will try a deep penetration, looking for short or long

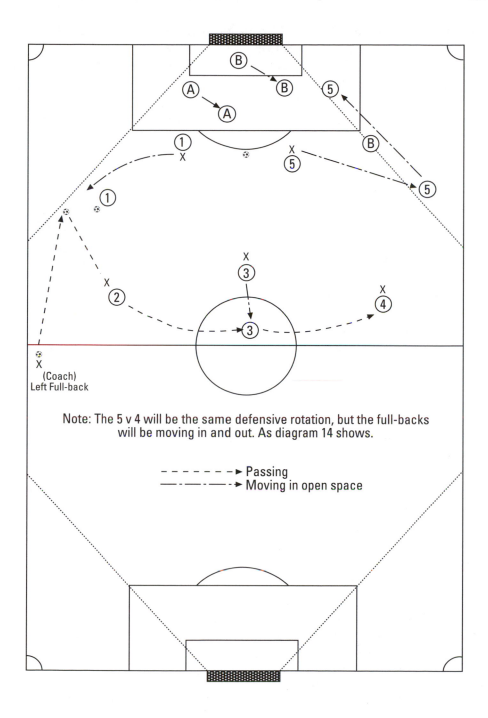

Note: The 5 v 4 will be the same defensive rotation, but the full-backs
will be moving in and out. As diagram 14 shows.

- - - - - - ▶ Passing
— · — · — · ▶ Moving in open space

Diagram 16: *5 v 2. Offensive half circulation V the inside defenders. a) flat line (flat 4).*

crossing. If the cross is allowed, this play is still a single circulation; but if the cross is not available, the double circulation will start with a pass back to the closest option, trying to create an opportunity to penetrate and finish when an inside *attacker is found.

*Note: This attacker could be a forward, outside midfielder or offensive midfielder as we said before - it depends on who did the deep penetration and after no available options, made the pass back to restart the circulation and moved inside to become an option to receive the ball back during this double circulation.

The progression starts with 6 v 0 and the example diagram 17 shows the circulation of the ball with the attackers. Ball starts with the full-back. Repetitions must be done starting from both sides.

The left full-back passes the ball to the attacker (1) moving in an open space. Attacker (1) passes the ball to attacker (2) who serves on a defensive diagonal to the attacker (3 - center midfield defensive). Attacker (3) serves the ball to attacker (4 - center midfield offensive). Attacker (4) passes to attacker (5 - right midfielder). Attacker (5) passes in an open space to attacker (6 - 2nd forward). Attacker (6) will penetrate as deep as possible looking for a crossing opportunity. If the cross is not there, the attacker (6) will pass the ball back to attacker (5) coming to support on a defensive diagonal. The attacker (5) will find the attacker (1) penetrating in the open space left by the attacker (6) and will finish the play.

The penetration off the double circulation in this example happened in the first option between attacker (5) and attacker (1), but if this option is not available, the circulation should keep going until a successful option for a good pass in open space for penetration comes up.

Start to add the defenders:
Use the 6 v 2 - 6 v 4 and finally the center defensive midfielder (5th defender). Spend the time necessary for your players to understand their roles (defensively and offensively)

Diagram 18 - 6 v 5 (Rotation of the defenders)
The same offensive movement as in diagram 17. Defensive rotation could adjust in the following way:

Defender (A- right full-back) comes to pressure attacker (1) who receives the ball. Defender (D - center defensive midfielder) comes to pressure the attacker (2), who has received the pass. When the ball is passed to the attacker (3) the defender (D) delays the pressure, waiting for the ball to be served to the attacker (4). Now defender (D) is pressuring attacker (4) and the defender (E - left full-back) is marking the attacker (5). When attacker (5) makes a deep pass to the attacker (6), defender (B- Sweeper or libero/the other inside defender) immediately moves in fast on the attacker (6) and tries to neutralize the play. Defender (E) runs inside the 18 yard box to cover defender (B). Defender (C - stopper) could go to pressure the attacker (6) instead of defender (B) if the defense is playing a flat four.

Defender (C) - must cover the attacker (1) penetration. Defender (E) has the last defender role and must pressure the attacker (5) when he receives the ball from attacker (6) starting the double circulation and the other defenders move inside to pressure ball side players.

The 6 v 5 must be followed by the 6 v 6, where the real pressure on the attackers will give you an opportunity to explain, practice and correct all the possible variations offensively (Circulation and time of penetration) and consequently the defensive rotation (playing with the libero or flat four).

In many soccer schools around the world the 7 v 6 becomes part of the team tactics.
We prefer to include this tactical situation in group tactics, and the major reason is to give the coach the opportunity to:
   a. Explain the offensive function of the outside full-backs in single and/or double circulation.
   b. Teach the importance of the outside full-back cover by the center defensive midfielder, and the center defensive midfielder by the opposite outside midfielder when in offensive penetration.
   c. Be able to have a very clear picture of his team defensively; analyzing deeply the speed of the rotation of the defenders trying to neutralize the offensive circulation (Reinforcing the players' communication).

One of the most effective ways to penetrate into the offensive zone during the game is utilizing the lateral parts of the field. Because of the excessive development of defensive tactics and the tremendous physical power of many teams, the only way to identify an open space in that zone is by moving the attackers and the outside midfielders inside, carrying their marks, and opening space to the full-back moving forward to become the attacker responsible for the crossing.

We show in diagram 19 the variation of the outside full-back coming to the attack, after a single circulation, and finding himself as the best offensive option.

7 v 0 - The ball starts with the right full-back (1a). As an attacker (1a)

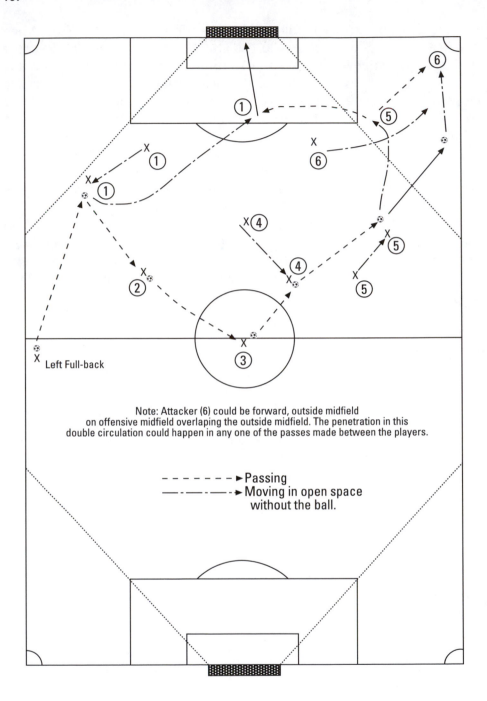

Left Full-back

Note: Attacker (6) could be forward, outside midfield
on offensive midfield overlaping the outside midfield. The penetration in this
double circulation could happen in any one of the passes made between the players.

– – – – – – ▶ Passing
— · — · — · ▶ Moving in open space
without the ball.

Diagram 17: *6 v 0*

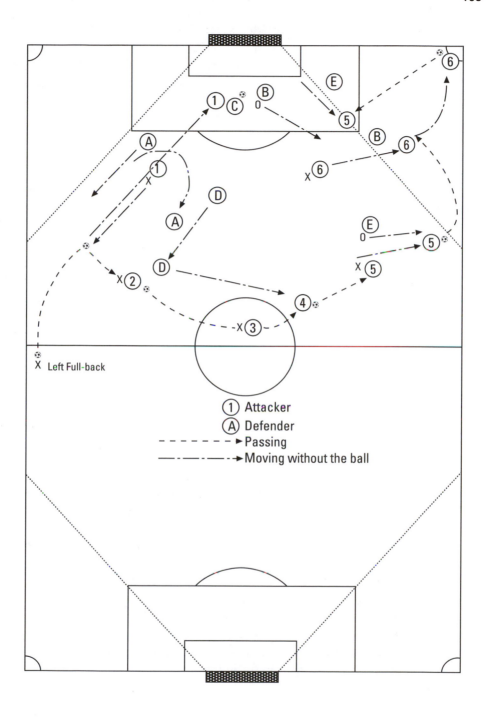

Diagram 18: *6 v 5 - Defensive rotation.*

serves the attacker (2 - center midfield defensive). Attacker (2) passes to attacker (3 - center midfield offensive) moving to an open space. Attacker (3) passes the ball to attacker (4 - left midfielder), and starts the penetration without the ball to the far post zone. Attacker (4) finds the attacker (1b - left full-back) moving to the open space in an offensive diagonal, and the pass is made. To cover the back of this full-back and allow him to attack without worrying about his back, the attacker (2) will slide outside and do this covering function. At the same time the attacker (7 - right midfielder) moves inside to cover the gap left by the attacker (2) and follows the attack to support at the top of the 18 yard box in case of a rebound. Attacker (1b) will dribble to the end line looking for a crossing situation. Attacker 5 (in this case the left forward) becomes the near post finisher. The attacker (6 - in this case the right forward) becomes the penalty kick spot finisher and attacker (3) becomes the far post finisher. Attacker (1b) crosses the ball.

In diagram 20 we will explain the double circulation with the opposite full-back doing the penetration and crossing.

7 v 0 - The single circulation was shown in diagram 19, and the left full-back had an opportunity to cross the ball. We will show in diagram 20 the starting of the double circulation. Because the full-back could not find the crossing opportunity, he plays the ball back and the double circulation starts, ending with the opposite full-back.

Attacker (1b - left full-back) cannot find the opportunity to cross the ball, and decides to pass to attacker (4 - left midfielder). Attacker (4) finds attacker (2 - center midfield defensive) moving inside in an open space. The left full-back must move back to cover that zone (two full-backs must never push up at the same time). Attacker (2) passes to attacker (7- right midfielder) moving outside in an open space. Attacker (7) serves the ball to attacker (1a - right full-back) pushing up to penetrate or moving deeper to cross the ball. Attacker (7) will move forward to support the attacker (1a) and attacker (2) will cover (1a), who is pushing up. The attackers (3), (5) and (6) will move out of the 18 yard box to bring the defenders with them and consequently find open space for a new penetration.

After the concept of offensives have been observed, you should introduce, practice and correct the defensive aspects of **7 v 6**. The progression should be as always:

7 v 2 • Light pressure. Identify good communication between the two inside defenders, and establish how to work in flat four or with a libero.

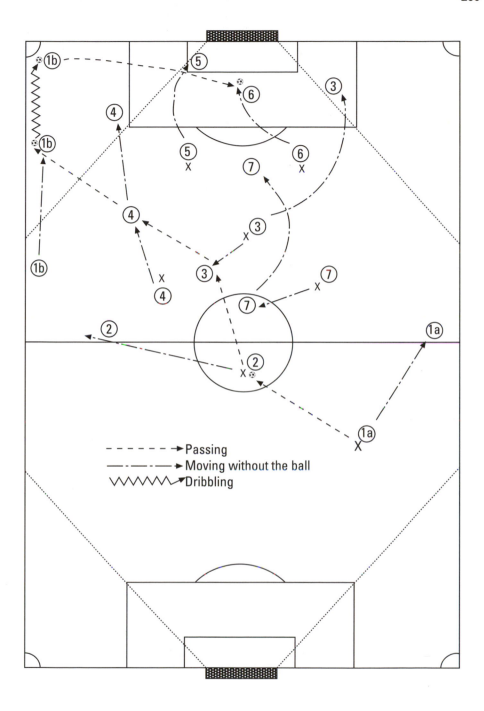

Diagram 19: *Offensive function of the full-back (single circulation).*

Passing

Moving without the ball

Dribbling

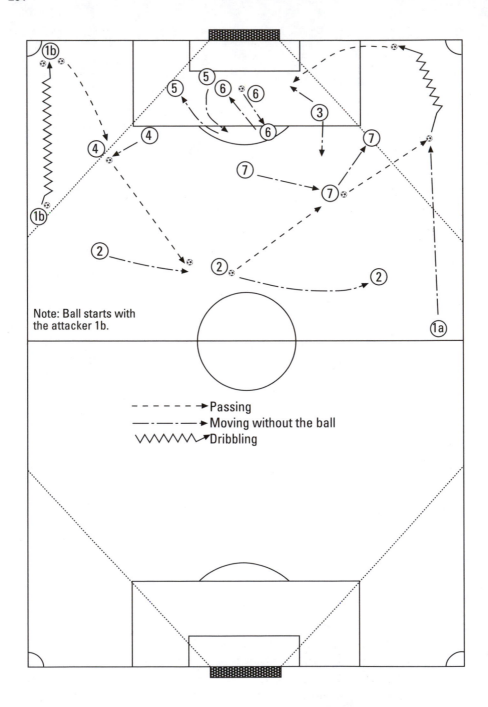

Note: Ball starts with
the attacker 1b.

- - - - - - → Passing
— · — · — · → Moving without the ball
⋁⋁⋁⋁⋁⋀→ Dribbling

Diagram 20: *Double circulation: offensive function of the opposite full-back.*

The **7 v 4** will be covering the same points as before in terms of covering and marking.

We prefer to introduce the concept of man-on-man and zone concepts when working in a **7 v 6** group tactics situation:

In diagram 21a we see the excessive concern to the side of the ball. The ball is with the LFB who is marked by the RFB. The libero will not have any-one to mark, but will be covering each one of the other players and in case of a breakaway he must be the one to pressure that attacker, trying to delay the play to give time to the defense to reorganize. The CMD and the RMF (opposite outside midfielders) will be in a covering situation, and when the circulation starts the defenders will rotate with enough speed to be reorganized to stop the penetration on the other side.

In the diagram 21b the same defensive organization is done, and as you can see; the CMD and LMF are the far away players without markers, and of course will be covered by the closest defenders.

In both diagrams we show the rotation of the defenders in marking in their specific ZONE always remembering the 1st defender is the closest man to the ball, and the 2nd defender must always cover 2nd attacker and support 1st defender. The players must move side to side relative to the speed of the ball and verify who could be the most dangerous and take that zone. Defensive players should rarely leave their zone. If a for-ward moves from the center to the outside zone, the inside defender who is marking that inside forward must follow him until meeting another for-ward coming to that inside zone. The inside defender will communicate with the outside defender and they will switch their marks.

When playing with flat four in the back, the level of communication among the defenders must be frequent and quick, not allowing the for-ward to receive the ball in the gap left when switching positions.

Before you move to the Team tactics situation we recommend you practice the 7 v 7 situation. It is one of the most realistic situations to ana-lyze all the different aspects, defensive and offensive.

After the 7 v 7 we will move to **THE TEAM TACTICS**.

TEAM TACTICS CONCEPTS:

To understand the progression we will discuss five major concepts. These concepts have been studied, analyzed, and have been applied in youth clubs, high schools, colleges in North America, and at pro-level in some Brazilian clubs. Many players and coaches have been through the cycle of education and have been successful. These concepts are based in the extensive work and study with the top youth and professional coaches in Brazil, and focus on what North America and the rest of the world should

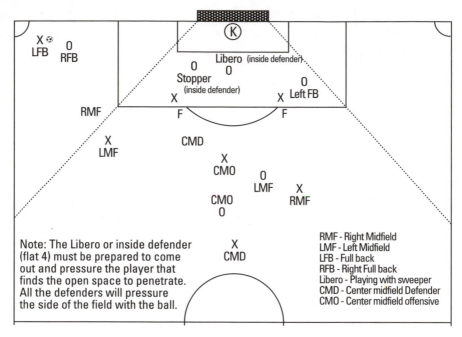

Diagram 21a: *Zone marking - left attacker.*

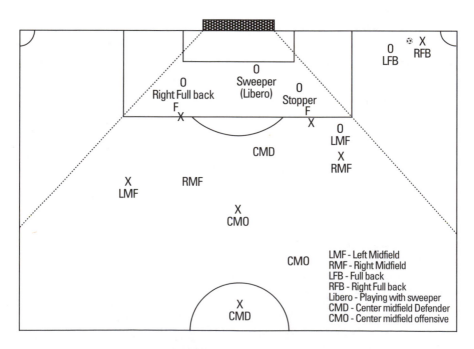

Diagram 21b: *Zone marking - right attacker.*

add to their coaching expertise. The progressive team tactics cycle has as a major mission to clarify what has been misunderstood about the Brazilian soccer philosophy and its concepts.

Basic important team tactic concepts to be introduced in this book:

I. The four basic aspects of Brazilian soccer.

II. 1 - Offensive Concepts.

a. Building the attack from the back (Defensive sector)
b. Building the attack from the back (Midfield sector)
c. Building the attack from the back (Attack sector)
d. Developing the team compactness.
e. Making the correct first decision after intercepting the ball
f. Developing the team's pace.
g. Horizontal and Vertical triangulation (offensive penetrations)
h. Circulation of the ball.
i. Making decisions inside the 18 yard box.

III. Variations of offensive patterns.

IV. Defensive Concepts:

1. Understanding the different kinds of pressure on the ball (In dead ball situations).
2. Defensive rotation of the players (ball in movement)

V. Cycle of the game.

I. THE FOUR MAJOR ASPECTS OF BRAZILIAN SOCCER

Even today, on the cement futesal courts of Brazil, the youth Brazilian players are still learning these basic aspects without the constant supervision of coaches. Here, the younger players must learn how to move the ball quickly and correctly, avoiding injuries or being blamed for making mistakes from the older players. In this natural process of quickness in their decision making and movement of the feet, the young Brazilian players develop these basic aspects. But in North America this process does not exist. The excessive supervision and controlling of games are factors that produce the lack of creativity and it will interfere in the speed of the game, destroying its beauty.

The first step in developing your team is cultivating this natural ability to perform the four basic aspects of Brazilian soccer without having to think before doing it. These aspects must start to be developed at the age of 10 or 11 and with any level of technical skills. The Brazilian soccer philosophy is based on trying to achieve the opposite goal as fast as possible, playing very safely with short passes on the ground, keeping possession of the ball as long possible. To make sure these concepts happen, the players must learn at young ages to make quick decisions with the ball, avoiding injuries and creating unpredictable counter-attacks as fast as possible. You have to develop these basic aspects before you can move up to any other tactical concept.

These aspects are:
1. Ball on the ground permanently, except in situations such as:
- Long switching point of attack
- Long crossing
- Outside the 18 yard box shot.

To increase the speed of the attack is very important. The players can establish a common speed of the ball. Keeping the ball on the ground will facilitate ball control and allow easier decisions with less touches on the ball, less chances of injuries and less mistakes and of course, maximum security.

2. Triangle passes:
We find in North America the constant application of passes in square. This kind of pass is a waste of time in a counter-attack, because the passer always forces the receiver to slow down the attacking speed, increasing the pressure from the defenders, and the probability of mistakes. Square passes often become 50/50 balls because the distance to the marker and the player receiving the ball is equal, not allowing enough time for the receiver to control it much earlier without the pressure. It is much faster to serve the ball in triangles. The receiver can more easily adjust his speed to the ball before receiving it, while always trying to move the ball forward. A player should always have at least 2 options to pass the ball: to a player in a defensive and a player in an offensive diagonal.
The passes in triangulation are divided in: Horizontal (the penetration of the attackers is through the outside part of the field) or Vertical (penetration through the middle) - which is used depends on what kind of penetration in the attack the player will be looking for and if the ball is intercepted in the middle or if the attack comes from the defensive back.

3. Minimize the number of touches on the ball.
Everybody recognizes Brazil for its fast soccer. The key to this speed is the low number of touches on the ball. It is recommended that keeper and defenders always play two touches (fast and very safe). Midfield should try to move it in one or two touches if it is possible (faster and very safe); they are responsible for linking the defense to the attack, and many times a mistake can cost a counter-attack. Forwards should try to play one touch

when building up the attack (very fast, not so safe), they should be able to use their improvisation and creativity skills, applying as many touches as necessary when in 1 v 1 situation or try to penetrate in 1 or 2 touches in collective penetration.

4. Reception of the ball always facing the opposite side where the ball comes from.
This will give the receiver an opportunity to read the full field and make the pass away from the pressure zone. He should support after making the pass, running in the opposite direction from where he made the pass. It is a very Brazilian soccer characteristic to use the outside foot to make a pass and move to the attack in an open space to receive it back in give and go situations. A player should not make the pass and stop the supporting run.

Development of these basic aspects:
    a. In your first practice make sure all your players are divided into two teams. One of the major problems we find in North America is the misunderstanding about the number of players to practice. At least once a week you should have the full 11 v 11 situation or the full scrimmaging related to the age group you are working with. We recommend that you invite some older players to combine with your 17 or 18 players.

    The full 11 v 11 allows you to observe if your players understand the concept of space to receive the ball in diagonal, have enough time to turn to pass to the opposite side away from the pressure, etc.
The progression will be:
11 v 11 or the number of players related to your age group.
    1. 15 minutes playing with just ball on the ground except in crossing or shooting outside the 18 yard box.

    2. 15 minutes of keeping ball on the ground and only passes in defensive or offensive diagonals will be allowed.

    3. 15 minutes - with the ball on the ground, passes in diagonal and minimize the number of touches to two, always following the pass to support the receiver.

    4. 15 minutes - finally, add the 4th aspect; the receiving of the ball, always facing the opposite side where the ball has been played. A free scrimmaging (no restrictions) is recommended after this progression.

II. 1- OFFENSIVE CONCEPTS

We will show in the next part of this book the progressive building up to teach your players how to play without the ball, better utilizing the open space to force the opposing team to get confused in their marking, creating gaps for fast penetrations.

We will divide the education progression of this concept in three sectors (thirds).

    a. Building the attack from the back (defensive sector)
    b. Building the attack from the back (midfield sector)
    c. Building the attack from the back (offensive sector)

a. BUILDING THE ATTACK FROM THE BACK (DEFENSIVE SECTOR)

As we mentioned before the most common defensive system line-ups in soccer are:

1. The four defenders in line (Flat 4). More than 70% of the clubs and National Teams around the world play in this system.

It is based on two inside defenders without specific functions. Both can be the first defender against the inside forward or the last defender covering the other 3 defenders. This positioning requests very good communication between both inside defenders. They should have the same technical ability to destroy the attack and build the counter-attack.

The inside defender will become the marker related to the side the ball comes from.

When the ball comes from a goalkick it is important to identify one inside defender as the marker of the inside attacker and the other one will drop back at least six yards (space necessary from the last defender and inside forward to provide enough time to control the ball and restart the game) becoming responsible for any escaping ball.

2. The line of defenders with a libero (Sweeper/Stopper)

The stopper is recognized as the marker of the inside forward all the time. It is a very effective way to play against forwards who do not move constantly. It is recommend for youth soccer teams in development in North America because of the lower level of communication and skills this line-up could request.

3. Three defenders in the back.

Very high risk defensively, but very appropriate to increase the offensive power. Commonly a 4 man defensive line moves to a 3 man, pushing up one of the inside defenders to center defensive midfielder, and the central defensive midfielder will push up to the offensive midfielder, and finally this one will become the 3rd forward, switching systems from 4-4-2 to

3-4-3 (or 3-5-2 when requesting extra cover in the midfield sector) establishing the full high pressure.

It very uncommon to see teams in North America apply the slow building up from the back because of the lack of understanding of the basic steps of the movement of the players without the ball in an open space and because of the normal risks and mistakes the team has to go through, until the players feel comfortable with it. It is going to take time for all the players to understand their tactical functions and adjust their technical skills to this philosophy.

It is recommended that the team practice and play against easier competition for a few weeks to identify the appropriate level of security and speed of the ball to be played. Make sure the team understands the applicability and importance of the "Four Major Aspects of the Brazilian Soccer Philosophy". After they feel comfortable about it, you will be able to work on the Tactical building up from the back, step-by-step. This concept can be taught when they become 12 or older, with the understanding of learning how to move to the open space without the ball (positioning). Be patient and they will understand.

Progression:

Divide all your players in 4 groups + Keeper(s). Each group should be in one of the 4 basic defensive positions. Two inside defenders and 2 outside defenders (right/left)

Our basic system will be 4-4-2 with the libero. You can adjust to flat four if you prefer.

1. 2 Keepers + 4 defenders (attacking) - 2 full size goals, on the soccer field related to the age group. Coach will be in the half of the field taking shots at the keeper. The keeper will restart the play to the opposite side the ball came from. The four defenders will be in defensive position. Step 1 (defensive). Diagram 22.

Important observations to be made in this situation:

- Keep the sweeper always in diagonal to the stopper to avoid the ball bouncing over both.

- Sweeper should be closer to the right side attacker, because normally the attackers are better with the right leg and try to penetrate in that side of the field. If the left side becomes a problem, we recommend the necessary adjustment.

- When playing with the libero, the other three defenders normally will be in line to help the off side trapping situation.

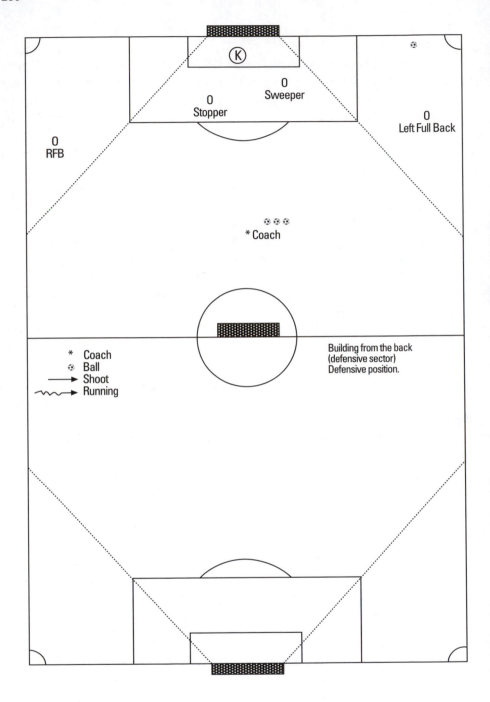

Diagram 22: *Building from the back - Step 1 (defensive) 1/2 field.*

Progression:
In offensive position to restart the attack. Step 2 (defensive). (Diagram 23), the closest inside defender (in this case the stopper) should move to the opposite side from where the ball comes from, running backwards facing the ball and receive it from the keeper. The RFB will move forward to open the space, carrying the pressure with him. The other inside defender (sweeper) will show up on an offensive diagonal. The keeper will be on a defensive diagonal and the opposite full-back (LFB) will move inside to cover the gap on an offensive diagonal to the sweeper. The inside defender who receives the ball (stopper in this case) will receive it facing the RFB and will make the pass.

Step 3 (Defensive) Diagram 24: Outside defender (RFB) will pass the ball to the nearest inside defender (sweeper in this case) moving forward on a defensive diagonal to the RFB. The other inside defender, must come back inside and cover the sweeper, pushing up to support the RFB. The Sweeper will receive the ball facing the opposite side and make the pass to the left fullback. LFB goes as deep as possible and crosses the ball to the RFB moving to the far post and the sweeper moving forward to the penalty kick spot. They will try to score.

Note: The closest inside defender to the weak side must be the one to move wide in diagonal to the keeper and start the build up. As soon as that outside defender receives the ball and makes the pass, he must go back to the center and protect the other inside defender.

- In the next step of this build up we will add the center defensive midfielder (CMD). This player is responsible for linking the four defenders and keeper to the midfield and forward lines. Step 4 (defensive) in diagram 25 the ball starts from the keeper passing to the inside defender (sweeper). The other inside defender will move in defensive diagonal, supporting the keeper. The full-back (RFB in this case) will push up, the CMD will show on an offensive diagonal. The other full-back (LFB) will move inside (to create outside space for individual penetrations) on an offensive diagonal to the CMD. The ball is passed from the wide inside defender to the CMD, and after the pass, this inside defender will move back to the inside of the 18 yard box to become the last defender and request the team to push up. The CMD will serve the ball to the opposite full-back (LFB). LFB goes to the end line and crosses the ball. The CMD penetrates in the middle of the box and the RFB does the penetration at the far post.

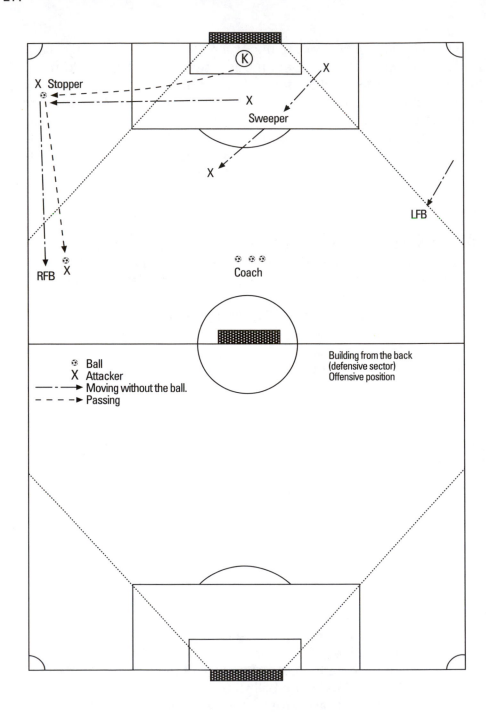

Diagram 23: *Building from the back - Step 2 (defensive) 1/2 field.*

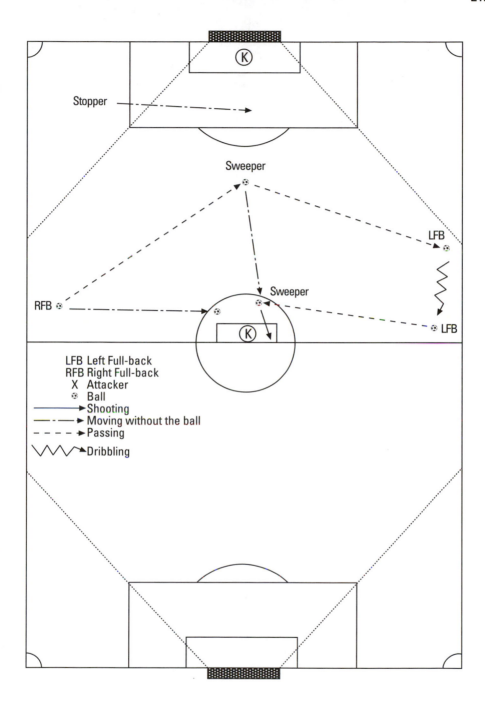

Diagram 24: *Building from the back. Step 3 (defensive) 1/2 field.*

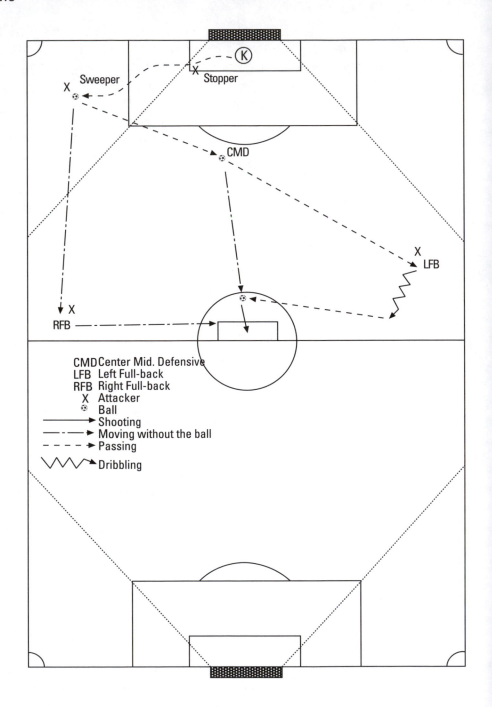

Diagram 25: *Building from the back - CMD Role. Step 4 (defensive) 1/2 field.*

Note: If the team is under high pressure, we recommend that the inside defender who received the ball from the keeper carry it to the top of the 18 yard box and try to attract the pressure. When the pressure starts to come, this defender will play the ball back to the other inside defender on a defensive diagonal, and this player will quickly switch the point of attack to the other outside full-back and start the counter-attack.

Another common variation to break the pressure will be the inside defender (sweeper in this case) serving the ball to the outside full-back (RFB). RFB serves on a defensive diagonal to the CMD. CMD serves the opposite outside full-back. This player goes to the end line and executes the cross. RFB and CMD will do the penetration. (Diagram 26). (variation of the Step 4 - defensive).

Progression to be developed:
- 5 v 0 - no pressure
- 5 v 2 - some pressure
- 5 v 5 - no pressure at all.
- 5 v 5 - light pressure.
- 5 v 5 - real game condition

In this progression the ball should start on one side and the players can only score if the ball is crossed from the opposite side and the teams must preform the build-up situation.

b. BUILDING FROM THE BACK (MIDFIELD SECTOR).

In this sub-chapter we will understand the relation between the five defenders and the three offensive midfielders (right and left midfielder and the center offensive midfielder).

In the Step 1 (midfield) diagram 27 the ball starts with the keeper serving the inside defender (sweeper).

Sweeper serves the CMD. CMD switches the ball to the CMO (Center midfielder offensive). CMO switches to the opposite full-back (LFB). LFB dribbles to the end line and crosses the ball. CMD supports the full-back. The CMD does the penetration in the middle and the opposite fullback penetrates to the far post.

Notes: The CMO will always be moving in an offensive diagonal to the opposite side of where the CMD received the ball.
- If the CMD is on man-on-man marking, the best way to neutralize this situation is by pushing up the CMD, and dropping the CMO to become the link from the defensive line to the attack line.

- CMO and CMD must learn how to find an open space to receive the ball in the middle. We recommend teaching them to commit to the opposite side first, before showing up to receive the pass.

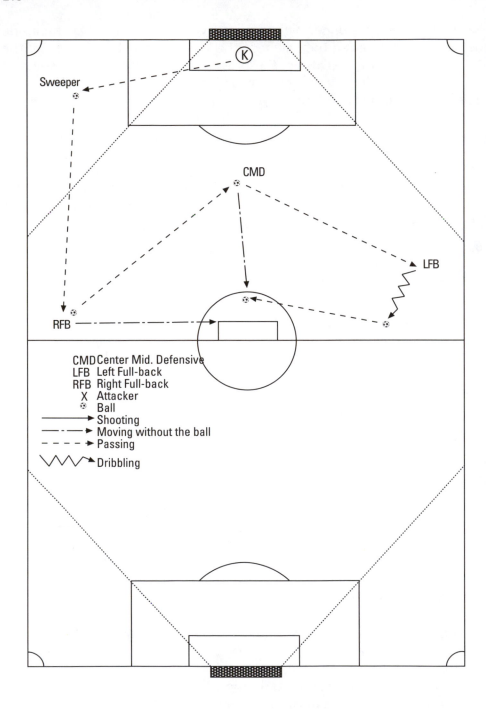

Diagram 26: *Variation of building up with the CMD. (Options of the Step 4) 1/2 field.*

*Center offensive midfielders:
- Link the ball from the defensive line to the attacking line or the midfield line.
- Show up on an offensive diagonal to the CMD when building up from the back. Must always be to the weak side.
- Should have good speed for penetration with the ball.
- Should be a good play maker.
- Should penetrate to the weak side of the attacker's running.
- Support the 2 attackers in switching the point of attack defensively or the two outside midfielders in switching the point of attack offensively.
- He is 70% offensive - 30% defensive in general.
- Responsible for the team's pace. Slowing down or accelerating the speed of the game, depending on the opportunity for quick counter-attack.

In the next step we will be adding the two outside midfielders. Before we explain the movement of the players, we should understand their basic roles in this position.

*Outside midfielders:
- Support the outside full-backs and the CMD on an offensive diagonal.
- Responsible for the zone of the field between the outside line and the center line.
- Do not move too wide without a direct option, to avoid neutralizing the lateral open space for fast penetration.
- Become the third attacker in low or high pressure.
- Should be a good play maker.
- Perform fast outside penetration.
- Cover the CMD central zone when the opposite full-back is pushing to the attack.
- He is - 50% defensive - 50% offensive.
- Should be on an offensive diagonal for any throw in.
- Become the middle men (penalty kick area) in the three attackers penetration when a fullback is crossing the ball.

Support the penetration of the full-back, becoming the defensive diagonal option

*** The full-back will serve the outside midfielder in case there is no option to cross the ball.*

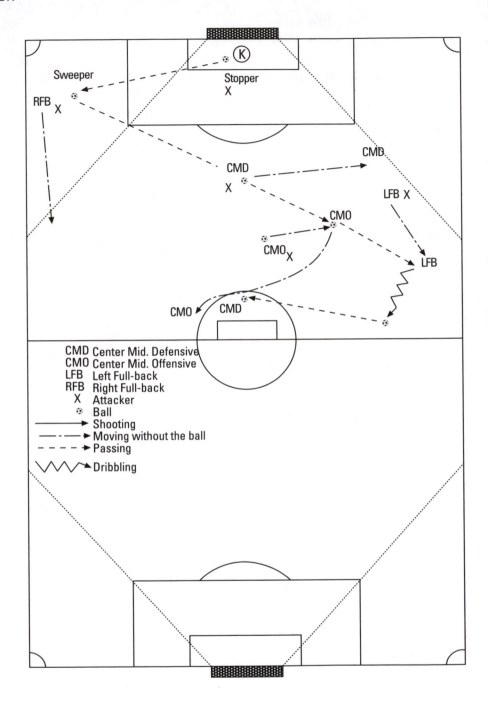

Diagram 27: *Adding the center midfield offensive. 1/2 Field. Step 1 (Midfield).*

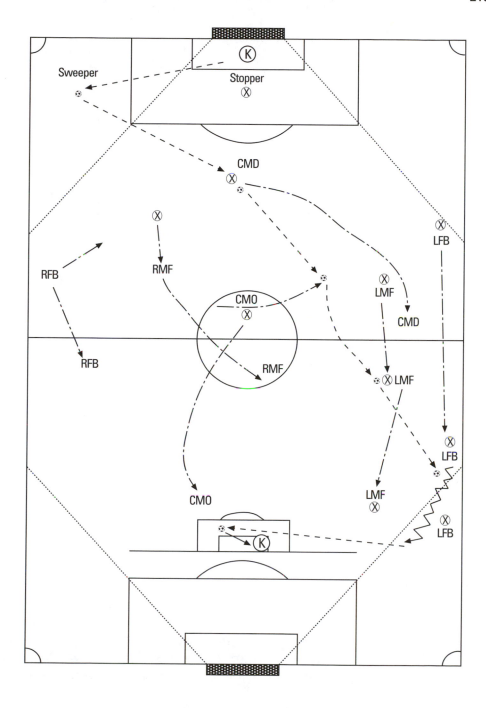

Diagram 28: *Adding the (2) outside midfielders. 3/4 Field. Step 2 (midfield).*

Step 2 (Midfield)

In diagram 28 we will observe the role of the outside midfielders linking the switching point of attack, all the way to the opposite full-back.

Progression:

3/4 of the field - 2 keepers. Ball starts from the keeper to one of the inside defenders moving outside (in this case the sweeper). Sweeper passes to the CMD (offensive diagonal).

CMD passes to CMO again on an offensive diagonal. CMO will serve the ball to the LMF moving in open space. LMF passes the ball to the LFB moving in open space for the cross.

Notes:

* CMD will move outside to cover the outside full-back penetration.
* CMO will penetrate without the ball as the far post attacker.
* RMF (outside midfielder opposite to the side the team is attacking) will slide inside to cover the gap left by the CMD.
* LMF will show up on a defensive diagonal to support the LFB in case a crossing situation is not available.

RFB will stay in the middle zone covering any opposite player, such as the stopper and the sweeper who stay at half field, anticipating any long ball or neutralizing any counter-attack situation.

Progression:
• 9 v 0 = No pressure
• 9 v 4 = Some pressure
• 9 v 9 = Light pressure
• 9 v 9 = Game condition
• 9 v 9 = Applying the four basic aspects of Brazilian soccer

c. BUILDING THE ATTACK FROM THE BACK.

The last sector of the field to be analyzed will be the attack. Playing with two forwards does not mean the Brazilian teams do not play offensively. As we said before, it is very important that players learn how play without the ball. The two forwards will have much more space to move, creating space for themselves or for the midfielders or outside full-backs coming from the back.

* Some of the forward's roles:
  • Both forwards should stay together, around 10 yards apart, waiting to see which side will be available for penetration.

- Identify when to play with his back to the opposite goal, receiving and holding the ball for a teammate's penetration.

- Identify when to get closer to the midfielders to apply a penetration with vertical triangulation.

- Make the correct decision when inside the box

- Perform constant movement off the ball.

- Try to create whenever possible the 1 v 1 situation and be prepared to finish correctly.

- Know how to apply pressure (low or high).

In the Step 1 (attack) diagram 29 we will be adding the 2 forwards and have the final picture of the development of the concept of building the attack from the back.

Full field - 2 goals - 2 keepers:
Ball starts with the keeper who passes to the inside defender moving outside (in this case sweeper). Sweeper to CMD. CMD passes to CMO. CMO passes to the LMF. LMF serves the ball in open space to F②. F②will do the penetration as deep as possible, looking for a crossing situation. Step 2 (attack) if a crossing situation is not found the ball will be passed to the outside midfielder (LMF). The LMF can penetrate or serve on a defensive diagonal to the CMD. CMD will quickly switch the point of attack by passing to the opposite outside full-back, who will go for the cross. Diagram 30.

Some changes will happen with the positioning.
- CMD will slide outside to cover the right full-back pushing up.
- RMF will drop back to support the RFB on a defensive diagonal.
- F② will move inside to become the far post attacker.
- F① will move away from the pressure and cover the penalty kick spot zone, replacing the RMF.
- CMO will become the near post attacker.
- The LFB will drop back and inside to help the sweeper.
- LMF will cover the space left by the CMD.

Note: If the crossing becomes impossible again, the switch and position-ing will be the same as before, except if the opposite full-back (LFB) moves up to do the crossing. In this case the positioning should be adjusted as in diagram 30.
Progression.
    1. 11 v 0

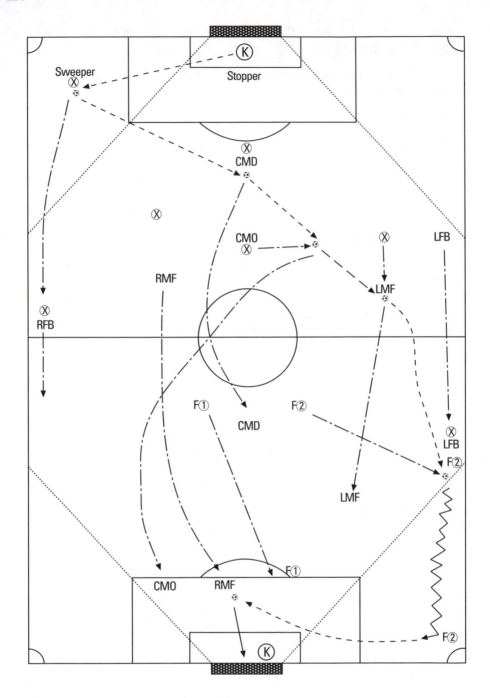

Diagram 29: *Building from the back (offensive sector). Step 1 (attack).*

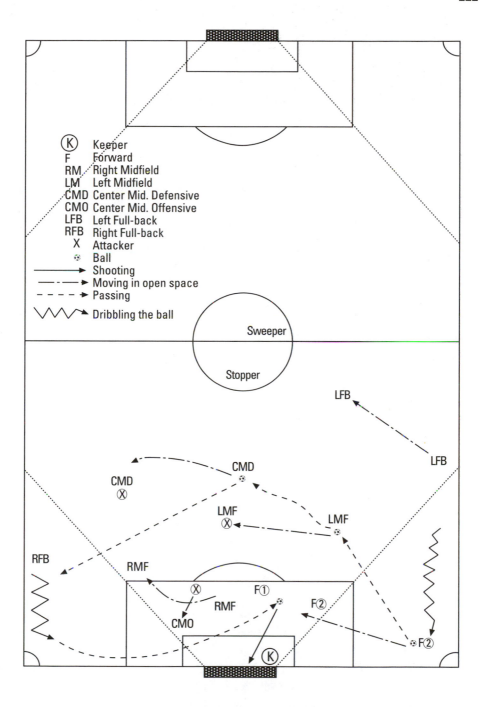

Diagram 30: *Circulating the ball when crossing was not available. Step 2 (attack).*

2. 11 v 5
3. 11 v 11 - light pressure
4. 11 v 11 - game condition.

The last step will emphasize on the four basic aspects of Brazilian soccer during the game condition and applying the building up.

d. DEVELOPING THE TEAM COMPACTNESS.

Your team now understands the concept of building from the back; but to have a real connection between each one of the positions, especially without your players being very skillful, it is important that all the players be able to identify the team's speed with and without the ball.

This speed can create a gap between the sectors (defensive, midfield and attack), and these gaps can be exploited very effectively by the opposing team originating the counter-attack. The definition for compactness in soccer is, "the consistent offensive and defensive movement of the full team as a unit, keeping distance between the team's last defender and the first attacker (40 forty U14 and above, 30 yards - U13 and under, 20 yards - 10 and under yard); not allowing any open space for penetration or consecutive passes from the opposing team".

Progression:
Two goals - Full field - 2 Keepers.
Players in their specific positions - moving up and down the field.

Note: You will probably have 17 to 22 players to work with. The extra players must be in the position you normally would play them.

The sweeper will do the commands saying:

push up	• All the players will move together to the offensive positioning.
stop	• When the sweeper arrives at the half field line.
push back	• All the players move back to their defensive positioning.

A gradual progression will be necessary until the players understand the team's speed and positioning without the ball (team shape), in both defensive (diagram 31) and offensive positioning. (diagram 32).

The players must place themselves in permanent diagonals, with a distance (around 6 yards) that allows them to receive the ball away from the pressure, with time to switch the point of attack and make the best decision available. The positions we show on diagrams 31 and 32 are the original points of that position.

In defensive positioning (diagram 31) - The sweeper must be on a diagonal to the stopper, to avoid the ball bouncing over both players. The sweeper should slide a little more to the left side, because normally you will find more effective right leg forwards than left, and it is better to defend the attacker's stronger side more aggressively. If an opponent has a stronger left side attacker, the change of side is recommended.

In our methodology the outside midfielders must be positioned between the outside line and the middle of the field (diagram 31), and the reasons are: To allow open space for outside penetration, give opportunity to the full-backs to use that outside space to push up to the attack and help the inside midfielders in neutralizing the opponents inside penetrations.

From this basic positioning the players will move in defensive or offensive diagonals, depending on where the ball and pressure are.

To better understand the formation we will build up this concept with four steps.

1. Walking 40 yards

   Players will move together counting aloud the 40 yards (or the respective age group distance)

   The sweeper will ask for everyone to move forward by saying "push up". When he gets to half field, the command will be "stop" (at this time, all the players must have the six yard distance they had when they started the walk); the coach should observe if the distance is not kept and correct it. The players must come backwards always facing the opposite goal and where the ball is.

2. Jogging 40 yards following the sweeper command.

3. Dribbling with the ball (each player in his specific position). Dragging the ball backwards.

4. In this step we will explain the importance of triangle passes in helping to identify the team's speed with the ball, and learn the first best decision to make when the ball comes to a player in any position. In our educational philosophy the ball controlled inside must go outside to the opposite side from where it comes from. If the ball is outside it should go inside to try to switch the point of attack. And always after the pass a support movement must be available from the passer, except if the receiver has no pressure at all and is able to turn to the opposite direction and keep playing.

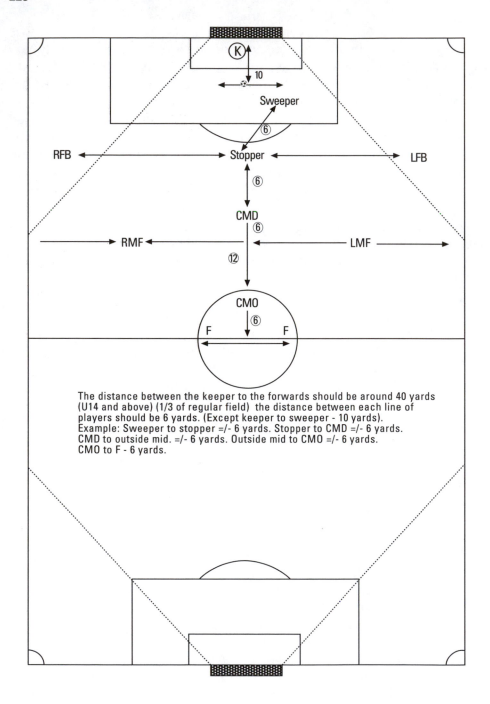

The distance between the keeper to the forwards should be around 40 yards (U14 and above) (1/3 of regular field) the distance between each line of players should be 6 yards. (Except keeper to sweeper - 10 yards). Example: Sweeper to stopper =/- 6 yards. Stopper to CMD =/- 6 yards. CMD to outside mid. =/- 6 yards. Outside mid to CMO =/- 6 yards. CMO to F - 6 yards.

Diagram 31: *Defensive positioning compactness.*

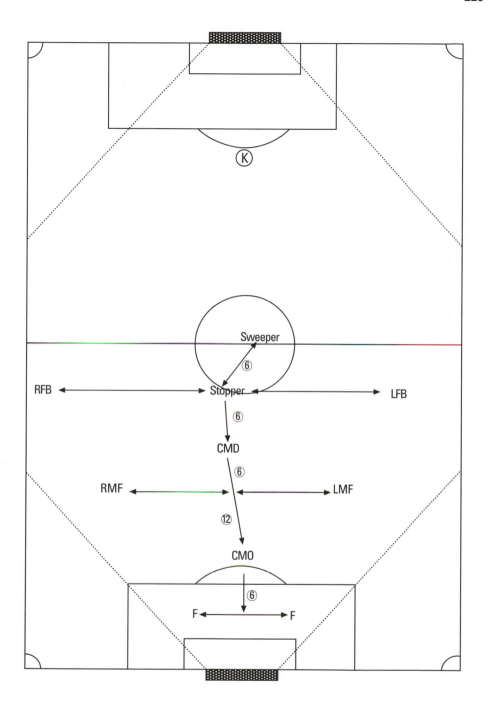

Diagram 32: *Offensive positioning for compactness.*

e. MAKING THE CORRECT FIRST DECISION AFTER INTERCEPTING THE BALL.

It is very common for players to get confused about the best decision to make after intercepting and/or controlling the ball. Many times they will play in a hurry (without thinking) instead of with quickness (thinking), and bad decisions will jeopardize the linking of passes and consequently the quality of the build-up. To increase the quality of this first decision, we always recommend that the inside players look for an outside option (relieving the player from the excessive traffic of players coming from the middle to pressure the ball) and if the ball is with an outside player, he must start the switching of the point of attack by passing to the middle on an offensive or defensive diagonal (relieving the pressure on the ball by the excessive number of defenders moving to that outside area) building up a new counter-attack through the middle or through the opposite out-side from where the ball starts.

Note: The idea of educating our players about the first decision is to help them to prepare their body for that specific decision. In other words: If possession is gained inside - the best first decision is passing outside (out-side penetration). If possession is gained outside - the best first decision is inside (switching the point of attack).

In diagram 33a (defensive shape) the players will be moving from the defense to the attack.

In diagram 33b (offensive shape) the players will be in their attacking position.

The sweeper will use the same commands and the players must keep the basic distance among themselves as they did when moving without the ball.

The players will be passing back to each other until the sweeper commands to stop. **Example:** Sweeper will pass the LFB and LFB will pass back to the Sweeper moving on an offensive diagonal, and back to the LFB again until they get to their offensive positioning point. (Sweeper point will be half field).

In this build-up the first decision will be:

- Keeper to Keeper (passing the ball to each other)

- Sweeper (when playing with the libero) or inside defender (when playing in flat four) to the left full-back.

- Stopper (playing with the libero) or inside defender (when playing in flat four) to the right full-back.

- CMD to the RMF
- LMF to the CMO
- Forward to forward.

Note: After the players understand the importance of the first best decision, the next step is to show how many decisions will become available after the ball control. We will be calling these the " best decisions available in each position", and they are related to the direction the ball is coming from and the sector of the field you are playing. (Offensive sector requires the players' improvisation many times because of the excessive pressure - The defensive sector requires excessive caution because of the risks of losing the ball). These are the best options recommended after the first decision in each position is made:

- Sweeper (if playing with the libero) or inside defender (if playing the flat four)- to the outside full-back.

- Stopper to the outside full-back.

- Outside full-backs to the CMD (defensive/offensive diagonal) or in line to the outside midfielder or to the forward penetrating in open space.

- CMD (defensive diagonal to the outside midfielders or CMO (offensive diagonal) or to the stopper.

- Outside Midfielders to the CMO or forwards (offensive diagonal) or CMD (defensive diagonal).

- CMO to the forwards (offensive diagonal) or to the opposite outside midfielder (defensive diagonal).

- Forward to the other forward (offensive diagonal) or to the CMO (defensive diagonal).

f. DEVELOPING THE TEAM'S PACE
The players have identified their first decision and the best options available to play the ball quickly, unpredictably and safely, but it is now necessary to identify how the team is going to be able to link as many passes as necessary to achieve its goal. To make this happen the next concept to be developed is the team's pace when attacking related to the speed of the ball.

Team's Pace: It is the quickness of the counter-attack of the team as a unit, related to the speed of the ball and the consistent distance of six yards between each one of the player lines (diagram 34). The team's pace

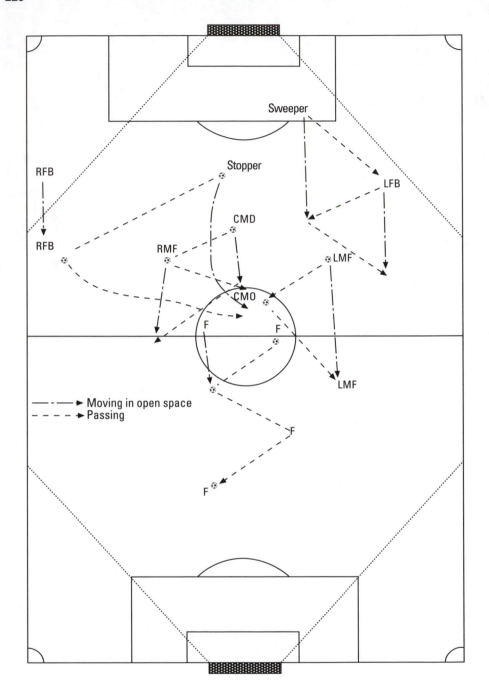

Diagram 33a: *Defensive shape. Taking the correct first decision. Triangulation - Identifying the team's speed with the ball.*

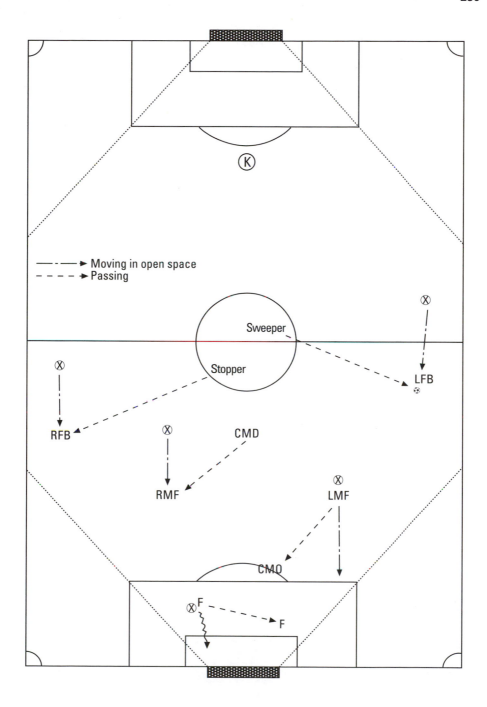

Diagram 33b: *Offensive shape. Taking the correct first decision, Triangulation. Identifying the team speed with the ball.*

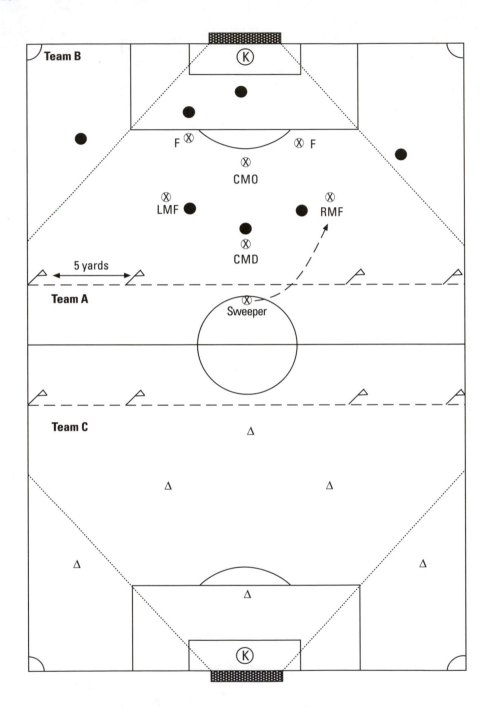

Diagram 34: *Developing the pace in a game condition.*

will always require diagonal positioning (defensive or offensive) when receiving the ball This facilitates the speed of the ball and decreases the time for the defenders to organize to intercept and counter-attack. This makes the build up, becoming as we said before, unpredictable and safe.

This progressive educational concept will be done in the same team shape as when developing the compactness.

Educational progression: The full group of players positioned in the position they normally will be playing. You can have 2 players in the same position, and the passing patterns are the same as used in the concept of making the first decision.
• Keeper to Keeper
• Sweeper to LFB
• Stopper to the RFB
• CMD to the RM
• LM to the CMO
• Forward to forward.

The players will follow the sweeper's (last defender) commands to push up, stop, and push back, as was done before when developing the first decision. The team will move at two touch speed (many times it is necessary to give the team enough confidence to try in the next game) - making give and go passes on an offensive diagonal and moving to support after the pass.

The next step will be moving forward in two touches, but with reception with the inside foot and the pass in diagonal made with the outside foot. Finally the ball will be wall passed at one touch speed.

In diagram 34 you will be able to develop the team's pace concept in a game condition.

With the group divided in three teams; you should have at least seven players on each team (and the keeper). The seven positions to observe during the attacking situation are:
(1) defenders: Sweeper
(4) midfielders: CMD/CMO/RM/LM
(2) forwards.

Objectives of this game:
1. Teach the players how to establish the team pace (consistent team speed when building from the back on counter-attack.)
2. Teach the players that applying defensive diagonal passes is many times the most efficient and secure way to build a quick counter-attack through the opposite side of the field.

3. Reinforce the importance of the defenders utilizing outside penetration as a great option when building from the back.

4. Comprehension of the importance of the team compactness related to the speed of the ball. Example: It is not the best maneuver for the forwards to push to the attack in a hurry, breaking the compactness and becoming predictable options for long passes.

Note: It is important to observe that the players must move the ball quickly and not run too much with it. Ask the players to be patient with their decisions. Do not force the offensive passes. Circulate the ball from side-to-side on defensive or offensive diagonals until a good option for quick penetration is found.

Explanation of the game:
Team A will be attacking against team B. They have two minutes to score or team B will become the attacking team versus team C. During the same two minutes team B will try to intercept the ball and build a counter-attack with outside penetration.

The rules of the game are:
1. Any player from the attacking team can penetrate at the attacking zone. But nobody from the defending team can penetrate inside the neutral zone to pressure the ball.

2. Any attacker can pass the ball back to the player in the neutral zone (it is the secure area). Any player can be that defender (like a point guard in basketball) to switch the point of attack.

3. The only way the defensive team can become the attacking team is if they cross the neutral zone line dribbling the ball through the two flags located on each side of the mid-line 5 yards apart.

4. As we said before - two minutes is the maximum time the two teams can play against each other.

5. If the attacking team scores they will get two points and will be playing against the C team. If the defending team does not allow a goal, and crosses the neutral zone line dribbling, they will get one point and become the attacking team.

6. If no decision is made during the two minute game, the defending team will become the attacker, but will not get any points. The duration and frequency of this game is related to the

level of understanding you want to accomplish with your team during that practice.

g. HORIZONTAL and VERTICAL TRIANGULATION
(offensive penetrations)

One of the major problems in soccer in many countries, especially in North America, is the lack of exciting plays and goals, and we believe the biggest reason is the excessive defensive mind of the coaches, worrying about the result instead of promoting the fun, creativity, beauty and real competitiveness in playing offensive systems.

We will find two basic ways to attack.
a. Building from the back (as we have shown before) when the ball is dead and starts with the keeper.
b. The quick counter-attacks: When the ball is intercepted by one of your players in any sector of the field and the opposite team is defensively disorganized.

We have four basic ways to develop a quick counter-attack.

1. THE LONG BALL over the opposite midfield, trying to find your target player in deep penetration, away from the pressure. This counter-attack is quick but unsafe and becomes too predictable if it is done from the defensive sector directly to the offensive sector. We recommend this kind of counter-attack when the pass is made from the midfield to the attack sector and the receiver is at least five yards away from the defensive pressure.

2. HORIZONTAL TRIANGULATION (OUTSIDE PENETRATION):

This kind of penetration in counter-attack is applicable when the ball is intercepted in any sector of the field and the opposite team is not organized enough to react. The passes must be safe in horizontal triangulation, utilizing the same side of the field, without switching the point of attack. The passes will be wall passes (one touch) and/or give and go (two touches) from the defensive to the offensive half, and the receiver will be always facing the passer. In this kind of penetration the 1st forward (player that intercepted the ball) must wait until the pressure gets closer (around three to four yards) to make the pass and start the cycle of continuous one or two touches until the endline, passing to a forward or any other player in position to finish that penetration.

This first offensive pass will identify the success, or not, of the penetration. A too early pass will give an opportunity to the 1st defender to pressure the ball and allow the 2nd defender to intercept it.

In diagram 35 you will be able to identify the areas to apply the

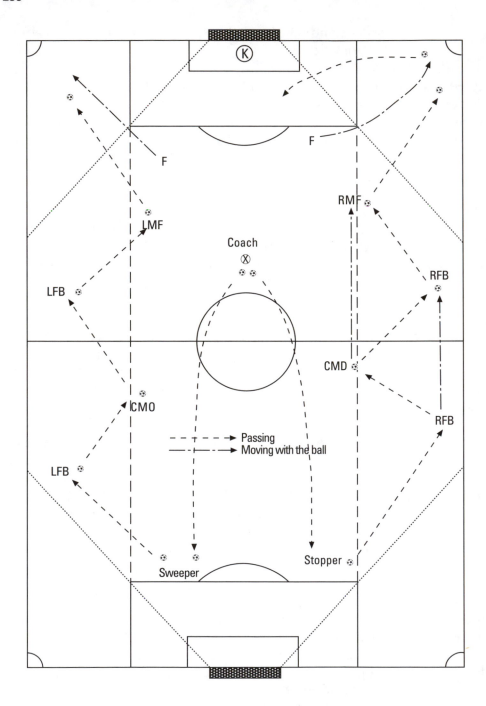

Diagram 35: *Horizontal triangulation (Outside penetration).*

outside penetration with horizontal triangulation.

Educational progression:
Divide the field into two sides (with an imaginary line from goal to goal).
   The coach will kick a long ball to the inside defenders (sweeper/stopper). Each time, one of them will intercept the ball and start the counter-attack situation with an outside penetration.
These positions will be part of the build up at the right side:
Stopper • RFB • CMD • RMF • RFB

These positions will be part of the build up at the left side:
Sweeper • LFB • CMO • LMF • LFB

Speed of the penetration to develop this educational progression:
   a. 2 touches
   b. 2 touches (inside trapping - outside foot passing)
   c. 1 touch

   The number of repetitions is related to the level of the quality of the execution the coach wants to achieve in that practice.
   The final step to develop this concept will be a game condition of 11 v 11.

3. VERTICAL TRIANGULATION (INSIDE PENETRATION).
This is the way to counter-attack when the ball is intercepted at the defensive sector and the outside penetration is not available. Inside penetration has been one of the most efficient ways to counter-attack against man on man marking.
   On diagram 36 we show the lines of players that help to determine the vertical triangulation.
The basic player lines are:
Line 1   •   Sweeper
Line 2   •   Stopper (inside defenders in flat four formation) and outside full-backs
Line 3   •   CMD
Line 4   •   Outside midfielders (right and left)
Line 5   •   CMO
Line 6   •   Forwards

   The inside penetration is based on the constant passes in vertical triangulation: first an offensive pass, jumping one of the player lines, then a defensive pass to the line that was jumped over. **Example:** Diagram 36.

237

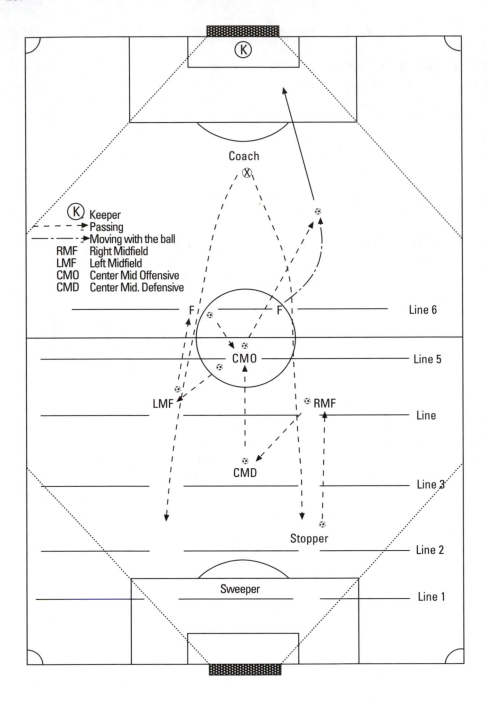

Diagram 36: *Vertical triangulation (Inside penetration) • Line of players.*

The coach will send a long ball. Sweeper (line 1) or stopper (line 2) intercepts the ball and identifies an opportunity to play through the middle. The ball is passed to the right midfield (line 4) - The RM will pass the ball back to the CMD (line 3). The CMD will pass the ball to the CMO (line 5). The CMO will pass the ball back to the LM (again line 4). LM will pass to the forward (line 6). The forward will try to penetrate or will pass back to the CMO (again line 5).

The CMO will serve the ball to the opposite forward (line 5), who does the final penetration. The variations that can be created are numerous, and the player in the open space will be the key point to maintain a fast and safe penetration, unpredictable to the opposite defense.

Educational progression.
Important points to educate the players when building up this concept:
1. The passes must always be on the ground.

2. The defensive receiver (player closer to his own goal) must always receive the ball facing the opposite side from where the ball comes from.

3. The offensive receiver (player closer to his opposite goal) must always receive the ball with his back facing the opposite goal.
   • The offensive receiver must control his body with good balance, waiting for a heavy physical pressure from the defender. We recommend that the receiver use the sole of the foot to trap the ball (this leg extension does not allow the defender to steal the ball, forcing him to commit to one side trying to take the ball). As soon as the defender commits to the ball, the attacker can penetrate to the other side.

5. The vertical triangulation will be necessary if the defender does not commit to one of the sides.

6. The offensive receiver must hold the ball long enough to find the defensive receiver in open space.

7. The offensive receiver must always keep arms up and the back bending back for better protection of the body against injuries and protecting the ball.

8. The one touch speed is the most effective to neutralize the man on man pressure.

9. The passer must always move to the open space to the opposite side where the ball was passed, becoming the support player.

Progression:
The Coach sends a long pass. The inside defenders (sweeper/stopper) intercept it and start the cycle of passes building the penetration.
These are the steps to be followed:
1. Situation 8 v 0 plus keeper.
2. 8 v 2 • Light pressure - Allow 3 touches to each player.
3. 8 v 2 • Light pressure - Allow maximum 2 touches.
4. 8 v 2 • 1 touch situation.
5. 8 v 8 • maximum 2 touches.
6. Final scrimmaging (11 v 11) • 2 touches.
7. Free touch scrimmaging • Requesting the players to only apply the inside penetration.

Note: Experiment with this concept in your next competition.

4. COMBINATION OF VERTICAL AND HORIZONTAL PENETRATION.
It is the most common way to counter-attack. You will identify the key players on your team and let them establish what will be the best variations of counter-attack based on the space available to the penetration. The attack can originate with inside penetration and become an outside penetration or vice versa.

You as a coach should be the one to read and identify the best options available and let your captain know your ideas. Your ideas along with the suggestions of the players could generate a very successful game plan.

Factors to be analyzed to identify the best game plan:
1. Your original game plan. Try to keep as close as you can to the actual game plan as in your practice game plan.

2. Try to collect the maximum information you can about the opposite team, to identify if inside or outside penetration will be the best option.

3. Their marking system.

4. Strong and weak players.

5. Collect any other information which could be helpful (see game analysis in Chapter: Planning).

h. CIRCULATION OF THE BALL

Knowing that a player touches the ball no more than three minutes in a ninety minute game, it is important to teach the players how to move without looking for the open space. To find this player in an open space, the other players will be circulating the ball at a speed that can be fast, safe and very unpredictable, allowing for very effective penetration.

To assure the success in this educational concept, it is very important first of all to reinforce the four basic aspects of Brazilian soccer, which are:

1. Ball on the ground as often as possible, except when a player is away from the pressure and available for a long ball pass, or crossing or shooting from outside the 18 yard box.
2. Minimize the number of touches, especially at the defensive and midfield sectors.
3. After receiving the ball, always switch the point of attack.
4. The passes must always be in diagonal and the passer must move to the opposite side of that pass to support the receiver.

In diagram 37 we show the importance of the correct positioning on defensive or offensive diagonals away from the pressure. The three players with the most responsibility for keeping the constant circulation of the ball with speed and safeness and identifying the best option for a quick counter-attack in outside or inside penetration are:

Sweeper (playing with the libero) or one of the inside defenders (playing in flat four), the CMD and the CMO.

Note: The stopper will become the link player when the sweeper is out of position to do the support.

We can recognize these three positions as being like the point guards in basketball. They will always be dropping back to support in defensive diagonal or moving forward to support in offensive diagonal.

Progressive education of this concept:
Important points to be observed:
Defensive positioning.
Half-field (related to the age group) • 8 v 7 (and keeper).
The eight offensive positions will be;
Defenders: Sweeper • Stopper
Midfields: CMD/CMO • Right and Left midfielder
(2) Attackers:

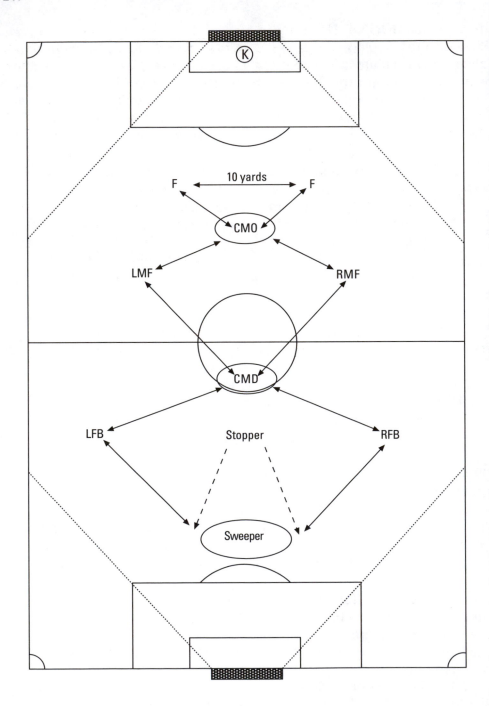

Diagram 37: *Circulation of the ball - Basic positions.*

In diagram 38 we show a good example of a game condition conducive to developing the players' understanding of the importance of circulating the ball quickly, safely and as unpredictably as possible, holding it as long as necessary to find a very effective option.

Observing that the ball starts with the stopper, the LMF shows on an offensive diagonal in open space. At the same time the ball is passed to the LMF, the other players will be moving to the open space, such as: the CMD will move in defensive diagonal; the CMO will move in offensive diagonal; one of the forwards will move to the offensive open space to receive the ball in line, and finally the LMF will slide to the center to cover the gap in the middle. The attacking team will try to score, and the defensive team will try to neutralize the penetration and build a counter-attack using the outside penetration. To get a point and become the attacker team, they must dribble the ball through the two flags placed in each outside part of the half field.

The ball will be circulating, and if an offensive option is not available, the pass should be in defensive diagonal.
This drill should be developed at different speeds of the ball:
1. Play with three touches
2. Play with two touches
3. Play with two touches, but only outside foot passes.
4. Play with only one touch.

Finally bring the game to 11 v 11 game situation and emphasize the constant circulation of the ball and the movement of the players in open space.

i. MAKING DECISIONS INSIDE THE 18 YARD BOX.
One of the most exciting aspects of Brazilian soccer is the facility to achieve the opposite team's goal with a high number of attackers and be able to find the space to move the ball inside the 18 yard box. Brazil scored more than 70% of their goals during the last World Cup inside that area. This is the last offensive concept to be covered in this chapter. We will explain the decisions to be made in a game-situation inside the 18 yard box.

In diagram 39 we show the organization of the drill to develop this very important concept.

Remember we have been developing all the necessary steps to bring the ball to this sector with speed very safely, providing options to make the final penetration or finishing unpredictable.

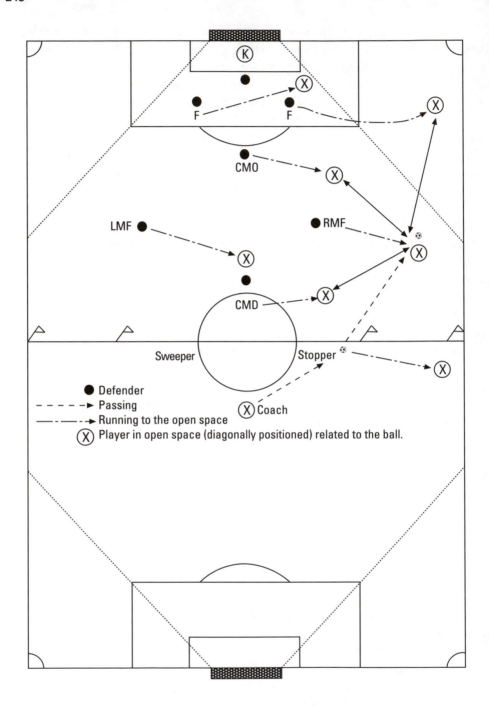

Diagram 38: *Circulation of the ball.*

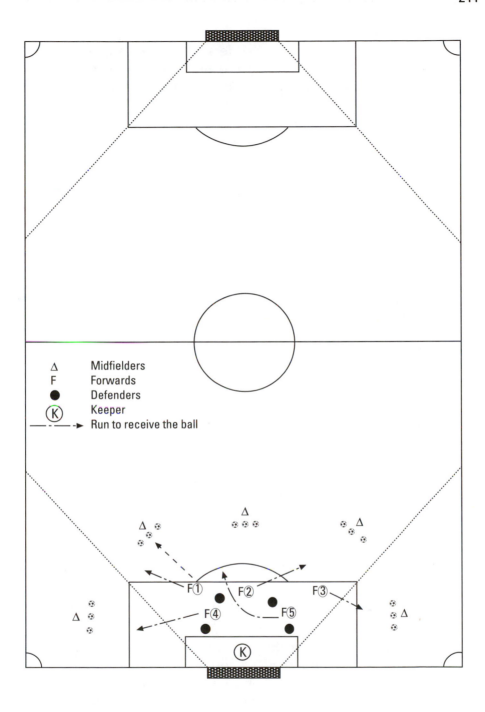

Diagram 39: *Making decisions inside the 18 yard box.*

Educational progression:
Divide players into 3 groups: 4 defenders, 5 forwards and 5 midfielders + keeper - you can always improvise the number of players, Ex: 5 v 4 or 4 v 3 - but always remember to have an extra forward - It is important we see the success of the attack when starting to develop this concept - Later the number of attackers can be equal to the number of defenders - Plus we want to develop the defensive concepts with our players in terms of marking, covering, delay and or tackling the ball.

The forwards and the defenders will be inside the 18 yard box and will be wearing different color vests. The midfielders will be outside the 18 yard box serving the ball to the forwards.

Understanding the function of each one of the group of players;

Defenders: Must be one player less than the forwards at the beginning of the drill. They must stay inside the box, trying to intercept or neutralize any option that could be taken by the attackers. They must place the ball out of the 18 yard box to count as a saved ball (emphasize the players' communication).

Forwards (Attackers): They must have an extra player during the beginning of this drill.

Each forward will have a number (from 1 to 5 or to the total number of forwards). On the coach's signal all the forwards move in different directions to meet the midfielders (without leaving the 18 yard box). The only player asking for the ball will be the player whose number is called. **Example:** Player number 3 will move as fast as possible to the opposite direction where the anterior ball was played, relieving the pressure on the reception of the ball, and will only receive it after asking for it through a vocal contact. Each forward will receive the ball in order and the total of balls to be served to each forward must be at least four. The forwards must receive the ball, and be directed by the midfielder serving it about what kind of pressure they have behind them. The important decisions to be taken by the forwards in communication with the midfielders:

1. If the forward receives the ball in an open space, and the pressure is away; the midfield command will be 'turn'.
   The forward should turn as fast as possible and finish that ball (always on the ground and to the opposite side where the keeper is).

2. If the forward receives the ball and the defender has the chance to intercept it, the midfield command will be 'man on', and

the forward should pass the ball to the midfielder, who must take a shot.

3. If the forward receives the ball and the defender is delaying, waiting for the his decision, the midfield command will be to the forward to try to play. The possible options in this case will be to:
   a. hold the ball with the sole, and wait until the defender tries to take the ball, turning on him and finish the play.
   b. hold the ball with the sole, look for an open teammate and try a fast give and go and quickly finish the play.

Midfielders: Will be positioned three yards out of the 18 yard box. Each midfielder should have at least four balls next to him. The midfielders will be positioned in common areas for rebounding balls. They must warn the forwards about what kind of pressure they have coming behind them. If the ball is passed back to the midfielder to take the shot, we strongly recommend to use the outside part of the foot for strong curve balls. No balls can be added to the total of four balls for each midfielder, to force the forwards to always move to different directions, avoid always using the same player for passing.

Important points of this drill:
- The forwards must move, always looking for an open space, and then call for the ball.

- If in a 1 v 1 situation, the forward must hold the defender with his body and try to turn and take the shot.

- If there is an extra defender in pressure, the forward should hold the ball and look for a forward moving to an open space to receive the ball or to a midfielder to finish.

- Patience is an important characteristic for a great forward. Remember, the defender is in a panic to clear the ball, and many times he will foul, giving a penalty.

Everybody should repeat this drill at east two times. After the group does one time, the functions of the players must switch. The attackers become midfielders. Half of the midfielders become attackers. The other midfielders become defenders. This drill will help to develop all the characteristics of each position for all the players.

The final step will be a 11 v 11 situation, requesting the players to apply all the points of the concept of making decisions inside the 18 yard box.

III. VARIATIONS OF THE OFFENSIVE PATTERNS

This sub-chapter will give you an idea why Brazilian soccer can become so unpredictable and able to confuse any kind of pressure. We will describe some of these offensive pattern variations that could occur when your team is starting the attack from the back or when they have intercepted the ball from the opposite team's counter-attack. Our major goal is to give a direction to the coaches about these Brazilian soccer tactical offensive patterns, and show that any coach with creativity can teach the players how to move to the open space and receive in correct position to make the team a successful unit. We described earlier in this chapter how to develop the concept of building the attack from the back. The basic build from the back is the most important concept to be developed during the educational process to build numerous offensive patterns. You should be patient and slowly introduce the numerous options available. To facilitate the learning process of these options we should consider some factors such as:

1. The ability to teach your players about the importance of the movement without the ball.

2. Understand the correct offensive and defensive positioning.

3. The applicability of the four basic aspects of Brazilian soccer, done with the maximum possible speed of the ball. In other words, your team should be able to move the ball even under pressure in two and many times only one touch.

Some of the most common tactical patterns utilized by the Brazilian teams.

We have three basic situations to build the attack and they are related to the area of the field where the final penetration is happening.

1. Penetrations started and finished on the same side of the field.

2. Penetrations started on one side and finished on the other side of the field.

3. Penetrations started from outside of the field and finished through the middle of the field.

Important information:

a. The diagrams will show the patterns for building from the back, but the same variations must be applicable if the ball is intercepted in the midfield or offensive sector (thirds).

b. We will be showing the build up of the offensive patterns from one side, but both sides must be practiced and be part of the options available during the game.

1. PENETRATIONS STARTED AND FINISHED AT THE SAME SIDE OF THE FIELD

Pattern 1 (Diagram 46)

Keeper passes the ball to the inside defender (sweeper), moving backwards facing the ball, to the open space of the opposite side from where the ball is coming from. Inside defender passes to the outside fullback (Right) in line. RFB passes in a defensive diagonal to the CMD. CMD passes the ball back to the RMF - RMF passes the ball to the forward (1) moving in an open space - Forward receives the ball and goes as deep as possible looking for a short or long cross. (*) (**)

In this pattern the three finishers inside the 18 yard box will be: CMO (far post) - LMF (left midfield/Penalty kick spot) Forward (2) (near post).

The RMF will do the defensive support - CMD does the middle field cover.

The opposite full-back (LFB) will be marking one of the opposite forwards and/or covering the far post and will be prepared to neutralize the counter-attack through that side. The stopper (or the other inside defender) will be marking the inside forward.

Sweeper (inside defender) will be free of marking somebody, but prepared to neutralize any counter-attack.

Pattern 2 (Diagram 47)

Keeper passes the ball to the inside defender (Sweeper) moving backwards facing the ball, to the open space of the opposite side from where the ball is coming from. Inside defender passes to the outside fullback (right) in line.

RFB passes the ball on an offensive diagonal to the RMF. RMF passes to the forward (1) penetrating in an open space at the same side. Forward (1) dribbles the ball to the end line looking for short or long cross.

In this pattern the three finishers inside the 18 yard box will be: CMO (far post) - LMF (left midfield/Penalty kick spot) Forward (2) (near post).

The RMF will do the defensive support to the (F1) - CMD does the middle field cover.

The opposite full-back (LFB) will be marking one of the opposite forwards and/or covering the far post and will be prepared to neutralize the counter-attack through that side. The Stopper (or the other inside defender) will be marking the opposite inside forward.

Sweeper (inside defender) will be free of marking somebody, but prepared to neutralize any counter-attack.

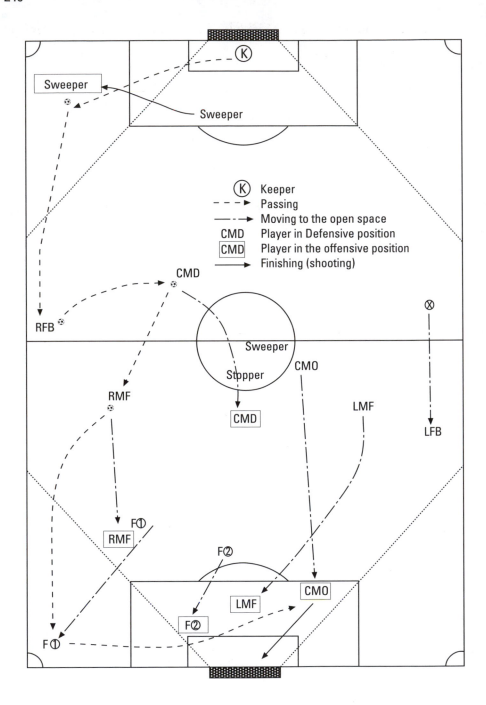

Diagram 46: *Pattern 1 • Penetration started and finished on the same side of the field.*

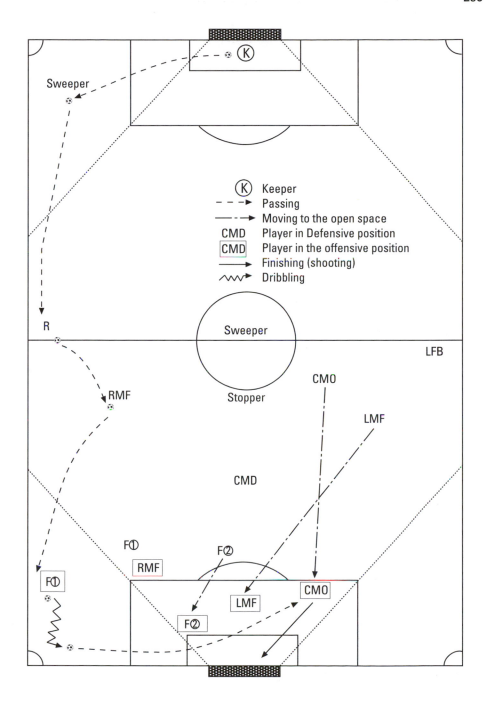

Diagram 47: *Pattern 2 • Penetration started/finished on the same side of the field.*

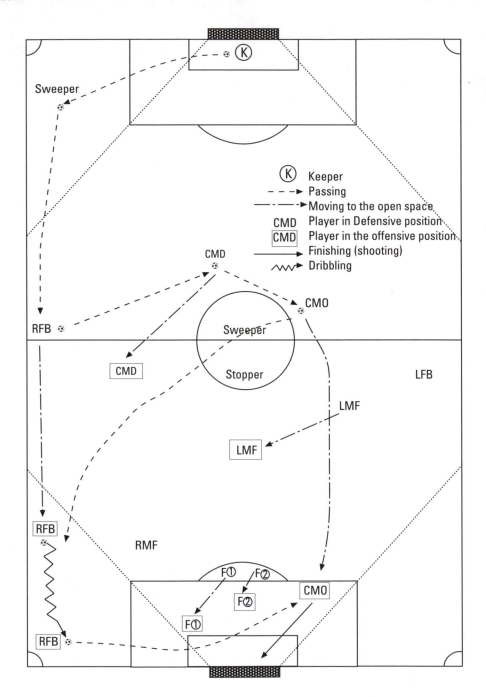

Diagram 48: *Pattern 3 • Penetration started/finished on the same side of the field.*

Pattern 3 (Diagram 48)

Keeper passes the ball to the inside defender (sweeper), moving backwards facing the ball, to the open space on the weak side. Inside defender passes the ball to the RFB. RFB passes the ball on a defensive diagonal to the CMD. CMD switches the point of attack, passing the ball to the CMO on an offensive diagonal. CMO switches back the point of attack, sending a long ball pass back to the RFB. RFB does the final penetration looking for a short or long cross. (*) (**)

In this pattern the three finishers inside the 18 yard box will be: CMO (far post) - Forward (2) (Penalty kick spot) Forward (1) (near post). The opposite outside midfielder (LMF) will slide to the middle of the field to cover the open space left by the CMD. The RMF will do the defensive support to the RFB - CMD will cover the RFB penetration. The opposite fullback (LFB) will be marking one of the opposite forwards and/or covering the far post and will be prepared to neutralize the counter-attack through that side. Stopper (or the other inside defender) will be marking the opposite inside forward. Sweeper (inside defender) will be free of marking somebody, but prepared to neutralize any counter-attack.

Pattern 4 (Diagram 49)

Keeper passes the ball to the inside defender (sweeper), moving backwards facing the ball, to the open space on the weak side. Inside defender passes the ball to the RFB. RFB passes the ball to CMO moving on an offensive diagonal. CMO passes the ball to the RMF on an offensive diagonal. RMF passes the ball to the RFB pushing up from the back to do the final penetration for a short or long cross. (*) (**)

In this pattern the three finishers inside the 18 yard box will be: CMO (far post) - Forward (2) (penalty kick spot) Forward (1) (near post). The opposite outside midfielder (LMF) will slide to the middle of the field to cover the open space left by the CMD. The RMF will do the defensive diagonal support to the RFB - CMD will cover the RFB penetration.

The opposite full-back (LFB) will be marking one of the opposite forwards and/or covering the very far post and will be prepared to neutralize the counter-attack through that side. Stopper (or the other inside defender) will be marking the opposite inside forward.

Sweeper (inside defender) will be free of marking somebody, but prepared to neutralize any counter-attack.

Notes:

(*) • The player in final penetration should opt for a short cross (ball to be crossed is located inside the 18 yard box should be on the ground, back to the penalty kick spot) or long crossed (ball to be crossed located out-

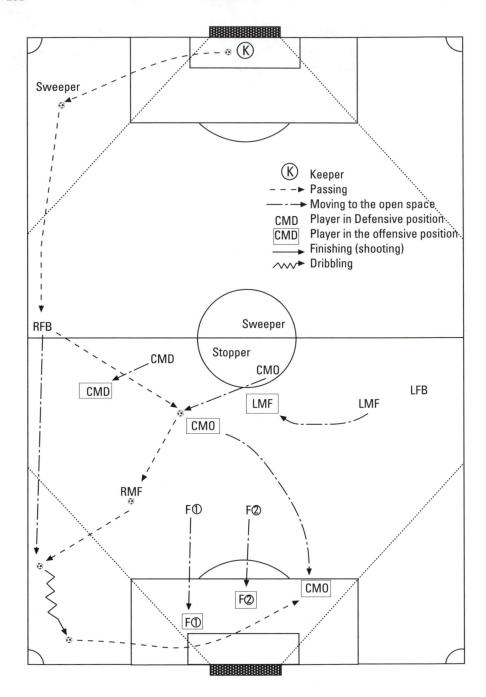

Diagram 49: *Pattern 4 • Penetration started/finished on the same side of the field.*

side of the 18 yard box should be in the air to the far post zone).

(**) • If a cross is not available when the attacker gets to the end line, he should turn and play the ball back to the support player (on a defensive diagonal, starting the circulation of the ball, switching the point of attack.)

(***) • When the CMD is marked in a man-on-man situation, the CMO will push back to do the building up through the middle and the CMD will push up, switching functions and creating a confusion in the marking.

Abbreviations of the positions:

RFB   • Right full-back
LFB   • Left full-back
CMD • Center midfield defensive
RMF • Right midfielder
LMF   • Left midfielder
CMO • Center midfield offensive
F   • Forward

2. PENETRATIONS STARTING ON ONE SIDE OF THE FIELD AND FINISHING ON THE OTHER SIDE OF THE FIELD.

Diagram 50 - Pattern 1

Keeper passes the ball to the inside defender (sweeper), moving backwards facing the ball, to the open space on the weak side. Inside defender passes the ball to the CMD moving in an open space to receive it. CMD passes the ball to CMO moving in an offensive diagonal in open space. CMO passes the ball to the LMF in offensive diagonal. LMF passes the ball to the Forward (1). Forward (1) does the penetration looking for a short or long cross. (*) (**)

In this pattern the three finishers inside the 18 yard box will be: CMO (far post) - RMF (penalty kick spot) - Forward (2) (near post).

The LMF will do the defensive diagonal support to Forward (1) - CMD will cover the middle of the field.

The opposite full-back (RFB) will be marking one of the opposite forwards and/or covering the far post and will be prepared to neutralize the counter-attack through that side. Stopper (or the other inside defender) will be marking the inside forward.

Sweeper (inside defender) will be free of marking somebody, but prepared to neutralize any counter-attack.

Diagram 51 - Pattern 2

Keeper passes the ball to the inside defender (sweeper), moving backwards facing the ball, to the open space on the weak side. Inside defend-

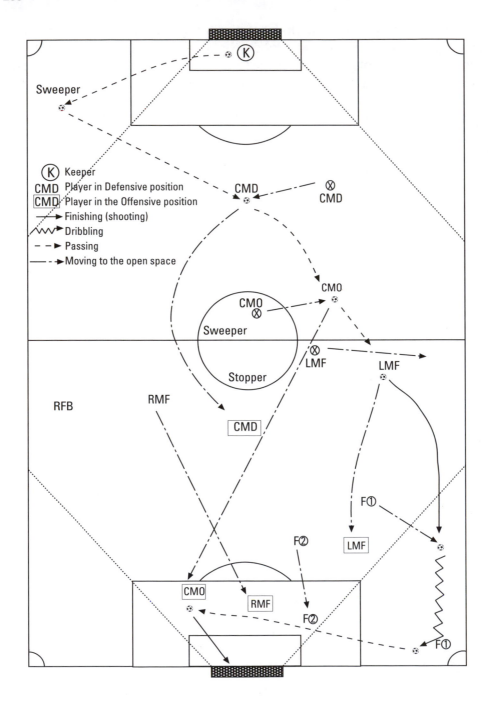

Diagram 50: *Pattern 1 • Penetrations starting on one side of the field and finishing on the other side.*

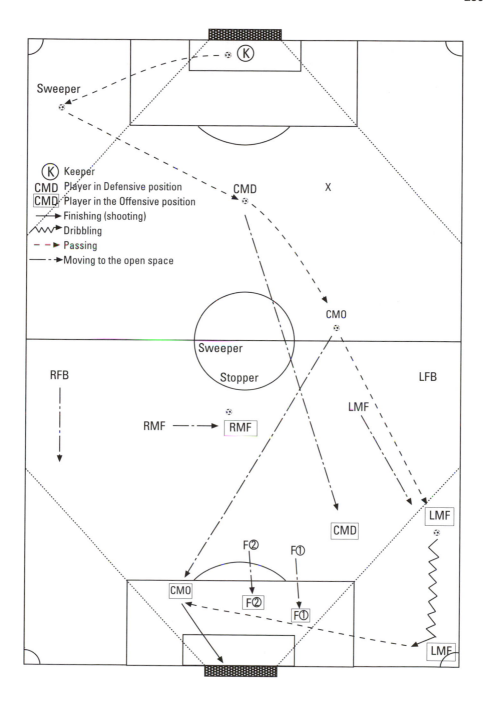

Diagram 51: *Pattern 2 • Penetrations starting on one side of the field and finishing on the other.*

er passes the ball to the CMD moving in an open space to receive it. CMD passes the ball to CMO moving in an offensive diagonal in open space. CMO passes the ball the LMF in an offensive diagonal. LMF does the penetration looking for a short or long cross. (*) (**)

In this pattern the three finishers inside the 18 yard box will be: CMO (far post) - F(1) (near post) - Forward (2) (penalty kick spot).

The CMD will do the defensive diagonal support to LMF - RMF will slide to the middle to cover the gap left by the CMD.

The opposite full-back (RFB) will be marking one of the opposite forwards and/or covering the far post and will be prepare to neutralize the counter-attack through that side. RFB will be prepared to push up in case the point of attack is switched. Stopper (or the other inside defender) will be marking the inside forward.

Sweeper (inside defender) will be free of marking somebody, but prepared to neutralize any counter-attack .

Diagram 52 - Pattern 3
Keeper passes the ball to the inside defender (sweeper), moving backwards facing the ball, to the open space on the weak side. Inside defender passes the ball to the CMO (***) moving in an open space to receive it. CMO passes the ball to CMD moving in offensive diagonal in open space. CMD passes the ball the LMF moving in an open space. LMF passes the ball to the LFB moving to the attack from the back. LFB will do the penetration looking for short or long crossing.

In this pattern the three finishers inside the 18 yard box will be: CMD (far post) - F(1) (near post) Forward (2) (penalty kick spot).

The CMD will cover the LFB pushing to the attack. LMF will do the defensive diagonal supporting the LFB. The RMF will slide to the middle to cover the gap left by the CMD.

The opposite full-back (RFB) will be marking one of the opposite forwards and/or covering the far post and will be prepared to neutralize the counter-attack through that side.

Stopper (or the other inside defender) will be marking the inside forward.

Sweeper (inside defender) will be free of marking somebody, but prepared to neutralize any counter-attack.

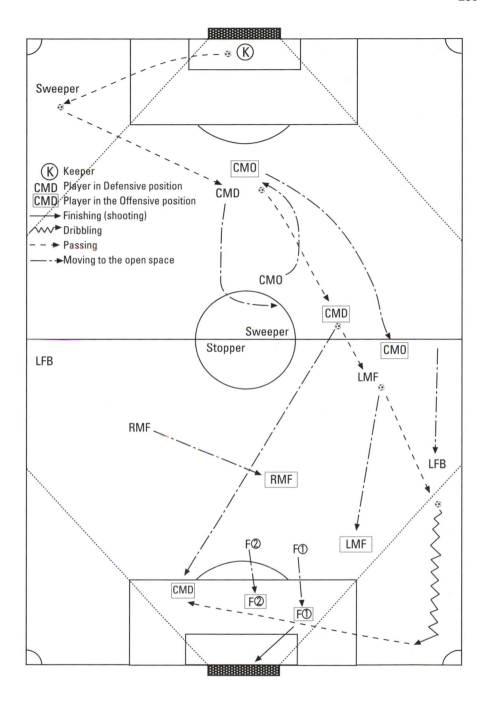

Diagram 52: *Pattern 3 • Penetrations starting in one side of the field and finishing on the other side of the field.*

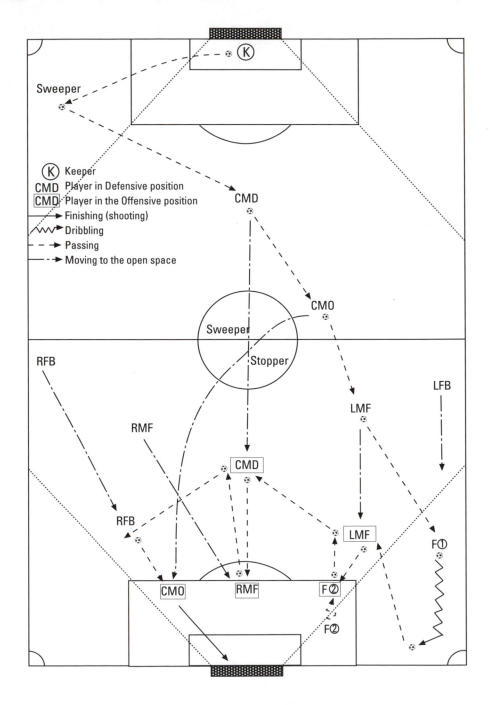

Diagram 53: *Penetration starting from the outside of the field and finishing through the middle.*

3. PENETRATION STARTING FROM THE OUTSIDE OF THE FIELD AND FINISHING THROUGH THE MIDDLE.

Diagram 53 - Pattern 1

Keeper passes the ball to the inside defender(sweeper/stopper), moving backwards facing the ball, to the open space on the weak side. Inside defender passes the ball to the CMD moving in an open space to receive it. CMD passes the ball to CMO moving in an offensive diagonal in open space. CMO passes the ball to LMF on an offensive diagonal. LMF passes the ball to the Forward (1). Forward (1) does the penetration looking for a short or long cross. (*) (**)

In this pattern the three finishers inside the 18 yard box will be: CMO (far post) - RMF (penalty kick spot) Forward (2) (near post).

In this situation the cross is not available. Forward (1) passes the ball back in a defensive diagonal to the LMF, starting the circulation of the ball. LMF will receive the ball turning to the opposite side and looking for the Forward (2) coming out of the 18 yard box (with his back to the opposite goal) prepared to receive the ball. Forward (2) will make the best decision available (see the concept- making decisions inside the 18 yard box). If a good option is not available to F(2), he turns and penetrates to build the final attack. The ball may be passed back to the LMF, who could take the shot or pass the ball in a defensive diagonal to the CMD. CMD will try to serve to the RMF moving out from the box and back to the opposite goal. The RMF can build the attack if that option is available.

Again no option is available. The RMF will pass back to the CMD, who will keep circulating the ball to the opposite outside full-back (RFB). The RFB will serve the CMO coming out to do the same circulating as before with the F(2) and the RMF. The original positions will be changing together with the circulation of the ball. The LMF will do the defensive diagonal support to Forward (1) - CMD will cover the middle of the field.

The opposite full-back (LFB) will be marking one of the opposite forwards and/or covering the far post and will be prepared to neutralize the counter-attack through that side, or assist the attack when the circulation of the ball is done.

Stopper (or the other inside defender) will be marking the inside forward.

Sweeper (inside defender) will be free of marking somebody, but prepared to neutralize any counter-attack.

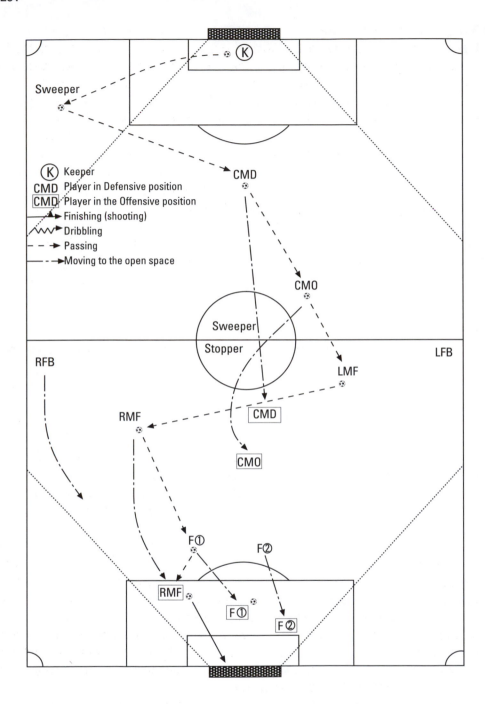

Diagram 54: *Penetration starting from the outside of the field and finishing through the middle.*

Diagram 54 - Pattern 2

Keeper passes the ball to the inside defender (sweeper), moving backwards facing the ball, to the open space on the weak side. Inside defender passes the ball to the CMD moving in an open space to receive it. CMD passes the ball to CMO moving in an offensive diagonal in open space. CMO passes the ball the LMF in an offensive diagonal. LMF does a long pass, switching the point of attack to the RMF penetrating in the open space. Many options can be created in this offensive variation. In this diagram we show the give and go between the RMF and Forward (1), and the RMF does the final penetration. In this pattern the three finishers inside the 18 yard box will be: RMF (near post) - F(2) (far post) Forward (1) (penalty kick spot).

The CMD will cover the middle. CMO does the follow up in diagonal defensive to the RMF or any one of the forwards. The right full-back (RFB) will support the RMF defensively, or can become the offensive diagonal for deep penetration and crossing.

LFB will be covering any forward in that zone and be prepared to push up in case of the point of attack is switched.

Stopper (or the other inside defender) will be marking the inside forward.

Sweeper (inside defender) will be free of marking somebody, but prepared to neutralize any counter-attack.

IV - DEFENSIVE CONCEPTS

In soccer, Brazil has been recognized as a country with a very offensive mind, but disorganized defensively. This tradition has changed since the success in the 1994 World Cup, when Brazil had only three goals scored against, and were extremely organized defensively when building their counter-attacks.

Brazilian's National team coach Carlos Alberto Parreira was criticized for the excessive number of defenders, playing with Mauro Silva as the center defensive midfielder (basically a second stopper), but the major objective of the coaching staff was to win the tournament, and bring the reputation back to Brazil, not to just play attractive soccer for the fans and jeopardize success. Zagallo maybe will be playing with the same defensive organization that was done in 1994, with only one difference. He will allow Dunga or Juninho to push up more often and deeper, supporting the two forwards with more consistency.

We will be covering the two major important defensive concepts of Brazilian soccer.

1. Understanding the different kinds of pressure (in dead ball situations).

2. Defensive rotation of players (pressure on the ball when in movement)

These concepts will be observed during the 1998 World Cup in France.

Before we go through the defensive concepts, we should understand the basic roles of each position of the defense. Remember these roles must be followed when your team is with and without possession of the ball.

a. Outside full-backs:
- Stop penetrations through the flanks.
- Create penetrations coming from the back.
- Cover the inside gaps when the ball is on the opposite side.
- Support the outside midfielders or attackers when in deep penetration for crossing.
- Be able to take shots when the ball rebounds from the opposite side cross.
- Remember and apply the concepts of delay and tackling when in counter-attack.
- Be in offensive diagonal when ball is on the opposite side, between the forward and the outside midfielder.
- Cover inside the 18 yard box when the libero or inside defender is pressuring the player who penetrated behind.
- Move wider and up as fast as possible to restart the counter-attack.

b. Libero (Sweeper) or inside defenders (playing the flat four system):
- Anticipate any ball sent to the target player inside the 18 yard box.
- Provide cover, marking and/or pressure to any other player in the defensive zone.
- Organize the balance and shape of the players in front.
- Delay counter-attack, forcing the attackers to go outside.
- Intercept through-balls.
- Cover very closely the other inside defender or the stopper.
- Organize offside trapping.
- Build up the counter-attack as soon as possible.
- Coordinate the players when organizing the build-up from the back offensively.

c. Role of the stopper or inside defender (when playing the flat four system):
- Organize the balance and the shape in front.
- Be prepared for the libero off side trapping.
- Be in position (angle) to recover as fast as possible.

- Mark the inside forward.
- Be in position to neutralize any kind of reception or penetration of the inside forward.
- Identify the correct time to switch players with any other defender in zone marking.
- Start a quick counter-attack through the middle.

d. Center midfield defensive.
- He is the closest defender to the opposite goal.
- Play 70% of the time defending (or supporting the attack) and only 30% building the counter-attack.
- Cover the outside full-back's penetration.
- Link the defensive line to the midfield/attack lines.
- Help to organize the balance and the shape of the other midfielders.
- Distribute early and with good accuracy.
- Establish the pace of the game.

1. UNDERSTAND THE DIFFERENT KINDS OF PRESSURE ON THE BALL (In dead ball situation)

One of the most important concepts to be taught to the players is the importance to always identify the opposite player who could create a dangerous penetration in his zone.

We have explained before the importance of understanding the concepts of marking and covering. We have shown the difference between man on man and zone marking.

Now it is time to identify the importance of unity in defensive organization.

We have four basic team pressures on the ball:
a. High pressure
b. Full high pressure
c. Low pressure
d. Medium pressure

These are applicable when the ball is dead and everyone has the opportunity to move together to neutralize the possible options and be able to counter-attack on the mistakes of the opposite team.

Important points to be considered in any one of these kinds of pressure:

1. Always come back to your zone and identify the player you are responsible for as soon as the ball is out of the game.

2. Return to your position, always backwards, facing the opposite goal to avoid surprises.

3. If the player is too tired to come back with enough speed, this player should quickly delegate somebody to do so.

4. Make sure the keeper or last defender communicates with the rest of the group to avoid having somebody from the opposing team free and able to jeopardize the defensive team organization.

5. The distance to be kept between the marker (defender) and the receiver (attacker) must be the length of the arm if that attacker is very skillful. If the attacker is faster rather than skillful, a distance of at least two yards must be kept to avoid long balls being sent behind the defender, creating a dangerous penetration; as soon as this fast player receives the ball, the defender will delay first and then tackle the ball. If the player to be marked has skills and is faster than the defender, anticipation skills will be required.

6. The players must understand and stick with the tactical plan when working on pressuring the ball - Any wrong commitment from one of the players and the team unity is gone.

7. Always remember that if the first goalkick taken by the opposite team is going to bounce around a specific area, the next ones will do the same. Be prepared to take control of the space in that zone as soon as possible to be in position to intercept the next goalkick.

a. HIGH PRESSURE

In diagram 40 we show the defensive positioning aimed at closing any gaps or space for penetration or ball control from the other team. Explanation of the position in diagram 40 in 4-4-2 system and the major functions:

Keeper: must push up to the top of the 18 yard circle.

Sweeper: will be on the half field line without any pressure.
He will:

a. Establish the off side trapping when necessary.

b. Be prepared to cover any one of the defensive players in case the defensive team unity is broken, especially the full-backs.

c. Coordinate the team in balance and shape, identifying any problem before the ball comes back to the game.

d. Pressure the ball when the opponent can not find any option available for short passes or building from the back forcing him to send long balls.

Stopper: Will be responsible for the inside forward.

Outside Full-backs: The full-back on the same side where the ball will start must take care of the other forward (the LFB on diagram 40), allowing the opposite full-back to move forward and take the responsibility to mark the outside Midfielder (LMF on diagram 40).

CMD: will be responsible for his player in that zone (normally the most offensive inside midfielder).

Outside midfielders: The one on the side where the ball will restart must mark the player in that zone. The other outside midfielder will push up to pressure the closest outside full-back, becoming the 3rd forward.

CMO: Will be responsible to mark the most defensive inside midfielder.

Forwards: One of the forwards will move to pressure the outside full-back on the side the ball will be. The other forward will stay between the two inside defenders, delaying the pressure and waiting for one of them to commit to dribbling the ball because of the lack of options, allowing that forward to establish in this case a real pressure.

Important: On diagram 40 we show how to pressure in the 4-4-2, because that is the way Brazilian teams play. But the system to be applied when pressuring the opposing team is related to their system. Example: Your team is high pressuring a 3-5-2 system. Against the 4-4-2 system you moved your outside midfielder to pressure the outside full-back, but against the 3-5-2 you will keep that midfielder marking somebody in the middle, with the outside full-back still pushing up to the midfield to mark the 5th midfielder.

The two forwards will pressure the three defenders, and one of the inside defenders (stopper) and one of the outside full-backs will neutralize the two forwards. The other defender (Sweeper) is free to cover any unexpected situation.

When to apply high pressure:
1. The opponent is excessively technical and builds their attack from the back. The idea is to force them to hurry in their decisions and commit mistakes close to their goal, giving you an opportunity to score a goal. Do not start the game on high pressure if you do not know the opposing team - Give yourself at least fifteen minutes to evaluate the group and after that establish the best pressure to be applied.
2. Normally the last 15 minutes of the1st half, and/or the last 15 minutes of the 2nd half of the game if your team is losing.

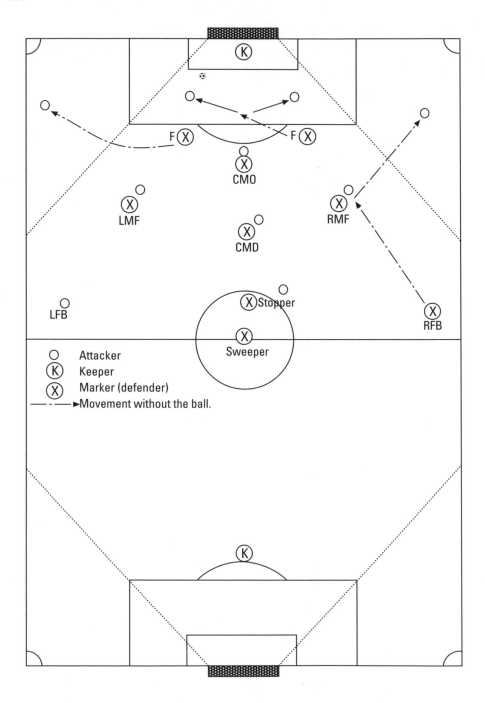

Diagram 40: *High pressure marking.*

3. The opposite team is technically weak and finds it difficult to start from the back and their long balls are not strong enough to cross half field.

b. Full high pressure.

Your team is losing or must get the score and there are about 15 minutes left in the game. This situation will require the risk to move your team to full high pressure. This pressure will basically become man on man marking, and this is really the biggest risk. It is the most intensive pressure to apply against the opposite team, and at the same time the most dangerous in terms of allowing counter-attacks.

On diagram 41 we show the position to be taken for each one of the players.

Keeper: must move up to the 30 yard line, becoming the sweeper, and will be responsible for covering the defenders against any penetration and coordinating the balance and the defensive shape of the team.

Sweeper: will become the last defender, but with the responsibility for marking the inside forward.

Stopper: will push up and become responsible for the most offensive inside midfielder.

Outside full-back: The ball side outside full-back will be responsible for marking the other forward. The opposite full-back will push up to the midfield, marking that outside midfielder.

CMD: Will push up to mark the most offensive inside midfielder.

CMO: Will push up to mark the inside defender away from the ball (becoming the 4th attacker).

Outside Midfielders: The one at the side of the ball will stay back, marking the outside midfielder in his zone. The other midfielder will push up to pressure the closest opposite outside full-back.

Forwards: One will move outside to pressure the full-back on the strong side. The other will pressure the closest inside defender to the ball.

c. Low pressure.

It is today the most common kind of pressure, where you allow the opposite team to build from the back, give them 3/4 of their half (some teams will allow less, some will allow more) creating a situation that they have control of the space. As soon as they push the ball up to the space allowed, they will recognize that a short pass build up is no longer a

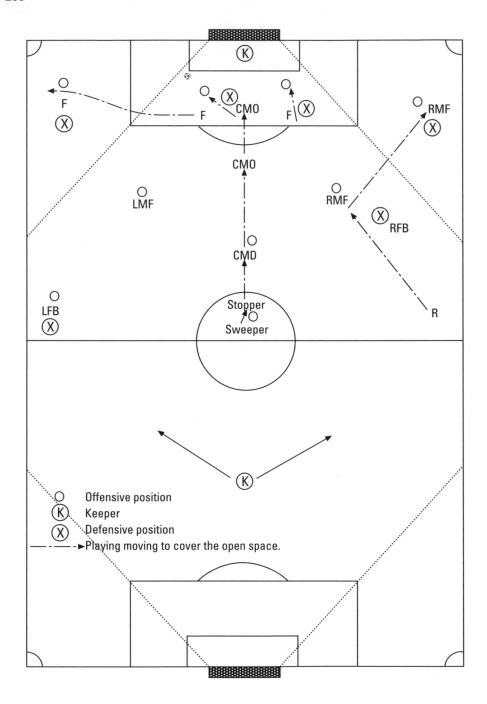

Diagram 41: *Full high pressure.*

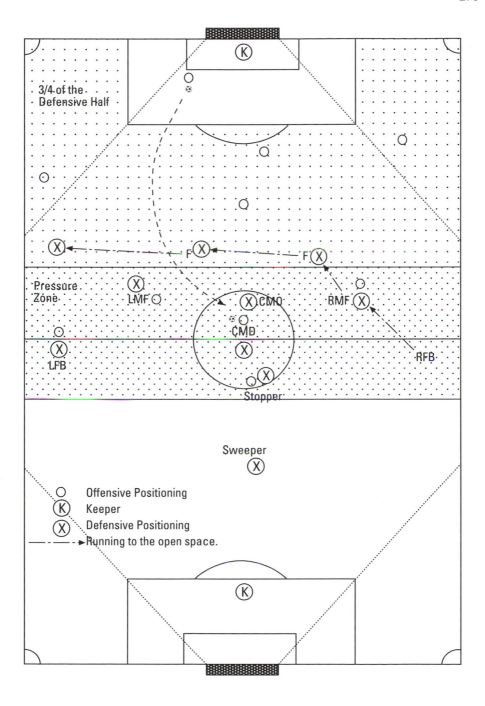

Diagram 42: *Low pressure.*

solution, and will be forced to send a long ball, which is usually an unsafe pass, very predictable and easily intercepted.

In diagram 42 we show the low pressure positioning of the players defensively and it is always related to the offensive organization of the opposite team. The idea is to concentrate all the pressure in the midfield zone (pressure zone - more or less from the top to the bottom line of the central circle).

Keeper: On top of the 18 yard box, preparing to come out in case of any mistake from the defense.

Full-backs: Using diagram 42 as the example, the RFB pushes up to mark the closest outside midfielder. The other full-back (the ball side) will be marking the forward moving to that zone.

CMD: Will be marking the closest inside midfielder.

CMO: Will not be responsible to mark anybody, but will be observing the penetration of the defensive inside midfielder moving up to the pressure zone, or will become the second player on double man pressure on the ball in case an open space is found by the attacker receiving the ball, who must be stopped before crossing the midfield line.

Outside midfielders: As in diagram 42, the LMF is marking their RMF, because that is the side the ball is restarting. The other outside midfielder (right) will push up to the offensive line, and he will be responsible to rotate together with the two forwards to establish a wall to the side where the ball should start. No specific match-ups will be established.

Forwards: They will not have a player to mark, but will be responsible, together with the outside midfielder pushing up, for establishing a wall, and they should wait until the ball comes close to the pressure zone to really tackle the ball and stop any option of penetration that could be available.

Low pressure is recommended:
1. In the first 15 minutes of the game, to give time to you and your players to study the opponent's strong and weak points; their tactical system and specially their defensive pressure.

2. When winning the game, and the opposite team is basing their counter-attack options in long ball passes. You will drop the team, organize defensively, and build the counter-attack when their defense is pushing up and not well organized.

3. Against teams with the direct soccer philosophy, establishing the players speed to pressure the ball's receiver. The right pressure becomes a high risk pressure, because the breakaway situations could happen accidentally.

4. When playing against low level teams, who drop all the players to their defensive half, and the excess of players in that small area do not allow any open space for your attackers' penetration. Dropping back the attackers and increasing the space to play, they will probably try to build from the back, by sending long balls which are predictable and easily defended.

Note: After we pressure the opposing team and take possession of the ball, the next step will be to make the fastest and best decision possible to allow your team to score in counter-attack. All the offensive patterns to be applied will be related to where the open space is available and where the ball was intercepted.

Here are some of the best decisions to be made for each one of the positions, as soon as they have control of the ball.

Keeper: Serve the inside defenders moving outside or full-backs starting to push up, or even the CMD moving to an open space.

Sweeper/Stopper: Serve the outside full-backs. Switch sides when necessary.

Full-backs: Serve the forwards moving outside or center midfielder running diagonally for the support to the outside midfielder moving to an open space, or to the inside defender on a defensive diagonal.

CMD: Serve right or left outside midfield or the outside forwards when possible.

Outside Midfielders: Serve the center midfield defensive or offensive and/or the outside forward.

Forwards: When the forwards intercept the ball and see the opportunity to penetrate directly to the goal and score, they must take it. If the forward penetrates outside, he should look for crossing.

d. Medium pressure

It is applicable when the opposite team has the long ball pass as their major option to build their attack, their defense being very conservative in pushing up to the attack. It can also be used against teams that keep their defense too deep, creating a big gap to their midfields, allowing your

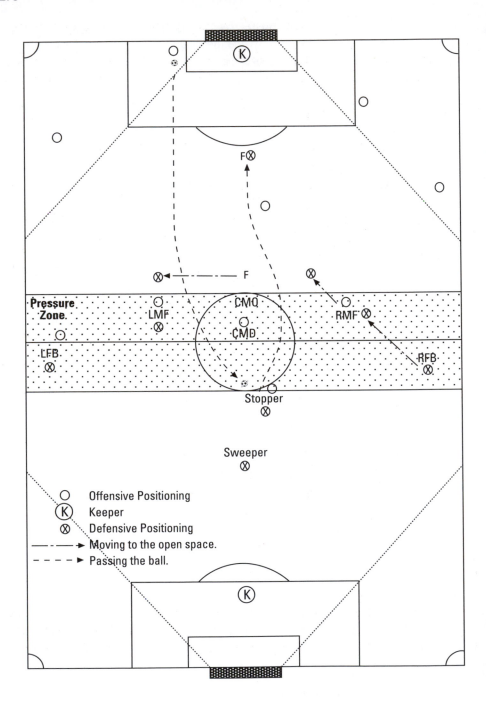

Diagram 43: *Medium Pressure.*

team to use that space to establish the target point to quickly counter-attack.

The important point in this pressure is that the defensive receiver of this long ball pass tries to head back or pass back to the forward who did not drop back to low pressure.

On the diagram 43 we show the medium pressure defensive organization related to the offensive decisions they could make.

The medium pressure is a variation of the low pressure, and the only difference is that the forward who stays up, closer to the opposite goal, tries to establish a faster counter-attack upon the slow pushing up of the opposite defense, as we explained before.

The receiver of the ball will look for the deeper forward as the target point. This deep forward will receive the ball, and could take one of these three options:

1. Hold the ball, allowing the midfield and defense to push up and establish a very effective compactness with correct balance and shape.

2. Play back in one touch and turn on the defender to receive the ball back and do the final penetration.

3. Hold the ball, waiting for the last defender to commit to the steal, and do the penetration to the opposite side of the defender's pressure.

Progressive education of this concept: (different kinds of pressure)

1. Explain the concept and its variations on the blackboard.

2. Show the moves without the ball on the field using cones or soccer balls - This will promote the cycle of questions and answers that helps the teaching process.

3. Time to go to the field!

3a. 11 v 0 situation.

Coach punts the ball to the team organized on the pressure positioning he is interested in developing in that practice. **Note:** Walk-thru each one of them very carefully, and do not cover more than two variations of pressure on the same day.

3b. 11 v 2 and Keeper

Now the opposite keeper and the two defenders will try to build from the back or punt the ball (on the coach's command). The sweeper or keeper of your team will call for the adequate pressure related to the coach's command. The defenders will take care of the ball and build up the attack through the space available for inside or outside penetration.

3c. 11 v 6 and Keeper
The same progression as in 3b. The six attacking players will be the four defenders and two midfielders to establish a better understanding of the different kinds of pressure.

3d. 11 v 11
Walk-thru the adequate arrangements in terms of each one of the pressures and its important points. The coach must designate the way the offensive team should build their attack and the keeper and/or the sweeper (inside defender) must organize the kind of pressure to neutralize that situation.

The final step will be a free scrimmaging, where each one of the team captains identifies how to attack and how to defend in each situation.

Note: During a game you can request the change of the pressure as many times as you feel is necessary to keep the game momentum to your side. It is very important you learn how to read the game, and this will happen by coaching and applying all these concepts as often as possible.

UNDERSTAND THE DEFENSIVE ROTATION OF THE PLAYERS
Your players are capable of reading what kind of pressure to apply against the different options of attacking when the ball is dead. Now it is time to develop the concept of neutralizing the opposite team's counter-attack. Your team had a good plan, but their defensive organization forced your players to make a mistake and you lost possession of the ball. That is when we must introduce the concept of DEFENSIVE ROTATION of THE PLAYERS.

This is a defensive concept where you will focus on minimizing the time to organize the defensive shape and balance and bring a double man pressure on the ball every time possible.

In diagram 44 we show the movement of the players when the ball is lost at the outside left midfield zone.

In this rotation we do not have a specific positioning to identify the perfect way, but the most important points in this concept are that the players understand their role as 1st, 2nd or 3rd defender, and understand that one player will do the double man on the player with the ball and the rest will be positioned in defensive or offensive diagonals, marking their available options, and leaving the opposite side of the field just in covering situations, which must be done by the keeper and/or the last inside defender (flat four) or sweeper (playing with the libero).

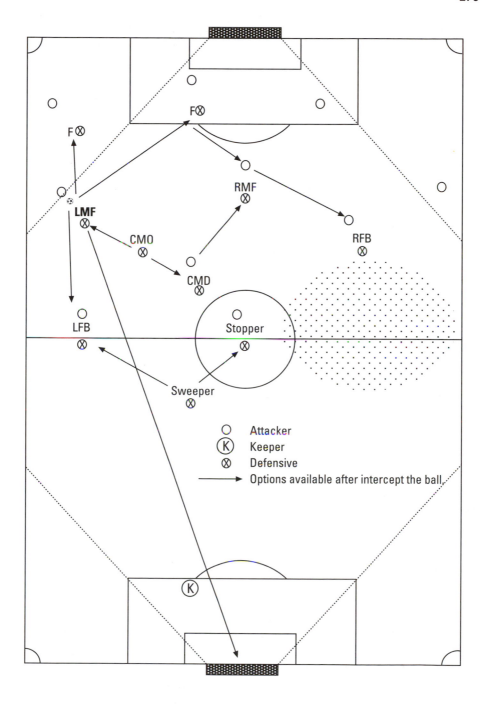

Diagram 44a: *Defensive rotation of the players (ball left side).*

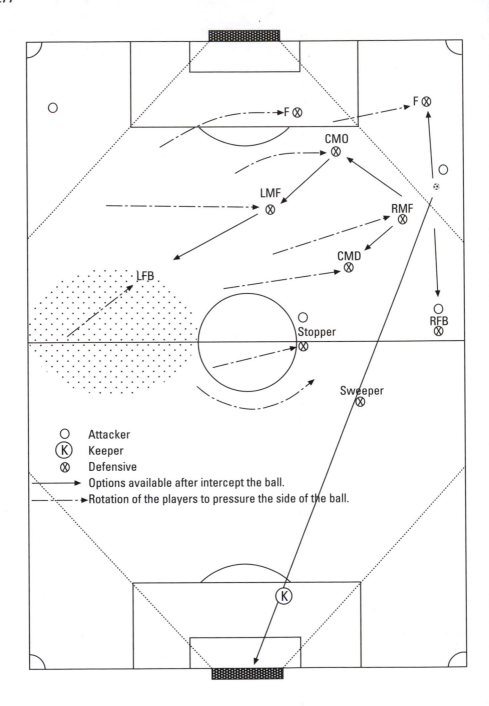

Diagram 44b: *Defensive rotation of the players (ball on the right side).*

Any team can do an organized pressure, but the mark of a good team is how quickly it reacts after losing possession. Let's use the diagram #44a as an example:

The team lost the ball at the left side zone, now the opposite RMF has the ball. The closest player to that ball (1st defender) was the LMF. The 1st action of the LMF is to establish the delay position to allow his team-mates to get organized defensively.

The CMO becomes the double man to pressure the player with the ball, and/or the 2nd defender (marking the 2nd attacker) if time is not available to have an extra player to help. All the players around that LMF will be responsible for marking any option available, and being prepared to show up in defensive or offensive diagonals as soon as the ball is inter-cepted, switching the point of attack and starting a quick counter-attack. To have the CMO free in diagram 44 we had the RMF sliding inside tak-ing care of their CMD and the opposite full-back (right in this case) will move up and inside and he will be responsible for the opposite outside midfielder.

On diagram 44b the ball is lost at the right side and the rotation is done as an unit.

IMPORTANT:

The players rotation is a concept based on the balance and shape of the midfield players. We show in diagram 45 how important the consis-tent support of the other midfielders is when one of them is pressuring the ball. It does not matter which midfielder will be on the ball, the most important thing is to have support on defensive and offensive diagonals pressuring the possible options that attacker could have. All the other players of the team will move together with the midfielders observing which players are responsible for switching the function of covering to marking and vice-versa, establishing a very effective defensive team unity to neutralize any option for penetration. The vital role to achieve success in this concept is a realistic analogy of the midfield players about their rotation related to the movement of the ball and the movement of their markers to an open space.

The basic shape is always the diamond, because of the constant oppor-tunities that can be created in diagonal passes defensively and offensively after intercepting the ball.

Progressive Education of this concept:

1. Explain the concept on the blackboard. Show a video with a Brazilian team playing.

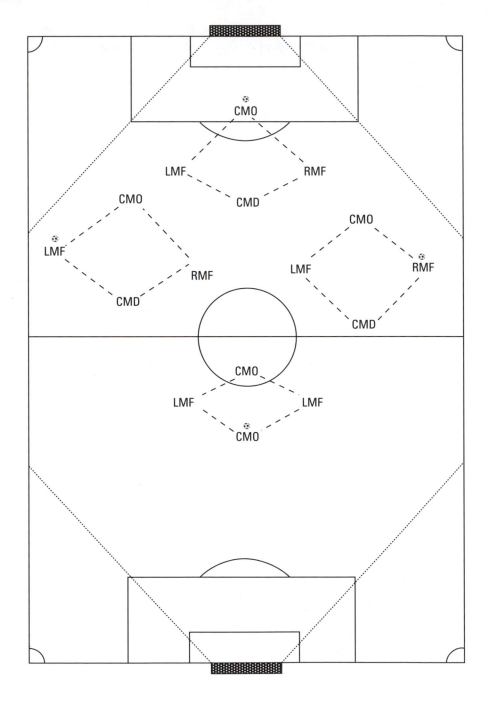

Diagram 45: *Midfield rotation. Developing the team's balance and shape.*

2. In 11 v 0 condition - The coach will move the ball to the right and left, forward and back and the team will follow the ball movement.

3. In 11 v 11 - Educate the players about the different situations that could happen. Observing the shape and balance of the mid-fielders and the support from the defenders and forwards.

4. 11 v 11 - In game condition the only way the team will score is after at least six players touch the ball. The players should rotate defensively trying to neutralize the penetrations in the following speeds of the ball:

   4a. Circulating the ball on speed of maximum 3 touches.

   4b. Circulating the ball on the speed of maximum 2 touches.

   4c. Circulating the ball on speed of only one touch.

5. 11 v 11 - Regular game condition, requesting the two teams to observe the correct rotation of the players defensively.

V. CYCLE OF THE GAME

It is the combination of the all important tactical concepts put together with the team unity and the full team understanding of when to apply, how to apply and finally, why to apply those concepts.

All these concepts will create the necessary excitement and the improvement of the quality of the players' performance.

You as a coach will teach:

1. The team pressure when without the ball.

2. Ways to attack and/or counter-attack. Variations of inside or out-side penetration.

3. How to identify the necessary defensive rotation of the players.

4. How to identify the necessary speed of the ball when doing the circulation.

5. How to identify the kind of pressure to apply.

6. Compactness of the team.

7. First decisions to be made when intercepting the ball and how to exploit the weak points of the opposite team.

Conclusion

As a Brazilian living in the United States, it took me some time to understand how to develop the game of soccer in terms which American players and coaches could relate to.

This book was part of the dream I had in the beginning of BRUSA's efforts to accomplish it's mission of bringing the Brazilian game of soccer to a fuller understanding in the United States.

Now we have written, in book form, the curriculum we have developed and taught for eight years in America. We have continued to train and prepare coaches and players in both Brazil and the United States. This publication is another step in the continuing cycle of education that BRUSA offers in promoting both the fun and the love for soccer.

Notes

REEDSWAIN BOOKS and VIDEOS
612 Pughtown Road
Spring City, Pennsylvania 19475 USA
1-800-331-5191 • www.reedswain.com

Notes

REEDSWAIN BOOKS and VIDEOS
612 Pughtown Road
Spring City, Pennsylvania 19475 USA
1-800-331-5191 • www.reedswain.com

Notes

REEDSWAIN BOOKS and VIDEOS
612 Pughtown Road
Spring City, Pennsylvania 19475 USA
1-800-331-5191 • www.reedswain.com

Notes

REEDSWAIN BOOKS and VIDEOS
612 Pughtown Road
Spring City, Pennsylvania 19475 USA
1-800-331-5191 • www.reedswain.com

Notes

REEDSWAIN BOOKS and VIDEOS
612 Pughtown Road
Spring City, Pennsylvania 19475 USA
1-800-331-5191 • www.reedswain.com

Notes

REEDSWAIN BOOKS and VIDEOS
612 Pughtown Road
Spring City, Pennsylvania 19475 USA
1-800-331-5191 • www.reedswain.com